POSTMODERN TIMES

TURNING POINT Christian Worldview Series
Marvin Olasky, General Editor

Turning Point: A Christian Worldview Declaration
by Herbert Schlossberg and Marvin Olasky

Prodigal Press: The Anti-Christian Bias of the American News Media
by Marvin Olasky

Freedom, Justice, and Hope: Toward a Strategy for the Poor and the Oppressed
by Marvin Olasky, Herbert Schlossberg, Pierre Berthoud, and Clark H. Pinnock

Beyond Good Intentions: A Biblical View of Politics
by Doug Bandow

Prosperity and Poverty: The Compassionate Use of Resources in a World of Scarcity
by E. Calvin Beisner

The Seductive Image: A Christian Critique of the World of Film
by K. L. Billingsley

All God's Children and Blue Suede Shoes: Christians and Popular Culture
by Kenneth A. Myers

A World Without Tyranny: Christian Faith and International Politics
by Dean C. Curry

Prospects for Growth: A Biblical View of Population, Resources and the Future
by E. Calvin Beisner

More Than Kindness: A Compassionate Approach to Crisis Childbearing
by Susan Olasky and Marvin Olasky

Reading Between the Lines: A Christian Guide to Literature
by Gene Edward Veith, Jr.

State of the Arts: From Bezalel to Mapplethorpe
by Gene Edward Veith, Jr.

Recovering the Lost Tools of Learning: An Approach to Distinctively Christian Education
by Douglas Wilson

A Fragrance of Oppression: The Church and Its Persecutors
by Herbert Schlossberg

The Soul of Science: A Christian Map to the Scientific Landscape
by Nancy R. Pearcey and Charles B. Thaxton

Postmodern Times: A Christian Guide to Contemporary Thought and Culture
by Gene Edward Veith, Jr.

POSTMODERN TIMES

A Christian Guide to Contemporary Thought and Culture

Gene Edward Veith, Jr.

CROSSWAY BOOKS • WHEATON, ILLINOIS

A DIVISION OF GOOD-NEWS PUBLISHERS

Postmodern Times:
A Christian Guide to Contemporary Thought and Culture
Copyright © 1994 by Gene Edward Veith, Jr.

Published by Crossway Books, a division of
Good News Publishers, Wheaton, Illinois 60187

 Published in association with the
Fieldstead Institute
P.O. Box 19061,
Irvine, California 92713

Cover illustration: Guy Wolek

First printing, 1994

Printed in the United States of America

Material from *Postmodernist Culture: An Introduction to Theories of the
Contemporary* by Steven Connor, copyright 1989, is reprinted by permission
of Basil Blackwell, Oxford, England.

Scripture taken from the *Holy Bible: New International Version®.*
Copyright © 1973, 1978, 1984 by International Bible Society.
Used by permission of Zondervan Publishing House. All rights reserved.

The "NIV" and "New International Version" trademarks are registered
in the United States Patent and Trademark Office by International
Bible Society. Use of either trademark requires the permission of
International Bible Society.

Library of Congress Cataloging-in-Publication Data
Veith, Jr., Gene Edward.
    Postmodern times : a Christian guide to contemporary thought and
culture / Gene Edward Veith, Jr.
        p.   cm. — (The Turning point Christian worldview series)
    Includes bibliographical references and index.
    1. Christianity and culture.   2. Postmodernism—Religious aspects—
Christianity.   3. Contemporary, The.   4. Sociology, Christian.
I. Title.   II. Series.
BR115.C8V37   1994   261—dc20   93-23646
ISBN 0-89107-768-5

03		02		01		00		99		98		97		96		95
15	14	13	12	11	10	9	8	7	6	5	4			

To
Sharon and Bob Foote

"When the foundations are being destroyed,
what can the righteous do?"

Psalm 11:3

TABLE OF

CONTENTS

PREFACE

*M*any people today are sensing that the modern era is over. In nearly every sphere, from academic fields to new social phenomena, the assumptions that shaped twentieth-century thought and culture are being exploded. As we enter the twenty-first century, it seems clear that Western culture is entering a new phase, which scholars are calling "postmodern."

What is less clear is whether the change is good or bad. On the one hand, the supreme example of a society built on modernistic materialism, atheism, and social engineering—the U.S.S.R.—has collapsed. Traditional American ideals of free market economics and individual freedom are sweeping the globe. Christianity, which not only survived communism but was a major force in its demise, has a new credibility, as old modernist critiques lose their force and multitudes worldwide discover the Word of God and turn to Christ.

On the other hand, society is segmenting into antagonistic groups. Tribalism, terrorism, and ethnic cleansing are splitting the globe apart. Americans fight "culture wars" over moral issues such as abortion and euthanasia and intellectual issues such as education and cultural diversity. Convulsed over "political correctness," universities no longer operate under the modernist assumption that one objective, rational truth exists. Even such basic questions as the value of Western civilization are up for grabs: Is the Western heritage one of human achievement and liberty, or is the Western heritage primarily racism, sexism, imperialism, and homophobia?

Diverse "communities"—feminists, gays, African-Americans, neo-conservatives, pro-lifers—now make up the cultural landscape.

These different groups seem to have no common frame of reference by which to communicate with each other, much less arrive at a consensus. In the meantime, families fall apart, AIDS kills thousands, and the mass culture puts us all in a TV daze.

So is the postmodern age good or bad from a Christian point of view? Perhaps we will have to say with Dickens, "It was the best of times; it was the worst of times." He was speaking, in *The Tale of Two Cities*, of the era of the French Revolution, in many ways the beginning of modernism. But his words seem to apply to every era. Every age has its greatness and its follies, its possibilities and its temptations. But these are always different from age to age. To embrace the opportunities and to avoid the traps, Christians should be in a continual process of "understanding the present time" (Romans 13:11).

The church has always had to confront its culture and to exist in tension with the world. To ignore the culture is to risk irrelevance; to accept the culture uncritically is to risk syncretism and unfaithfulness. Every age has had its eager-to-please liberal theologians who have tried to reinterpret Christianity according to the latest intellectual and cultural fashion. Enlightenment liberals had their rational religion and the higher criticism of the Bible; romantic liberals had their warm feelings; existentialist liberals had their crises of meaning and leaps of faith; there is now a postmodern liberalism (as we shall see). But orthodox Christians have also lived in every age, confessing their faith in Jesus Christ (as we shall see). They were part of their culture (you can recognize the distinct style of seventeenth, eighteenth, and nineteenth-century Christians, even when they say the same things). Yet they also countered their culture, proclaiming God's law and gospel to society's very inadequacies and points of need.

This book is a guide to the contemporary landscape—its dominant ideas, its art forms, its social configurations, and its spiritual assumptions. It describes various trends and comments on them from a Christian point of view.

Some Christians think that with the end of modernism, the postmodern era can mean a rebirth of classical Christianity. They speak of the postmodern age in glowing terms. While I agree with this perspective, I also see a new secular ideology replacing the modernistic worldview. Like modernism, this postmodernism is hostile to Christianity, but for different reasons. In this book I am critical of what I call "postmodern*ism*," although I see promise in being "postmodern."

Since I write here for the church as a whole, and not for academic specialists, I leave out the more technical aspects of postmodernist thought. The specific contributions of major figures of postmodern thought such as Lacan, Derrida, Foucault, and others, I am skipping. Nor am I plunging into the technical details of critical theory, hermeneutics, or other highly specialized kinds of discourse postmodernists generally use to thrash out their ideas. Other Christian scholars, particularly Roger Lundin and Clarence Walhout, have provided thoughtful and sophisticated treatment of such scholarship from a Christian point of view.

The origins of this book go back to a lecture I was asked to give, "Deconstructing Deconstruction," sponsored by Probe Ministries at the University of Texas. I owe a great deal to my colleague Dr. David Krenz (who should have written this book) for helping me to understand what the postmodern is all about. Nancy Pearcey, through our work with Charles Colson's "Breakpoint" radio program, has helped me, seventeenth-century scholar as I am, to keep a focus on contemporary issues.

I also appreciate the contributions of two fellow writers with whom I get together to drink coffee, read manuscripts, and talk. Rev. Harold Senkbeil has helped me understand the theological problems facing contemporary Christianity and the possibilities of developing a confessional alternative grounded in Reformation spirituality. Rev. Richard Eyer, a hospital chaplain, has opened my eyes to medical ethics and to the ways that Christianity is engaged in (literally) a life-and-death struggle with the new worldviews.

Thanks too to Marvin Olasky for commissioning this final contribution to the Turning Point Series, to the Fieldstead Institute for its support of this series, and to all of its other authors who have helped me in countless ways to see our times in light of the Word of God. I also owe a great debt of gratitude to my wife Jackquelyn and to Paul, Joanna, and Mary.

"THERE ARE NO ABSOLUTES"

Charles Colson tells about having dinner with a media personality and trying to talk with him about Christianity. Colson
told him how he had come to Christ. "Obviously Jesus worked for
you," his friend replied, but went on to tell him about someone he
knew whose life had been turned around by New Age spirituality.
"Crystals, channeling—it worked for her. Just like your Jesus."

Colson tried to explain the difference, but got nowhere. He
raised the issue of death and the afterlife, but his friend did not
believe in Heaven or Hell and was not particularly bothered by the
prospect of dying.

Colson explained what the Bible said, but his friend did not
believe in the Bible or any other spiritual authority.

Finally, Colson mentioned a Woody Allen movie, *Crimes and
Misdemeanors*, about a killer who silences his conscience by con-
cluding that life is nothing more than the survival of the fittest. The
friend became thoughtful. Colson followed with examples from
Tolstoy and C. S. Lewis on the reality of the moral law. The friend
was following him. Then Colson cited the epistle of Romans on
human inability to keep the law. His friend then paid close attention to the message of Christ's atoning work on the cross.

Although the friend did not become a Christian, Colson felt
that he finally had broken through at least some of his defenses. The
difficulty was in finding a common frame of reference. Because of
his friend's mind-set, the usual evangelistic approaches did not
work. "My experience," says Colson, "is a sobering illustration of

how resistant the modern mind has become to the Christian message. And it raises serious questions about the effectiveness of traditional evangelistic methods in our age. For the spirit of the age is changing more quickly than many of us realize."[1]

THERE ARE NO ABSOLUTES

It is hard to witness to truth to people who believe that truth is relative ("Jesus works for you; crystals work for her"). It is hard to proclaim the forgiveness of sins to people who believe that, since morality is relative, they have no sins to forgive.

According to a recent poll, 66 percent of Americans believe that "there is no such thing as absolute truth." Among young adults, the percentage is even higher: 72 percent of those between eighteen and twenty-five do not believe absolutes exist.[2]

To disbelieve in truth is, of course, self-contradictory. To believe means to think something is true; to say, "It's true that nothing is true" is intrinsically meaningless nonsense. The very statement—"there is no absolute truth"—is an absolute truth. People have bandied about such concepts for centuries as a sort of philosophical parlor game, but have seldom taken these seriously. Today it is not just some esoteric and eccentric philosophers who hold this deeply problematic view of truth, but the average man on the street. It is not the lunatic fringe rejecting the very concept of truth, but two-thirds of the American people.

Moreover, the poll goes on to show that 53 percent of those who call themselves *evangelical Christians* believe that there are no absolutes. This means that the *majority* of those who say that they believe in the authority of the Bible and know Christ as their Savior nevertheless agree that "there is no such thing as absolute truth." Not Christ? No, although He presumably "works for them." Not the Bible? Apparently not, although 88 percent of evangelicals believe that "The Bible is the written word of God and is totally accurate in all it teaches." Bizarrely, 70 percent of all Americans claim to accept this high view of Scripture, *which is practically the same number as those who say "there are no absolutes."*[3]

What is going on here? Perhaps those polled did not understand the question or the implications of what they claimed to believe. Some of the evangelical sceptics in the 53 percent may be solid Christians who were only parroting what they heard on television, oblivious to the theological implications of this pop philosophy. The polls may reflect ignorance or confusion. Even so, it amounts to the same thing. Holding mutually inconsistent ideas is a sure sign of believing that there are no absolute truths.

The rejection of absolutes is not just a fine point in philosophy. Many of those polled no doubt took the question as referring not so much to epistemology as to morality. Relative values accompany the relativism of truth.

Up until now, societies have always regulated sexuality by strict moral guidelines. This has been the case in all ages, for all religions, and for all cultures. Suddenly, sex outside of marriage has become routinely accepted. In 1969, well into the "sexual revolution," 68 percent of Americans believed that sexual relations before marriage are wrong. In 1987, a supposedly conservative era already frightened by AIDS, only 46 percent—less than half—believed that premarital sex is wrong.[4] In 1992 only 33 percent reject premarital sex.[5]

In issue after issue, people are casually dismissing time-honored moral absolutes. The killing of a child in the womb used to be considered a horrible, almost unspeakable evil. Today abortion is not just legal. It has been transformed into something good, a constitutional right. People once considered killing the handicapped, the sick, and the aged an unthinkable atrocity. Today they see euthanasia as an act of compassion.

These moral inversions are taking place not only in the secular world, but within what passes as Christendom. A recent study claimed that 56 percent of single "fundamentalists" engage in sex outside of marriage. This is about the same as the rate for "liberals" (57 percent). (Ironically, the church with the strictest teachings about sexual morality and the greatest emphasis on the role of good works in salvation may have the most permissive members. According to this study, 66 percent of single Roman Catholics are sexually active. American Catholics may be even more permissive than secular Americans. The study claims that while 67 percent of Americans accept premarital sex, 83 percent of Catholics do, in complete opposition to the teaching of their church.)[6] Along the same lines, 49 percent of Protestants and 47 percent of Catholics consider themselves "pro-choice" when it comes to abortion.[7]

Some 49 percent of evangelicals and a startling 71 percent of Catholics say they believe in euthanasia,[8] apparently assuming that "Thou shalt not kill" is not an absolute.

Certainly, opinion polls can be slippery, misleading, and subject to various interpretations. Other polls show that people have strong moral positions on other issues. As I will show, over-reliance on opinion polls is one of the signs of a particular kind of contemporary confusion.

And even if the polls are correct, they only confirm what the Bible says about sin. No one with a Biblical view of sin should be surprised to see that immorality is rampant throughout society and in churches and that Christians too fall prey to moral failure and hypocrisy.

Churches have always been packed with sinners, as is fitting (who else is there?). Christians admit their inability to keep God's Law, and so they depend solely for their salvation on the forgiveness won by Jesus Christ. Theologians have always recognized that church members, no less than the unchurched, need to be evangelized and discipled.

And yet the polls suggest something new. While people have always committed sins, they at least acknowledged these were sins. A century ago a person may have committed adultery flagrantly and in defiance of God and man, but he would have admitted that what he was doing was a sin. What we have today is not only immoral behavior, but a loss of moral criteria. This is true even in the church. We face not only a moral collapse but a collapse of meaning. "There are no absolutes."

THE SHIFT IN WORLDVIEW

What has happened? Once most people accepted basic Christian concepts. Now only a minority do. This moral and religious shift is not the only change we face. "We are experiencing enormous structural change in our country and in our world," says the Christian futurist Leith Anderson, "change that promises to be greater than the invention of the printing press, greater than the Industrial Revolution."[9] Christians dare not be blind to change of this magnitude.

As Francis Schaeffer and other scholars have shown, Western

culture has gone through many phases. One worldview follows another. In the eighteenth century the Enlightenment challenged the Biblical synthesis that had dominated Western culture. With the nineteenth century came both romanticism and scientific materialism. The twentieth century has given us Marxism and fascism, positivism and existentialism.

Today as we enter the twenty-first century, a new worldview is emerging. The "modern," strange as it is to say, has become old-fashioned. The twentieth century, for all of its achievements and catastrophes, is passing into history. The "modern ideas" that characterized the twentieth century no longer seem relevant. We are entering the "postmodern" age.

The term "postmodern" primarily refers to time rather than to a distinct ideology. If the "modern" age is really over, Christians have every reason to be glad. Ever since the battles between "modernists" and "fundamentalists"(and before), Biblical Christianity has been bludgeoned by the forces of modernism, with its scientific rationalism, humanism, and bias against the past. Today the assumptions of modernism, including those that have bedeviled the church in this century, are being abandoned. Christians can rejoice at the dawn of a postmodern age.

Modernism, however, is being replaced by the new secular ideology of postmodern*ism*. This new set of assumptions about reality—which goes far beyond mere relativism—is gaining dominance throughout the culture. The average person who believes that there are no absolutes may never have heard of the academic exercise of "deconstruction." The intellectual establishment may disdain the electronic world of television. Contemporary politicians may be unaware of *avant garde* art. Nevertheless, these are all interconnected and comprise a distinctly postmodernist worldview.

While modernist attacks on Christianity are losing their force, postmodernists are attacking Christianity on different grounds. For example, modernists would argue in various ways that Christianity is not true. One hardly hears this objection any more. Today the most common critique is that "Christians think they have the only truth." The claims of Christianity are not denied; they are rejected *because* they purport to be true. Those who believe "there are no absolutes" will dismiss those who reject relativism as "intolerant," as trying to force their beliefs on other

Allan Bloom's book

people. Postmodernists reject Christianity on the same grounds that they reject modernism, with its scientific rationalism. Both Christians and modernists believe in truth. Postmodernists do not. Whether modernism or postmodernism will prove the more hospitable to Christianity remains to be seen.

Scripture tells us of the importance of "understanding the present time" (Romans 13:11). "Most Christians," observes George Barna, "do not perceive the Church to be in the midst of the most severe struggle it has faced in centuries."[10] Many Christians, including theologians, are still battling modernism, unaware that the issues have changed. If Christians are to minister effectively in the postmodern world and avoid its temptations, they must understand the spirit of the age.

THE CURSE OF BABEL

Despite the endless claims of novelty, Christians know "there is nothing new under the sun. Is there anything of which one can say, 'Look! This is something new'? It was here already, long ago" (Ecclesiastes 1:9-10). Unbelief and sin have always been with us. The ancient pagans too were relativistic, in a way, and God's people have always been tempted to compromise their faith by selling out to the dominant culture. The Bible thus addresses the issues of the postmodern age with startling clarity.

The shift from modernism to postmodernism seems in fact a version of an ancient failure and an ancient curse. At one time, "the whole world had one language and a common speech" (Genesis 11:1). Exhilarated with their unity, their common understanding, and their technological ability, people said, "'Come, let us build ourselves a city, with a tower that reaches to the heavens, so that we may make a name for ourselves'" (11:4).

The culture that built the Tower of Babel parallels the modern age. Confident in their human abilities, their reason and scientific knowledge, the modernists had no need for God. To make a name for themselves, they not only built cities, they engineered new social and economic orders, such as socialism. Their technology, more advanced than the Babelites', enabled them to build not just a tower to reach the heavens, but spaceships to reach the moon.

God judged the pretensions of Babel. Noting their genuine

accomplishments and the vast potential of human achievement, the Lord saw that a united, technologically sophisticated human race would be nearly unlimited in their capacity for evil. "If as one people speaking the same language they have begun to do this, then nothing they plan to do will be impossible for them" (11:6). God mercifully thwarted this primitive but dangerous beginning (what "they have begun to do"). He shattered their self-deification and brought their famous tower to ruin.

In our own time, it has become clear that reason, science, and technology have not solved all of our problems. Poverty, crime, and despair defy our attempts at social engineering. The most thoroughgoing attempt to restructure society according to a rationalistic, materialist theory—communism—fell to pieces. Technology continues to progress at breakneck speed, but, far from reaching the heavens, it sometimes diminishes our lives.

God punished Babel by undermining the faculty that made possible their success—their language. The human race splintered into mutually inaccessible groups.

> "Come, let us go down and confuse their language so they will not understand each other." So the LORD scattered them from there over all the earth, and they stopped building the city. That is why it was called Babel—because there the LORD confused the language of the whole world. From there the LORD scattered them over the face of the whole earth. (Genesis 11:7-9)

This is exactly what has happened with the fall of modernism. The monolithic sensibility of modernism, which seemed to have an unlimited potential, has fragmented into diverse and competing communities. People can no longer understand each other. There *of which the gang is a micro cosm.* are no common reference points, no common language. Totalitarian unity has given way to chaotic diversity. Scattered in small groups of like-minded people, those who speak the same language, human beings today are confused.

God's people can only agree with the judgment on the Tower and the curse of Babel. They will likewise agree that modernism is idolatrous and will rejoice in its fall. The curse of Babel, while appropriate, was a punishment for sin. When Christ atoned for the sins of the world, the curse for sin was removed. When the Holy

Spirit was poured out upon the church, the curse of Babel was undone.

> When the day of Pentecost came, they were all together in one place. Suddenly a sound like the blowing of a violent wind came from heaven and filled the whole house where they were sitting. They saw what seemed to be tongues of fire that separated and came to rest on each of them. All of them were filled with the Holy Spirit and began to speak in other tongues as the Spirit enabled them.
>
> Now there were staying in Jerusalem God-fearing Jews from every nation under heaven. When they heard this sound, a crowd came together in bewilderment, because each one heard them speaking in his own language. Utterly amazed, they asked: "Are not all these men who are speaking Galileans? Then how is it that each of us hears them in his own native language? Parthians, Medes and Elamites; residents of Mesopotamia, Judea and Cappadocia, Pontus and Asia, Phrygia and Pamphylia, Egypt and the parts of Libya near Cyrene; visitors from Rome (both Jews and converts to Judaism); Cretans and Arabs—we hear them declaring the wonders of God in our own tongues!" Amazed and perplexed, they asked one another, "What does this mean?" (Acts 2:1-12)

What it means, among other things, is that the gospel is for the whole human race in all of its diversity, that through the Word preached by the apostles the Holy Spirit communicates faith to people of every language and culture. Far from being some unintelligible utterance, the tongues of Pentecost were uniquely intelligible—to everyone, no matter what their native language. The restoration of language was a sign of the Kingdom of God.

On Pentecost the Holy Spirit began gathering the Church from all nations (Acts 2:41). This Church was a different kind of community, neither unified in an autonomous humanism like the Tower-builders and the modernists, nor fractured into alien groups like the Babelites and the postmodernists. Rather, the Church is a balance of both unity and diversity, a single Body consisting of organs as different from each other as a foot and an eye (1 Corinthians 12), but unified in love for each other and faith in Jesus Christ.

Because of this larger perspective, God's people will see the futility of both the building of the Tower and the cacophony of voices that followed its abandonment. They will likewise recognize the limitations of both the modernists and the postmodernists. Once again, the issues will be sin, idolatry, and language.

OVERVIEW OF THE BOOK

This book is a walking tour of contemporary thought and culture. As such, it will range far and wide, examining academic philosophy and popular TV shows, art and politics, social changes and the new religions. Its purpose is to describe trends that Christians need to be aware of, commenting on them from the perspective of Biblical Christianity.

The first section on postmodern thought describes the new paradigms that characterize contemporary thinking, from the deconstructionism and post-Marxism of the universities to the relativism of popular culture. The section surveys the history of modernism and postmodernism, describes their consequences, and suggests a Christian response.

The next section explores the arts, in which the inner dynamics and implications of postmodernism are expressed most clearly. From the popular art forms of film and television to the experiments in art and literature of the *avant garde*, the new aesthetic testifies to the loss of both absolutes and humanness. On the other hand, some postmodern art, architecture, and literature, in their reaction against the modern, offer a model for how the traditions of the past can be brought back into the contemporary world.

The third section examines postmodern society, showing how our society is splintering into various factions, with the culture fragmenting into subcultures based on race, ethnicity, and sexuality. The chapter on politics shows how postmodernism reduces all social relationships to questions of power, threatening freedom and democracy. The fall of communism, however, suggests that democracy, a free economy, and Biblical absolutes may provide the basis for an alternative postmodern social order.

Although the entire book amounts to a theological commentary on contemporary culture, the final section concentrates explicitly on religion. It shows how the postmodernist worldview manifests itself not only in New Age religions, but tragically even within the evangelical church. The section closes by showing that to be truly relevant to the postmodern age, the church need not succumb to the spirit of the age; rather, the postmodern church has only to recover and apply its spiritual heritage.

This book is critical of postmodern*ism*, but remains open to the postmodern. It is as if there were two contrary postmodern positions, each vying for dominance. Is the true herald of the postmodern age the counterculture movement of the 1960s or the fall of the Berlin Wall? Who best represents contemporary America, Madonna or Ronald Reagan? Is Christianity declining as Americans descend into relativism and neo-paganism, or is it triumphing, emerging from Communist persecution and catching fire across the globe? The postmodern consciousness seems to make possible either a new radicalism or a new conservatism. Which version will prevail in the next millennium remains unclear.

This book may help Christians tip the balance. Certainly, the turmoil of the present time is characteristic of a transition from one epoch to the next. Whether Christianity will once again exert its influence on the culture, or whether Christianity will become further marginalized in the twenty-first century, Christians must pay close attention to the signs of the times.

In doing so, they will see that Biblical faith has survived every assault, even persecution, and has proven relevant to every age despite attempts to silence or to change its message. Conversely, each humanly devised worldview has proven inadequate and has been replaced by yet another set of assumptions. As modernism gives way to postmodernism, and as the twentieth century gives way to the twenty-first century (if Christ delays His coming), Christians will discover even more reasons to hold fast to the Word of God.

PART ONE

POSTMODERN THOUGHT

FROM THE MODERN TO THE POSTMODERN

A massive intellectual revolution is taking place," says Princeton theologian Diogenes Allen, "that is perhaps as great as that which marked off the modern world from the Middle Ages."[1] Signs of this revolution appear everywhere—on university campuses and on television screens, in the thought-forms of computer networks and in the lifestyles of average Americans. As the twentieth century draws to a close, there is a sense that a particular way of thinking is disappearing and that we are on the verge of something new.

Christian scholar Thomas Oden was one of the first to chronicle these changes. He maintains that the modern age lasted exactly 200 years—from the fall of the Bastille in 1789 to the fall of the Berlin Wall in 1989.[2] The French Revolution exemplifies the triumph of the Enlightenment. With the destruction of the Bastille, the prison in which the monarchy jailed its political prisoners, the premodern world with its feudal loyalties and spiritual hierarchies was guillotined. The revolutionaries exalted the Rights of Man. They dismissed Christianity as a relic of the past. During the course of the revolution, they installed the Goddess of Reason in Notre Dame Cathedral. In the modern period, human reason would take the place of God, solving all human problems and remaking society along the lines of scientific, rational truth.

The trust in human reason and the rejection of the supernatural took many forms, but nowhere did the modernistic impulse reach further or more ambitiously than in the invention of the Marxist state. Marxism, beginning with the assumption of "dialectical materialism," sought to find material, economic causes for all human problems. Marx reduced the human condition to issues of class struggle and economic exploitation. In doing so, he worked out a quasi-scientific alternative that would supposedly bring on an earthly paradise. Under communism there would be no private property. There would be no more exploitation. Under socialism individuals would find meaning by losing themselves in a larger group. The economy and all phases of society would be planned for the good of the whole.

Soviet leaders put these seemingly "enlightened" ideals into practice with the Russian Revolution. But instead of bringing a worker's paradise as the theory promised, oppression and brutality resulted, on a scale unparalleled in human history. Amazingly, the monolith of Soviet communism, though armed with secret police and nuclear weapons, crumbled when its people uncovered its lies and demanded freedom.

Christians could have predicted what would happen when human beings claim ultimate authority for themselves. The doctrine of original sin means that human beings left to themselves may profess noble-sounding ideals, but in fact they will commit horrific evil. The French Revolution offers an example, as the lofty rhetoric of the Rights of Man ushered in the guillotine and the Reign of Terror.

Now the assumptions of modernism have fallen apart, from Moscow to San Francisco. The Enlightenment is discredited. Reason is dethroned, even on university campuses. The Industrial Revolution is giving way to the Information Age. Society, technology, values, and basic categories of thought are shifting. A new way of looking at the world is emerging.

Thomas Oden contends that this postmodern era is an opportunity for orthodox, classical Christianity to make a come-back.[3] The failure of modernism means that the old secular critiques of supernatural Christianity have lost their force. Conservative Christianity has a new credibility in the postmodern world.

He is right. Postmodern Christians can proclaim the gospel to their culture with a new force and urgency. Nevertheless, the secular establishment is setting up some postmodern alternatives of its own. These views respond to the failure of the Enlightenment by jettisoning truth altogether. The intellect is replaced by the will.

Reason is replaced by emotion. Morality is replaced by relativism. Reality itself becomes a social construct. This emerging worldview challenges Christianity in different ways from the old modernism. Postmodern Christians will have to confront the views of post-modern non-Christians.

BEFORE THE MODERN

To understand the modern and the postmodern, we must first understand the premodern. To put it simply, in the premodern phase of Western civilization people believed in the supernatural. Individuals and the culture as a whole believed in God (or gods). Life in this world owed its existence and meaning to a spiritual realm beyond the senses.

This is the definition assumed by modernist theologians who are used to saying that since, of course, "modern man" can no longer believe in miracles, the supernatural events described in the New Testament must be reinterpreted for the "modern age." Since many in the twentieth century do in fact believe in the supernatural, it is clear that by the term "modern" they do not refer to chronology but to a state of mind. They accuse conservative Christians of holding premodern ideas due to ignorance, lack of education, and intellectual naivete. As one scholar puts it, evangelicals simply "have not heard the news of modernity."[4] This "news," this gospel of modernity, has such authority that other kinds of news, such as the gospel of Jesus Christ, are not even considered.

The premodern, however, deserves to be taken seriously. This phase of Western culture was not characterized by a single monolithic worldview. Rather, this complex, dynamic, and tension-filled era included mythological paganism and classical rationalism, as well as Biblical revelation.

The ancient Greeks themselves struggled with the conflict between their pagan religion, which grew out of the animistic nature religions of primitive cultures, and the rational philosophy of intellectual giants such as Plato and Aristotle. Socrates was forced to drink the hemlock because of his "atheism"—he rejected the mythological worldview, arguing that the stories of the so-called gods were nothing more than projections of human vices. There must be only one supreme God, he reasoned, the source of all truth, beauty, and goodness. Plato, the disciple of Socrates, went on to develop classical idealism, the view that the particulars of this world owe their form to transcendent ideals in the mind of God.

As Platonists explored the ideals and the universals of the mind, Aristotle turned his attention to the external world. He too rejected the mythological, reasoning that all causes must trace back to a First Cause, which itself is uncaused. This First Cause can only be a transcendent God, of whom there can be only one. Aristotle went on to investigate the tangible world, classifying plants and animals, and unveiling the purposes of physical objects and natural organisms. In his inquiries into human life, Aristotle affirmed the existence of objective values. Aristotle's analytical method—with his distinction between means and ends, his relation of form to purpose, and his discovery of absolute principles that underlie every sphere of life—pushed human reason to dizzying heights.[5]

The ancient Greeks began with a mythological paganism, but by the sheer power of intellect forged a different way of looking at their world. Certainly Greek society with its uneasy mixture of pagan mythology and classical rationalism was no utopia. Morally decadent, this society institutionalized infanticide, slavery, war, oppression, prostitution, and homosexuality.

But when Paul and the other apostles made their missionary journeys, the Greek world was ready for the gospel. Already those nourished by Greek culture had an inkling of the immortality of the soul, the reality of a spiritual realm, and the existence of only one transcendent God. Paul discovered in Athens an altar "to an unknown God." The Greeks had come to realize that there is a God, but they did not know Him. Their reason, highly developed as it was, had to give way to revelation. "Now what you worship as something unknown I am going to proclaim to you" (Acts 17:23).

When the Greeks converted to Christianity, they were introduced to the Bible. The Hebrew Scriptures gave them new ways of thinking about God and the creation, human beings and moral truth. The new religion squarely opposed infanticide, abortion,[6] and homosexual vice. (Liberals who think the New Testament condemnations of homosexuality, for example, were only an expression of the culture of the day are precisely wrong. Greek culture not only tolerated but encouraged homosexuality.[7] Greek military

minds reasoned that soldiers tied together by homosexual relationships would fight harder to defend their lovers. Even Plato
believed that women were inferior, and therefore, the highest love
would be expressed between men. New Testament sexual morality
was *countercultural*, as it must be today.)

Christianity both challenged and fulfilled the worldview of
the Greeks. The Biblical and the classical worldviews did not
always fit together, but they were not completely and in every detail
opposed to each other. They agreed that there was a transcendent
reality beyond this world, to which this world owed its meaning.
They agreed that the physical world was orderly and to some extent
knowable; they agreed on the objectivity of truth and on intellectual absolutes. The Greek perspective tended to rely too much on
human reason and to downplay human sinfulness. Nevertheless,
Augustine found that he could draw on Plato to help formulate his
rigorously Christian theology. In the Middle Ages, Thomas
Aquinas attempted to synthesize the Bible with Aristotle.

For over a thousand years, Western civilization was dominated by an uneasy mingling of worldviews—the Biblical revelation, classical rationalism, and even the remnants of native pagan
mythologies. Often Biblical truth was compromised by human reason and pagan superstitions. Other times the Christian worldview
emerged clearly and with authority.

During the Middle Ages (A.D. 1000-1500), Christian piety,
classical rationalism, and the folk-paganism of European culture
achieved something of a synthesis. Although medieval civilization
was impressive in its own terms, scholastic theology subordinated
the Bible to Aristotelian logic and human institutions, sacrificing
the purity of the Biblical revelation. Medieval popular culture further obscured the gospel message, often keeping much of the old
paganism under a veneer of Christianity, retaining the old gods but
renaming them after Christian saints.

In the 1500s and the 1600s, Western civilization returned to
its roots. The Renaissance challenged the somewhat muddled
medieval synthesis, as the West returned to both of its sources.
Renaissance humanism rediscovered and reasserted the Greeks; the
Reformation rediscovered and reasserted the Bible. Both classicism
and Biblicism came back to life in a purified form.

Myth, classicism, and Christianity—these three different

worldviews, in different configurations, defined the Western world for centuries. Not everyone was a Christian in the premodern world. Biblical Christianity was always in tension with its culture. Mythology and humanistic rationalism continually tempted the church.

Christianity should not be identified exclusively with premodern civilization, anymore than it should be identified with any other humanly devised institution. Still, after a while Christian assumptions—often shared by classical rationalism and even paganism—acquired a special authority. Most people assumed that God is real and must be taken into account. Good is in conflict with evil. Human beings are sinful, yet they are valuable and the objects of God's salvation. Nature is God's creation, but there is a reality beyond nature—the realm of the spirit, the source of all values and the true destiny of human beings. Neither humanity nor society nor nature is autonomous. All are utterly dependent on the sovereignty of God.

Then came the modern age. Human beings, sinful as we are, have always desired autonomy, to be free from all restrictions, to focus on this world instead of some world to come. The turning away from Biblical supernaturalism is sometimes traced to Renaissance humanism, with its antecedents in medieval scholastic theology and Greek classical rationalism. If so, such views have always been a temptation for the West. But however humanistic they may have been, medieval and Renaissance thinkers could not deny the ultimate reality of God.

In time, however, thinkers began to see Christian supernaturalism as old-fashioned. Human achievements in science and technology seemed to open up a new age of progress, rendering the wisdom of past ages obsolete. The modern world, properly speaking, began in the 1700s with the Enlightenment.

THE ENLIGHTENMENT

The emerging sciences had their origins in the Biblical view that nature is the good and orderly work of a personal Creator and in the classical view that absolute rational laws govern nature. In the 1700s the progress of science accelerated so rapidly that it seemed as if science could explain everything. Some saw no limits to the power of human reason operating upon the data of the senses.

This age of reason, scientific discovery, and human autonomy is termed the Enlightenment. Its thinkers embraced classicism with its order and rationality (although their version of classicism neglected the supernaturalism of Plato and Aristotle). However, they lumped Christianity together with paganism as outdated superstitions. Reason alone, so they thought, may now replace the reliance on the supernatural born out of the ignorance of "unenlightened" times.

This does not mean that Enlightenment thinkers entirely rejected religion. Rather, they sought to devise a rational religion, a faith that did not depend upon revelation. The result was Deism. According to the Deists, the orderliness of nature does, in fact, prove the existence of a deity, a rational mind that created the universe. This God is, however, no longer involved in the creation. He constructed nature in all of its intricacy and then left it to run like a vast machine. Miracles, revelation, and supernatural doctrines such as the incarnation and redemption are excluded on principle. According to this religion, human beings, armed with reason, are basically on their own.

The Enlightenment rejected Christianity but did affirm the existence of God, at least at first. There is, however, no real need of a God who is not involved in His creation. Eventually, the deity withered away. Enlightenment rationalism saw the whole universe as a closed natural system of cause and effect. Every phenomenon must be understood in terms of a cause *from within the system.*

Enlightenment thinkers at first related moral absolutes to their deity, going so far as to affirm the existence of an afterlife which rewarded good and punished evil. (In doing so, they rejected salvation by grace and instituted a new legalistic works-righteousness.) But soon people began to answer ethical questions in terms of the closed system, and a new approach to moral issues—utilitarianism—emerged. Utilitarians decided moral issues, not by appealing to transcendent absolutes, but by studying the effect of an action upon the system. Stealing is wrong, not because the Ten Commandments say so, but because stealing interferes with the economic functioning of society. Something is good if it makes the system run more smoothly. Something is evil if it interferes with the cogs of the vast machine. Practicality becomes the sole moral criterion. If it works, it must be good.

Utilitarianism is the view that justified slavery, exploitive child labor, and the starvation of the poor, all in the name of economic efficiency. Today this Enlightenment ethic is the view that favors abortion because it reduces the welfare rolls and sanctions euthanasia because it reduces hospital bills. Utilitarianism is a way of facing moral issues without God.

As Enlightenment science continued to gather momentum into the nineteenth century, the final tie to God dissolved. The Deists taught that while God is not, strictly speaking, necessary to everyday life, He *was* necessary to get everything started. Charles Darwin, however, argued that God was not even necessary to explain the creation. In describing "the origin of species" in terms of the closed natural system of cause and effect, Darwin removed the need for any kind of creator. Nature became completely self-contained. Science could now explain everything.

Eventually, thinkers discarded even Enlightenment classicism. The rationalism that had its roots in Plato and Aristotle assumed universal absolutes and nonmaterial truths. In the nineteenth century, however, the empirical supplanted the rational. According to nineteenth-century materialism, only what we can observe is real. The physical universe, as apprehended by our senses and as studied by the scientific method, is the *only* reality.

The philosophers known as the Logical Positivists went so far as to say that any statement that could not be verified empirically (such as theological, metaphysical, aesthetic, and moral statements) are meaningless. You cannot show me "God" or "justice"; therefore, they do not exist. Abstract philosophy is nothing more than a game of language. (It did not seem to matter to the Logical Positivists that their own criterion of meaning is also nonempirical and thus by their own standards must be meaningless.)

The heritage of the Enlightenment blossomed in diverse ways. Methodologies designed to dissect natural objects began to be applied to human beings. The "social sciences" were invented. Sociology purported to explain human institutions; psychology sought to explain the inner life of human beings, all in terms of a closed natural system accessible by empirical scientific methods.

Societies and economies were re-thought and re-engineered.

The American Constitution and free enterprise economics, like the natural sciences, had their origin in a Biblical worldview, though they dovetailed with Enlightenment theories. The social theories that excluded God went much further. Under the assumption that all problems could be solved by human planning, various schemes of socialism succeeded the noble ideals and brutal practices of the French Revolution. The most thoroughgoing attempt to remake society and human beings according to a rationalistic theory came through the imposition of Marx's dialectical materialism on a vast percentage of the world's population. Marxism eradicated private property, sought to liquidate religion, suppressed native cultures, and tried to abolish individualism in favor of a vast collective community.

The Enlightenment tradition tried to find ways of doing without the supernatural. Christianity was pushed into the background, put on the defensive. Many churches compromised, reinterpreting the faith according to Enlightenment dogmas. Liberal theology was invented. Nothing was excluded from the sovereignty of the human intellect.

VOICES OF DISSENT

Even as enlightened modernism marched from victory to victory, it provoked rebels. The Enlightenment sparked the reaction of romanticism. Materialism sparked the reaction of existentialism. In some ways these movements can be seen as phases of modernism. In another sense, they were anti-modern. Both romanticism and existentialism paved the way for today's postmodern worldview.[8]

Early nineteenth-century romanticism turned the rationalism of the Enlightenment upside down. Rather than seeing nature as a vast machine, the romantics saw nature as a living organism. Rather than believing with the Deists that God is far away and detached, the romantics believed that God is close at hand and intimately involved in the physical world. God is immanent in nature and in ourselves. Some went so far as to believe that God is identical to nature and to the self, rejecting the God of the Bible (who is both immanent and transcendent) in favor of a new pantheism. Whereas the Enlightenment assumed that reason is the most important human faculty, romanticism assumed that emotion is at the

essence of our humanness. The romantics exalted the individual
over impersonal, abstract systems. Self-fulfillment, not practicality,
was the basis for morality.

Whereas the Enlightenment followed the paradigms of the
physical sciences, seeking to apply them to all of life, romanticism,
as Nancy Pearcey has shown, followed the paradigms of biology.[9]
Nature was to be explained not merely in mechanistic terms, but
in terms of a "life force" which animates the entire universe as well
as the individual human being. By getting in touch with one's inner
feelings, by intensely experiencing all of life, and by opening oneself up to the splendors of the physical world, a person could
"become one with nature" and achieve unity with this life force
which animates all of existence. The life force was by no means the
personal God of the Bible, who is both in the world and beyond it.
The life force replaced Him and, like Deism, served as the basis for
a new secular religion.

Romantics criticized "civilization" as reflecting the artificial
abstractions of the human intellect. Children are born free, innocent, and one with nature. "Society" then corrupts them with the
bonds of civilization. Primitive tribes consist of "noble savages,"
who live close to nature and are thus uncorrupted by modern technology and materialism. The romantics glorified the past. They
sought not mere civilization, the achievements of human intellect,
but "culture," the natural soul of organic communities.

Romanticism cultivated subjectivity, personal experience,
irrationalism, and intense emotion. It encouraged introspection and
attention to the inner life. The romantics drew on Kant, who
argued that the external world owes its very shape and structure to
the organizing power of the human mind, which imposes order on
the chaotic data of the senses. Some romantics took this to imply
that the self, in effect, is the creator of the universe.

The self became not only the creator, but the lawgiver. Instead
of following external rules or even practical considerations, romanticism interiorized the moral life. The romantics did agonize over
their honor and their personal failures. But they ultimately understood morality in terms of the fulfillment of the self. Since the purpose of life is to "grow," like flowers and embryos, whatever
enriches the self must be good, and whatever diminishes the self
must be bad.

Such a view could inspire both heroic action and abysmal self-ishness. Byron gave his life on a quixotic mission to liberate Greece; he also defied "society's laws" by committing incest with his half-sister. Shelley deserted his family in an affair with Mary Godwin, who understood him better than his wife. After being abandoned, his wife committed suicide. This sort of romantic ethic manifests itself everywhere today—executives divorcing their spouses so they can have "trophy wives"; abortion advocates who argue that having a baby might interfere with a woman's self-fulfillment; euthanasia apologists who believe that those unable to pursue a self-directed life of "quality" are better off being killed.

Darwin's theory of evolution challenged romanticism just as it did Christianity. Darwin showed that nature was not the realm of harmony and goodness that the romantics idealized. Rather, nature is intrinsically violent. The "survival of the fittest," the raw struggle for survival in which the strong prey upon the weak, emerges as the fundamental law of nature, accounting for the very origins of species. In the latter half of the nineteenth century, romanticism faded before the hard-edged certainties of neo-Enlightenment materialism.

Materialism, though, is also hard to live with. The twentieth century saw a new worldview, one that accepted the bleak facts of materialism, while offering meaning for the individual. This worldview is existentialism.

According to existentialism, there is no inherent meaning or purpose in life. The blind automatic order of nature and the logical conclusions of rationalism may be orderly, but they are inhuman. As far as a human being is concerned, the mindless repetitions of natural laws are meaningless. The objective realm is absurd, void of any human significance.

Meaning is not to be discovered in the objective world; rather, meaning is a purely human phenomenon. While there is no ready-made meaning in life, individuals can create meaning for themselves. By their own free choices and deliberate actions, human beings can create their own order, a meaning for their life that they and they alone determine. This meaning, however, has no validity for anyone else. No one can provide a meaning for someone else. Everyone must determine his or her own meaning, which must

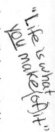

"Life is what you make of it"

remain private, personal, and unconnected to any sort of objective truth.

Existentialism provides the rationale for contemporary relativism. Since everyone creates his or her own meaning, every meaning is equally valid. Religion becomes a purely private affair, which cannot be "imposed" on anyone else. The content of one's meaning makes no difference, only the personal commitment—to give life meaning Sartre chose communism; Heidegger chose Nazism; Bultmann chose Christianity. Everyone inhabits his or her own private reality. "What's true for you may not be true for me."

Moral values, like other kinds of meaning, are created by the self. The best example of an existential ethic can be found in some of those who advocate abortion but call themselves "pro-*choice*." To them, it makes no difference what the woman decides, only that she makes an authentic choice whether or not to have the baby. Whatever she chooses is right—for her. "Pro-choice" advocates are not interested in *any* objective information that might have a bearing on the morality of abortion. Data about fetal development, facts about how abortions are performed, philosophical argumentation about the sanctity of life—all such objective evidence from the outside world is meaningless and can have no bearing on the woman's private choice.

Existentialism began in the nineteenth century, but by the middle of the twentieth century, it emerged as a major philosophical movement. Today existentialism is no longer merely the province of *avant garde* novelists or French intellectuals in cafés. Existentialism has entered the popular culture. It has become the philosophy of soap operas and television talk shows. Its tenets shape political discourse and are transforming the legal system. Existentialism is the philosophical basis for postmodernism.

THE END OF MODERNISM

In the early part of the twentieth century, an intellectual, literary, and artistic movement arose that went by the name of modernism. Although I have argued that the modern age began in the 1700s, both the achievements and the despair of the modern condition reached their peak in the twentieth century.

Modernism sought to create new forms of art for the new century. That these artists and intellectuals called themselves modernists did not mean they were enamored of the modern world. Many of them hated it. Although they despised romantic sentimentality, many modernists yearned for the past. Many were existentialists, determined to create their own meaning. A few, such as T. S. Eliot, even turned to Christianity. All of them sought to confront the twentieth century in an honest way and with artistic forms that could capture the modern condition. Some of them, though considered modernists, were ahead of their time and anticipated postmodernism.

Modernism, with its unstable mixture of positivism dampened by existentialism, dominated the intellectual and artistic worlds through the middle of the century. Then came something new—perhaps not exactly new, but a new application of ideas that had been latent for decades.

According to Charles Jencks, the end of modernism and the beginning of postmodernism took place at 3:32 P.M. on July 15, 1972. At that moment the Pruitt-Igoe housing development in St. Louis, a pinnacle of modernist architecture, was blown up. Though a prize-winning exemplar of high technology, modernistic aesthetics, and functional design, the project was so impersonal and depressing, so crime-ridden and impossible to patrol, that it was uninhabitable.[10]

The demolition of the Pruitt-Igoe development is a paradigm for postmodernism. The modern worldview constructs rationally designed systems in which human beings find it impossible to live. This paradigm applies not so much to housing projects as to philosophical systems and ways of life. Christians could not agree more. The new secular solution, however, is not only to blow modernism to smithereens but to explode *all* stable forms, including Christianity.

Instead of erecting some other structure on the rubble, secular postmodernism concentrates on the explosion. The effort to help poor people by giving them a temple of modernism to live in did prove futile. While it may have been appropriate to dynamite modernism, most postmodern theorists refuse to provide a more habitable alternative. The low-income inhabitants of the Pruitt-Igoe housing project no longer have to live in a sterile, inhuman structure. Under postmodern ways of thinking, now they can be homeless.

Most scholars associate the postmodern shift with the counterculture of the 1960s. Many young people began questioning the fruits of modern civilization—technology, social regimentation, rational planning. They sought instead a way of life organically related to nature and free of moral and rational restraints. The Vietnam War epitomized for them the evils of capitalism, technology, and the traditions of American democracy. They experimented with drugs as a way of creating an ecstatic, mystical consciousness—in stark contrast to the demands of modern rationalism. They cast off sexual prohibitions to realize total freedom and to pursue a life of untrammeled pleasure.

Many scholars see 1968 as the turning point.[11] In that year, student demonstrations shut down universities throughout the world. The campus protests against the Vietnam War had a significant impact in the United States, but they were even more successful in Europe. Student revolts in Paris and other university cities had a profound effect throughout the intellectual world. The universities became radicalized. A new breed of intellectuals came to power whose goal was to dismantle the modern world.

The youth culture of the 1960s can be seen as simply a revival of romanticism, an infantile regression made possible by the affluence and permissiveness of the society they were rebelling against. The nineteenth-century romantics could rhapsodize about nature, but nineteenth-century Americans struggled with nature in order to survive. By the 1960s, though, the hard times seemed over. Young people, supported by money that their parents had earned, could wear flowers in their hair, complain about their parents' materialism, and criticize technology, while themselves under the influence of high-tech chemicals. The 1960s subculture, however naive and incoherent it might seem today, had a profound effect. It set the fashions. Its values began to permeate the nation's entertainment industry and the electronic media. The sexual revolution in particular took hold in all classes of society.

The youth movements of the 1960s also took a political turn. The Civil Rights movement had its roots in Christian activism, growing out of the social ministry and moral appeals of the Black churches. The movement appealed to the traditional American values of equality and Constitutional rights. The young people who looked on did not necessarily draw motivation from the church or from constitutionalism, but the Civil Rights movement fueled their idealism and convinced them that the whole society must be changed. More liberation movements followed the crusade for racial liberation. Feminism blossomed. Homosexuals began to define themselves as an oppressed minority group.

Marxists soon co-opted the youth culture's political idealism, seeking to channel the desire for social change and questioning of the status quo into a revolutionary movement. The student revolts of 1968 made Marxism politically correct throughout American and European universities. Marxist scholarship bloomed and achieved a new academic respectability, making its mark in disciplines ranging from sociology to literary criticism.

Ironically, at the very time that Marxism came in vogue in the West, Soviet communism brutally oppressed its own intellectuals, artists, and authors who were trying to break out of the Marxist straitjacket. There can be no greater proof of the youth movement's narcissism and the Western intellectuals' moral blindness than their continual invocation of the glories of 1968. This year of "the student revolution" was also the year Soviet tanks rolled into Czechoslovakia. Marxism proved its true nature by stamping out an outbreak of freedom; however, Western intellectuals looked the other way. While their fellow students in Russia and China went to jail or died for questioning Marxism, students in the West wrapped themselves in red banners and quoted the words of Chairman Mao.

Thomas Oden sees modernism ending not with the fall of the Pruitt-Igoe housing project, but with the fall of the Berlin Wall. Today's university postmodernists still refuse to acknowledge the failure of political radicalism. Oden sees them as being really "hypermodernists," pushing the assumptions of modernism, with its skepticism and contempt for moral authority, to new extremes.[12] Be that as it may, the new ideology is taking hold throughout Western culture.

THE ANTI-ENLIGHTENMENT

Modernism is now being challenged by a new way of looking at the world that seems to be taking hold in every aspect of the culture.

This new worldview's adherents label it "postmodernism." (We should distinguish between the adjective *postmodern,* referring to a period of time, and *postmodernism,* referring to this distinct ideology. If the modern era is over, we are all postmodern, even though we reject the tenets of postmodern*ism*.)

David Harvey presents a postmodernist's case against the Enlightenment:

> The Enlightenment project . . . took it as axiomatic that there was only one possible answer to any question. From this it followed that the world could be controlled and rationally ordered if we could only picture and represent it rightly. But this presumed that there existed a single correct mode of representation which, if we could uncover it (and this was what scientific and mathematical endeavours were all about), would provide the means to Enlightenment ends.[13]

According to the postmodernists, the problem with the Enlightenment is not its uncritical dependence upon human reason alone, but its assumption that there is such a thing as objective truth. "Generally perceived as positivistic, technocentric, and rationalistic, universal *modernism* has been identified with the belief in linear progress, absolute truths, the rational planning of ideal social orders, and the standardization of knowledge and production." On the other hand, Harvey continues, "fragmentation, indeterminacy, and intense distrust of all universal or 'totalizing' discourses (to use the favoured phrase) are the hallmark of postmodern thought."[14]

Key — Modernists, according to Harvey, attempt to "totalize chaos."[15] Faced with the inherent meaninglessness of life, modernists impose an order upon it, which they then treat as being objective and universally binding. Postmodernists, on the other hand, live with and affirm the chaos, considering any order to be only provisional and varying from person to person.

Such a description clearly shows that the new ideology rests upon the philosophical assumptions of existentialism. But it has other progenitors as well. Nancy Pearcey has shown how developments within science itself have undermined confidence in objective order and in knowable absolutes. Non-Euclidean geometry has raised the possibility that mathematics may be only an arbitrary mental game instead of reflections of absolute laws of nature. Einstein's theory of relativity in physics, as popularly misunderstood, suggests to the masses that "everything is relative." More seriously, quantum physics defies all of our abilities to imagine what it describes, seemingly violating the basic canons of logic or common sense. When experiments prove that light is either a particle or a wave, depending on how it is observed, it seems as if the fundamental law of noncontradiction is violated, as if reality is not rational.[16]

When the postmodernists say, "There are no absolutes," this is no frivolous claim. The course of modern secular thought has led them to this conclusion. The next chapter will show the basis of this claim—the critique of absolutes and the alternative modes of thinking replacing classical rationalism.

It is true that the Enlightenment is over. Secular rationalism has run into dead ends. Christians would agree that without God, there is no way to account for objective meaning. In the wake of Adam's Fall, sinful human beings are plagued with meaninglessness and intellectual limits (Ecclesiastes 1). The attempts to idolize human reason and to ignore its limits before the mysteries of God will necessarily fail. As we shall see, Christianity can share in the postmodernist critique of the Enlightenment.

And yet postmodernism will array itself against Christianity as well. Like modernism, Christianity and most premodern systems of thought such as classical rationalism also believe in absolute truth. As a "universal or totalizing discourse," Christianity would thus fall into the same category as the Enlightenment. Postmodernists will tend to treat Christianity and much premodern thought as varieties of modernism! Both Christianity and modernism will be dismissed on the same grounds: They claim to be true.

Ihab Hassan contrasts the values of modernism with those of postmodernism by offering a set of antitheses:[17] Modernists believe in determinacy; postmodernists believe in indeterminacy. Whereas modernism emphasizes purpose and design, postmodernism emphasizes play and chance. Modernism establishes a hierarchy; postmodernism cultivates anarchy. Modernism values the type; postmodernism values the mutant. Modernism seeks the *logos*, the underlying meaning of the universe expressed in language.

Postmodernism, on the other hand, embraces silence, rejecting both meaning and the Word.

Modernist art, according to Hassan, focuses upon the object of art as a self-contained, finished work; postmodern art focuses upon the process, the performance, of art. In place of the modernist concern for "creation/ totalization/ synthesis," the postmodernists are more interested in "decreation/ deconstruction/ antithesis." Modernists value selection and boundaries; postmodernists value combination and interconnections. Modernists cultivate presence; postmodernists cultivate absence. Modernists are interested in depth; postmodernists are interested in surfaces. Modernism emphasizes form; postmodernism is antiform.

Postmodernism attempts to re-order thought and culture on a completely different basis, accepting reality as a social construction and avoiding "totalizing discourse" altogether. What kind of edifice can be built on such a foundation, or rather on the rejection of all foundations? What does this mean for the value of human life, for the arts, politics, and religion? Indeterminacy, anarchy, mutants, absence, surface, antiform—are such postmodernist values merely an obsession of an intellectual elite, or are they permeating the entire culture and even the church? The rest of this book will attempt to answer these questions.

POSTMODERNISM AND CIVILIZATION

One of the first scholars to use the term "postmodernism" was the great historian Sir Arnold Toynbee. In the 1940s, Toynbee engaged in a magisterial study of the rise and fall of world civilizations. Toynbee's insights into history and the dynamics of his own time are startlingly prophetic.[18]

Based on his study of twenty-one world civilizations—ranging from ancient Rome to imperial China, from Babylon to the Aztecs—Toynbee found that societies in disintegration suffer a kind of "schism of the soul." They are seldom simply overrun by some other civilization. Rather, they commit a kind of cultural suicide. Disintegrating societies, he says, have several characteristics. They fall into a sense of *abandon*, "a state of mind that accepts antinomianism—consciously or unconsciously, in theory or in practice—as a substitute for creativeness."[19] In other words, people stop believing in morality and yield to their impulses at the expense of their creativity. They also succumb to *truancy*, that is, escapism, seeking to avoid their problems by retreating into their own worlds of distraction and entertainment.[20]

There is a sense of *drift*, in which people yield to a meaningless determinism, as if their efforts do not matter and as if they have no control over their lives.[21] There is a sense of *guilt*, a self-loathing that comes from their moral abandon.[22] There is a *promiscuity*, which Toynbee means not so much in the sexual sense, but as the indiscriminate acceptance of anything and everything, an unfocused eclecticism and uncritical tolerance. Toynbee describes this promiscuity as "an act of self-surrender to the melting pot . . . in Religion and Literature and Language and Art as well as . . . Manners and Customs," the triumph of a mass mind.[23]

One does not have to agree with Toynbee's monumental reading of history to experience in his analyses of the last throes of long-dead civilizations an unsettling shock of recognition. But when he turns to his own time, to the end of World War II and the beginnings of the cold war, Toynbee predicts the advent of postmodernism, not only using the term but describing what it will mean. Patricia Waugh summarizes his prediction:

> For Toynbee, the postmodern age would be the fourth and final phase of Western history and one dominated by anxiety, irrationalism and helplessness. In such a world, consciousness is adrift, unable to anchor itself to any universal ground of justice, truth or reason on which the ideals of modernity had been founded in the past. Consciousness itself is thus "decentered": no longer agent of action in the world, but a function through which impersonal forces pass and intersect. Art becomes not so much an expression of human spirit, but another commodity. Like knowledge, therefore, it can no longer be critical but only functional. Moreover, we are in the postmodern condition and, implicated in a culture where all knowledge is produced through discourse, we can no longer seek transcendence. There is no position outside of culture from which to view culture. There is no Kantian "view from nowhere," no conceptual space not already implicated in that which it seeks to contest. There can only be disruption from within: micropolitics, language games, parodic skirmishes, irony, fragmentation.[24]

The following chapters explore these concepts in more detail and consider whether this "consciousness adrift" is liberating, as many contemporary theorists claim, or whether it signals, as Toynbee believed, the end of Western civilization. Or will the civilization rejuvenate itself, as Toynbee acknowledged sometimes happens, by means of a religious awakening?

CONSTRUCTING AND DECONSTRUCTING TRUTH

*I*n his book, *Reality Isn't What It Used to Be: Theatrical Politics, Ready-to-Wear Religion, Global Myths, Primitive Chic, and Other Wonders of the Postmodern World*, Walter Truett Anderson hails the dawning of a conceptual shift as profound as any in human history.

According to Anderson, we are presently in the midst of a transition from one way of thinking to another. He cites three processes shaping this transition: (1) The breakdown of belief. Today there is no universal consensus about what is true. We are, he says, in "a kind of unregulated marketplace of realities in which all manner of belief systems are offered for public consumption." (2) The birth of a global culture. Anderson says, "All belief-systems become aware of all other belief systems." As a result, it is difficult to accept any of them as absolutely true. (3) A new polarization. Conflicts over the nature of social truth tear at our society. We have "culture wars," particularly battles over the critical issues of education and moral instruction.[1]

Anderson distinguishes between "objectivists" (those who believe that truth is objective and can be known) and "constructivists" (those who believe that human beings make up their own realities).

> The constructivists—whose thinking runs close to my own . . .
> —say that we do not have a "God's eye" view of nonhuman reality, never had, never will have. They say we live in a sym-

bolic world, a social reality that many people construct together and yet experience as the objective "real world." And they also tell us the earth is not a *single* symbolic world, but rather a vast universe of "multiple realities," because different groups of people construct different stories, and because different languages embody different ways of experiencing life.[2]

Anderson argues that in the postmodern age, the constructivists will be victorious, with profound and liberating implications for all of life.

This postmodernist ideology is more than simple relativism. Whereas modern existentialism teaches that meaning is created by the *individual*, postmodern existentialism teaches that meaning is created by *a social group and its language*. According to this view, personal identity and the very contents of one's thoughts are all *social* constructions. The old existentialism stressed the alienated individual, dignified in loneliness and nonconformity; postmodern existentialism stresses social identity, group-think, and fashion sense. Postmodern existentialism goes back to Nietzsche to emphasize not only will, but power. Liberation comes from rebelling against existing power structures, including oppressive notions of "knowledge" and "truth."

ANTI-FOUNDATIONALISM

The great intellectual systems of the past (such as Platonism, Christianity, Marxism, science) have always had specific foundations (rational ideals; God; economics; empirical observation). Postmodernism, on the other hand, is anti-foundational. It seeks to destroy all such objective foundations and to replace them with nothing.

Patricia Waugh summarizes this anti-foundationalism:

Central to the "postmodern condition," therefore, is a recognition and account of the way in which the "grand narratives" of Western history and, in particular, enlightened modernity, have broken down.

2 Tim. 4:

As is customary among postmodernists, Waugh speaks of objective systems of thought as "narratives," that is, stories. Truth-claims are defined as fictions. This rhetorical sleight of hand is more than an example of assuming what one is trying to prove; it is an example of the postmodern dictum that all truth is only a construction of language. She goes on:

> Counter-Enlightenment, of course, is as old as Enlightenment itself, but whereas in the past (in Romantic thought, for example), the critique of reason was accompanied by an alternative foundationalism (of the Imagination), Postmodernism tends to claim an abandonment of all metanarratives which could legitimate foundations for truth. And more than this, it claims that we neither need them, nor are they any longer desirable.[3]

In the past, when one framework for knowledge was thought to be inadequate, it was replaced by another framework. The goal of postmodernism is to do without frameworks for knowledge altogether. In postmodernist jargon, "metanarratives" are stories about stories, "large-scale theoretical interpretations purportedly of universal application";[4] that is to say, worldviews. Postmodernism is a worldview that denies all worldviews.

Metanarratives are seen as "totalizing discourses," which are associated with oppression.[5] In the words of the neo-Marxist Terry Eagleton:

> Post-modernism signals the death of such "metanarratives" whose secretly terroristic function was to ground and legitimate the illusion of a "universal" human history. We are now in the process of wakening from the nightmare of modernity, with its manipulative reason and fetish of the totality, into the laid-back pluralism of the post-modern, that heterogeneous range of lifestyles and language games which has renounced the nostalgic urge to totalize and legitimate itself. . . . Science and philosophy must jettison their grandiose metaphysical claims and view themselves more modestly as just another set of narratives.[6]

The belief in a universal humanity, usually thought of as an ennobling vision of human equality and dignity, is described in conspiratorial language as "secretly terroristic." Modernity, which for all its faults has at least made everyday life a little easier, is a "nightmare," a primitive superstition holding on to its "fetish." Even science is dismissed as "just another set of narratives." The alternative is "laid-back pluralism," a cosmic California amusing itself with "language games" (of which this passage is an illuminating example).

Postmodernism dismisses "foundationalism," defined as "the idea that knowledge is the reflection of truth and that we can discover a stable foundation for it in God, History or Reason."[7] God was left out of the picture as early as the Enlightenment, an omission no doubt responsible for the vulnerability of modernism to these kinds of attacks. Now reason is also rejected.

Postmodernists also seek to dissolve history. They no longer see it as a record of objective facts, but as "a series of metaphors which cannot be detached from the institutionally produced languages which we bring to bear on it." As a result, Patricia Waugh says, we can make no distinction between "truth" and "fiction." "History is a network of agonistic language games where the criterion for success is performance not truth."[8]

Since there is no objective truth, history may be rewritten according to the needs of a particular group. If history is nothing more than "a network of agonistic [i.e., fighting, contending] language games," then any alternative "language game" that advances a particular agenda, that meets "success" in countering institutional power, can pass as legitimate history. "Performance, not truth" is the only criterion. Scholarship becomes rhetorical manipulation. Truth does not have to get in the way.

This rejection of historical objectivity in favor of advocacy scholarship is currently in vogue throughout the intellectual establishment. "Revisionist scholars" villainize Christopher Columbus and other American heroes, and in doing so argue that the American heritage is not freedom but oppression. They decry the bias of "Euro-centric" scholarship and curricula, only to substitute aggressively "Afro-centric" scholarship and curricula. Histories are rewritten and whole disciplines are revised in accordance with feminist or gay agendas.

Postmodernist tenets may seem academic and somewhat arcane, but they are being taught throughout contemporary universities. The new generation of college graduates has been immersed in this kind of thinking. Our new teachers, journalists, lawyers, judges, and political leaders have been indoctrinated. Many of them are coming out convinced that there is no objective meaning and that truth is nothing more than an act of power.

Those who do not believe in truth are more likely, I believe, to lie. Those who believe that moral values are nothing more than the imposition of power may be more likely to use power to suppress their opposition, whether in enforcing politically correct postures in academia or, when they have political power, in acts of tyranny.

THE DECONSTRUCTION OF LANGUAGE

Postmodernists base this new relativism and the view that all meaning is socially constructed on a particular view of language. This set of theories, along with the analytical method that they make possible, can be referred to as "deconstruction."[9] Whereas intellectual movements of the past have been worked out in the fields of metaphysics or science, postmodernism as a coherent intellectual discipline has developed out of literary criticism (of all things). The same analysis that purports to show that works of literature can have no objective meaning can apply to everything else, including science, reason, and theology.

Postmodernist theories begin with the assumption that language cannot render truths about the world in an objective way. Language, by its very nature, shapes what we think. Since language is a cultural creation, meaning is ultimately (again) a social construction.

Contemporary scholars draw on the work of structural linguists, who have always noted a distinction between the "signifier" (the word) and the "signified" (the meaning). The connection between the two is arbitrary—in English we use the sound *dog* to refer to the animal that sheds on our carpet; in Spanish the sound *perro* refers to the same animal. There is no relationship between those particular sounds and the actual animal. This is why there can be different languages, each of which employs arbitrary symbols in a self-contained system.

Postmodernist linguists go further: The very meaning of

words is part of the self-contained system. When you look up the meaning of a word in a dictionary, you find more words. Words ultimately refer to other words. Much of our language consists of abstractions that refer to nothing observable, but to sheerly mental (and thus linguistic) concepts. (This preceding sentence, for example, depends for its meaning upon abstractions such as "much," "consists," "abstractions," "refer," and "concepts," and grammatical function words such as *of, that, to.*)

To be sure, some words point to ordinary objects, but ordinary objects too can be "signs," communicating cultural meanings just as surely as words do. What is the difference between a "dog" and a "wolf"? A dog is domesticated, at home in our culture; a wolf is wild. The connotations of "dog" are those of a childhood pet and "man's best friend." The connotations of "wolf" are those of childhood fears, the devouring monster of "Little Red Riding Hood" and the complex combination of fascination and terror that we have for the natural world outside human control.

Contemporary critics study and interpret the meaning of clothing, buildings, fashions, and other "nonverbal communication" in the same way that classical critics analyzed the meaning of literary texts. The "dress-for-success" books show how wearing a tie communicates social status for men. Office furniture can communicate authority (the executive protected behind a massive bunkerlike desk with the underling cringing before him in a naked folding chair); or office furniture can communicate informal collegiality (everyone sitting on sofas around a circle). Automobiles communicate the driver's personality and make a "social statement." A Cadillac signifies middle-class wealth; a BMW, yuppie sophistication; a pickup, down-home rural values; a Corvette, a taste for adventure; a station wagon, family values. Everyday social artifacts, from the brands we buy to the entertainment we enjoy, are means of communication, expression, and persuasion.

Every cultural artifact is thus construed as a "text." That is, every human creation is analogous to language. To use a postmodernist slogan, "The world is a text." Governments, worldviews, technologies, histories, scientific theories, social customs, and religions are all essentially linguistic constructs.

Postmodernist theorists speak of "intertextuality," that cultural life and intellectual life are nothing more than texts interacting with other texts, producing more texts. As human beings, we are unable to step outside the boundaries of our language; we cannot escape its limits or its demands. Since language is bound up with our culture, it is largely beyond our control, and we cannot truly even think for ourselves. To a large degree, our language thinks for us.[10] There is no "transcendental *logos*," no objective meaning, no realm of absolute truth that exists beyond the bounds of our human language. To use another postmodernist slogan, we are incarcerated in a "prison house of language."

Given that language is a prison, the deconstructionists seek to undermine the walls so that we can break out. Deconstructive linguists argue that language is intrinsically unstable. Meaning is slippery and changeable; the very meaning-system of our language is clumsy and full of gaps and self-contradictions.

Linguistic meaning, they argue, rests on oppositions and exclusions. "Man" is defined as the opposite of "woman." "Freedom" excludes "slavery." Yet, because a word is defined in terms of what it excludes, each word carries with it a "trace" of its opposite. Every time we use the word *man*, we are excluding women. "Freedom" depends for its meaning on the concept of slavery—a totally free society would presumably have no word for the concept. Freedom would be taken for granted. To say, "Americans are free," calls to mind (to the deconstructionists) the ways that they are also enslaved.

Deconstructionists agree that meaning is a *social construct*. Societies construct meaning through language. Deconstructionists further assume that societies are inherently oppressive. These thinkers draw on Nietzsche, who contends that human life and culture are expressions of an innate will to power. They also draw on Marx, who reduces culture to class conflict and economic exploitation. And they invoke Freud, who interprets culture in terms of sexual repression. This assumption has non-Freudian variations such as feminist theory, which sees culture in terms of the conflict between genders and the oppression of women, and "Queer theory," which sees culture in terms of the suppression of homosexuals.

These theories are all different (and there is wide variation even among the practitioners of deconstruction), but they have in common the assumption that the true significance of culture lies beneath the surface, that institutions are really "masks" for a sinister, though perhaps unconscious, conspiracy. None of these approaches, for example, accept or reject religion on its own terms. They interpret religion as a coverup for something else. Freud sees religion as a system for suppressing sexuality, and feminists see it as a means of subordinating women. Religion, to Marx, is the opiate of the people, a ploy by the rich to keep the poor focused on Heaven so that they will obediently allow themselves to be exploited on earth. Nietzsche turns Marx upside down. Christianity is not a means of social control by the rich, but a "revolt of the slaves," a conspiracy of the poor and weak, who manipulate the rich and strong by making them feel guilty and by forcing upon them an ethic of love and compassion that interferes with the survival of the fittest.

Working from these mutually incompatible assumptions, the deconstructionists develop "a hermeneutics of suspicion." They approach a text not to find out what it objectively means, but to unmask what it is hiding.[11] Assuming that language is the arena of all power, deconstructionists seek liberation from this power by disrupting the authority of language.[12]

Deconstructionists cultivate what they call "subversive readings." Language does not *reveal* meaning (which would imply that there is an objective, transcendent realm of truth); rather, language *constructs* meaning. Although artificial linguistic constructions are designed to convey the illusion of truth, they are actually a cover for the power relationships that constitute the culture. Deconstructive critics scrutinize this process of meaning-building, uncover the linguistic contradictions, and expose the power-relationships that underlie the text. The meaning-making process is taken apart. The text is thereby "*de*constructed."

Deconstruction, while sometimes limiting itself to finding linguistic or literary contradictions, lends itself well to radical politics. The hermeneutics of suspicion sees every text as a political creation, usually designed to function as propaganda for the status quo. This is especially true of the texts that have the highest status, the "great works of literature," the "classics" that are promoted in school and are part of the "canon" of the civilization. These texts are "privileged" because they codify and justify the racism, sexism, homophobia, imperialism, economic oppression, sexual repression (take your pick) that is the hidden superstructure of the culture.

Consider, for example, the Declaration of Independence. "We hold these truths to be self-evident, that all men are created equal; that they are endowed by their Creator with certain unalienable rights; that among these are life, liberty, and the pursuit of happiness."[13] It could be deconstructed along these lines: Although the text speaks of equality, its language excludes women ("all *men* are created equal"). Although it speaks of liberty, its author, Thomas Jefferson, owned slaves. The surface meaning of equality and freedom is completely contradicted by the subtext, which denies equality and freedom to women and minorities. The passage enshrines the rights of the wealthy white males who signed the document, grounding their privileged status in God Himself. The Declaration of Independence can thus be deconstructed into just another power play, implying the opposite of its surface meaning.

A traditional reading of the Declaration of Independence might also note the discrepancy between the democratic ideals and the actual practice of eighteenth-century colonial America. Nevertheless, the reader would see the principle of God-given rights as objectively true. People do have objective and transcendent rights, having their origins in God Himself. That people were not universally given these rights or that the people who described them did not live up to their own ideals does not prove that the rights do not exist. If the moral absolutes described in the Declaration of Independence are objectively valid, society should be reformed to bring itself closer in line with these moral absolutes.

The ideals of the Declaration of Independence did in fact eventually lead to the abolition of slavery, to women's suffrage, and to ever-expanding democratic liberties. It is hard to see how the skepticism of deconstruction could have a similar impact, since there could be no absolute values to strive for, and any alternative values could be similarly deconstructed.

Literary texts are subject to the same inversions. Shakespeare's *King Lear*, about a father's mistreatment at the hands of his daughters, can be deconstructed as sexist patriarchal propaganda. The text gives hints that the reason the daughters turn against their father is that he first mistreated them. Shakespeare presents the daughters as villains, but in doing so, he inadvertently reveals them as feminist rebels against an oppressive patriarchal family structure.

Deconstructionists even analyze the metaphors inherent in scientific language. To speak of "natural *laws*" is to use a political metaphor; scientists who formulate "laws" are attempting to impose human political power on the natural order. Even technical theories, such as the "master molecule theory of DNA functioning," contain a gender bias ("master" is a male term). When scientists speak of "unveiling the mystery of the ocean" or "penetrating the secrets of nature," they are using sexual metaphors—undressing and raping the natural order, which is always conceived in feminine terms. The so-called scientific objectivity and all of Western science's technological achievements are "texts" that mask the male desire to subjugate, exploit, and sexually abuse "Mother Nature."

Deconstructionists speak of "interrogating the text" to uncover its hidden political or sexual agenda. The phrase is exquisitely accurate, calling to mind the way the KGB would interrogate writers to ferret out their secret political sins. Marx assumed that art existed to justify the existing political order; therefore, the old capitalist art must be overturned, and the new art must justify the new socialist order. Under communism artists who represented the old order, who refused to follow the canons of socialist realism, or who simply tried to create works of meaning and beauty were censored or sent to the Gulag. Under deconstruction, the "dead, white, European males" who have dominated the "canon" of Western civilization are similarly discredited and exiled.

DOING WITHOUT TRUTH

For the deconstructionists, *all* truth claims are suspect and are treated as a coverup for power plays. Reason, objective truth, science, and all "Western claims to serenely self-aware rationality" are challenged.[14] "Not only is *truth* abandoned," says Patricia Waugh, "but also the desire to retain *truth-effect*."[15]

Deconstructionism represents a new kind of relativism, one that is intellectually sophisticated, theoretically grounded, and methodologically rigorous. As it corrodes the very concept of absolute truth, deconstructionism provides the intellectual grounding for the popular relativism running rampant in postmodern society.

Today's universities, while ostensibly devoted to cultivating truth, now argue that truth does not exist. This does not mean that the universities are closing their doors. Rather, the universities are redefining what scholarship is all about.

Knowledge is no longer seen as absolute truth; rather, knowledge is seen in terms of rearranging information into new paradigms.[16] Human beings *construct* models to account for their experiences. These models—whether worldviews or scientific theories—are "texts," constantly being revised. These paradigms are useful fictions, a matter of "telling stories." "But the stories are now indistinguishable from what was once assumed to be knowledge: scientific 'truth,' ethics, law, history."[17]

Contemporary scholars seek to dismantle the paradigms of the past and "to bring the marginal into the center" (rewriting history in favor of those who have been excluded from power—women, homosexuals, blacks, Native Americans, and other victims of oppression).[18] Scholars attack received ideas with withering skepticism, while constructing new models as alternatives. Those who celebrate the achievements of Western civilization are accused of a narrow-minded "Euro-centrism"; this view is challenged by "Afro-centrism," which exalts Africa as the pinnacle of civilization. Male-dominant thought is replaced by feminist models. "Patriarchal religions" such as Judaism and Christianity are challenged and replaced with matriarchal religions; the influence of the Bible is countered by the influence of "goddess-worship." Homosexuality must no longer be considered a psychological problem; rather, homophobia is.

These new models tend to be adopted without the demands for rigorous evidence required by traditional scholarship. If Euro-centrism is a fault, one would think Afro-centrism would be similarly narrow-minded. If patriarchy is wrong, why would matriarchy be any better? But these quibbles miss the point of post-modernist scholarship. Truth is not the issue. The issue is power. The new models "empower" groups formerly excluded. Scholarly debate proceeds not so much by rational argument or the amassing of objective evidence, but by rhetoric (which scheme advances the most progressive ideals?) and by the assertion of power (which scheme advances my particular interest group, or more to the point, which is most likely to win me a research grant, career advancement, and tenure?).

As one postmodernist researcher admits, the goal of scholarship is:

> "no longer truth but performativity"—no longer what kind of research will lead to the discovery of verifiable facts, but what kind of research will work best, where "working best" means producing more research along the same lines. . . . The university or institution of learning cannot in these circumstances be concerned with transmitting knowledge in itself, but must be tied ever more narrowly to the principle of performativity—so that the question asked by teacher, student, and government must now no longer be "Is it true?" but "What use is it?" and "How much is it worth?"[19]

Whereas classical scholarship sought the true, the beautiful, and the good, the postmodernist academy seeks "what works." The traditional academic world operated by reason, study, and research; postmodernist academia is governed by ideological agendas, political correctness, and power struggles.

It is not clear whether the intellectual establishment's abandoning of truth has influenced the culture (by churning out the teachers, journalists, and other opinion-makers) or whether the intellectual establishment is simply rationalizing the values of the culture. At any rate, the arcane academic debates mirror the loss of truth and the rejection of absolutes characterizing postmodern culture.

Abstract ideas are not the only casualty. When the objective realm is swallowed up by subjectivity, moral principles evaporate. Other people—even spouses and children—are valued only for what they can contribute to my pleasure. Even external objects are sucked into the vortex of subjectivity. The old materialism sought to accumulate valuable objects; the new materialism is interested not so much with objects in themselves as with the status they bring and the experiences they represent. "From rock music to tourism to television and even education," points out Steven Connor, "advertising imperatives and consumer demand are no longer for goods, but for experiences."[20]

In this new intellectual climate, politicians make earnest promises, and then once they are elected, with astonishing speed and seemingly no sense of contradiction, they break them. Politicians, of course, have always broken their promises, but never with such shamelessness. Judges exercise ingenious "interpretive strategies" to throw out centuries of civilized law and to construct brand new legal principles reflecting current fashions. Journalists, taught that objectivity is impossible, write biased news stories and advance their own ideological agendas. Teachers, convinced that there are no objective truths to learn, teach "processes" instead, offering "experiences" instead of knowledge and encouraging their students to question existing values and to create their own.

Many people find this loss of truth liberating. If we construct our own reality, then there are no limits to our freedom. In the words of a writer paraphrasing the punk rock band Johnny Rotten and the Sex Pistols, "If nothing [is] true, everything [is] possible."[21]

How does one live without metanarratives? David Harvey cites four possibilities: (1) Accept the meaninglessness. Embrace the total openness of existence and live without truth. In the words of the Czech writer Milan Kundera, one can embrace the "unbearable lightness of being."[22] (2) Deny complexity. Take refuge in simplistic slogans and depthless images. This is the option taken by Andy Warhol and by those who surrender themselves to fashions and superficiality, playing their roles and having a good time. (3) Settle for limited action. Since nothing is universal, concentrate on your own little world. Find your own group identity. If you cannot change the world, change your neighborhood. (4) Construct your own language and thus command it. Knowing that all metanarratives are mere constructions, play the game yourself. Employ your own "hyper-rhetoric" as a way to assert your own power. This is the most dangerous, says Harvey, the way of schizophrenia and terrorism.[23]

DOUBTING THE INSTRUMENT

It is odd that a particular theory should be so influential when it is so vulnerable. Those who argue that "there is no truth" are putting forward that statement as being true. Such lines of thought are intrinsically contradictory.

Postmodernist theorists admit this paradox. Steven Connor notes the irony that there is now a consensus that consensus is impossible, that we are having authoritative announcements of the disappearance of authority, that scholars are writing comprehensive narratives on how comprehensive narratives are unthinkable.[24] One postmodernist philosopher says that the only role of the philosopher now is to "decry the notion of having a view while avoiding having a view about having views."[25]

C. S. Lewis has pointed out the fallacy of any theory that rejects the connection between thought and truth. "All possible knowledge . . . depends on the validity of reasoning."

> No account of the universe can be true unless that account leaves it possible for our thinking to be a real insight. A theory which explained everything else in the whole universe but which made it impossible to believe that our thinking was valid would be utterly out of court. For that theory would itself have been reached by thinking, and if thinking is not valid that theory would, of course, itself be demolished. It would have destroyed its own credentials. It would be an argument which proved that no argument was sound—a proof that there are no such things as proofs—which is nonsense.[26]

Lewis was writing in the 1940s, but his description of thought that "destroys its own credentials" anticipates deconstruction. Lewis believes such arguments are self-refuting, but deconstructionists are by no means deterred by such contradictions. After all, they claim that contradictions are inherent in all assertions of truth and in language itself. Deconstructionists revel in contradiction.

Some scholars, worrying about their own pretensions to objectivity and authority, are publishing new kinds of treatises. Since deconstructionists believe that the clarity of language is an illusion, their own writing tends to be dense, jargon-laden, and obscure, "demanding interpretation" on the part of the reader. Others are experimenting with new kinds of academic writing that are fragmented, impressionistic, and void of logical connections. This "open" style of academic writing is designed to be "democratically inclusive discourse," forcing readers to interpret what is being said and thus to take an active role in the creation of meaning.[27] One scholar, for example, intersperses his heavy-duty and jargon-ridden discussion of "the politics of style" with reproductions of advertisements and illustrations of Mickey Mouse. His purpose, he says, is "to induce in the reader that distracted, drifting state of mind we associate with watching television."[28]

Thus the life of the mind has a new model—not Socrates searching for truth through dialogues in the marketplace, not Augustine contemplating his own life in light of Scripture, not Newton scrutinizing nature with mathematical rigor, not the scientist working in the lab or the historian sifting through archival evidence. The new model for intellectual achievement is a dazed couch potato watching TV.[29]

Perhaps an even better model is the virtual reality helmet. The much-heralded union of computers, television, and video games will enable us to put on a helmet that will create the illusion that we are in the middle of a computer-generated world. When this technology is perfected, we will be able to take part in multi-sensory fantasies, as if we were the main character in a science fiction movie. Some people are even looking forward to virtual reality body condoms which will offer pre-programmed sexual fantasies.[30]

According to the postmodernists, all reality is virtual reality. We are all wearing helmets that project our own separate little worlds. We can experience these worlds and lose ourselves in them, but they are not real, nor is one person's world exactly the same as someone else's. We are not creating our own reality, however. Rather, we accept a reality made by someone else. Just as the corporations that manufacture the virtual reality technology program the fantasy, the so-called objective world that we experience is actually programmed by large, impersonal social institutions. Despite our heroics in fantasy land, zapping space aliens and freeing the holographic princess, we are only playing a game. We are actually passive and at the mercy of our programmers.

No matter what the intellectual elite says, truth, of course, exists. Postmodernist theorists cite new scientific concepts—such as Heisenberg's Uncertainty Principle, the theory of relativity, the New Physics, and chaos theory—to bolster their relativism. Nevertheless, real scientists are not relativists. If there are no metanarratives, why are the New Physicists working on a unified field theory (the attempt to explain gravity, electricity, and the other natural forces in terms of one grand design)? If there can be no objective data from the external world, why do New Physicists want to build expensive particle accelerators?[31] While much of the university collapses into skepticism, scientists and engineers continue making discovery after discovery.

Yet if postmodernism is a reaction against the Enlightenment and its cultivation of objective truth, one of the casualties may be science itself. As C. S. Lewis warns:

> Men became scientific because they expected Law in Nature, and they expected Law in Nature because they believed in a Legislator. In most modern scientists this belief has died: it will be interesting to see how long their confidence in uniformity survives it. Two significant developments have already appeared—the hypothesis of a lawless sub-nature, and the surrender of the claim that science is true. We may be living nearer than we suppose to the end of the Scientific Age.[32]

The dizzying achievements of science and technology were products of the modern age and may not survive its passing.

Similarly, moral judgments keep asserting themselves, no matter how often postmodernists attempt to evade them. The very claim that certain power structures are oppressive, repeated over and over in postmodernist scholarship, implies a moral principle, that it is not good to oppress people. As C. S. Lewis observes, "Whenever you find a man who says he does not believe in a real Right and Wrong, you will find the same man going back on this a moment later. He may break his promise to you, but if you try breaking one to him, he will be complaining, 'It's not fair.'"[33] Postmodernists, more than most people, complain about how various power structures are unfair, and they are always demanding sensitivity, tolerance, and justice. Do they not realize that they are appealing to transcendent, authoritative moral absolutes? Do they mean what they say, holding honestly to the implications of their own theory, or is it a mask for some other agenda? In other words, can we deconstruct deconstructionism?

DECONSTRUCTION AND CHRISTIANITY

Thus far, I have been criticizing deconstructionism. Now, in an example of a postmodern paradox, I would like to defend it (to a certain extent).

Many Christian scholars argue that the collapse of the modern and the advent of the postmodern age will bode well for a return to orthodox Christianity. The intellectual culture is admitting that it has no foundation for truth; this may be a genuine opportunity for Christians who do have a foundation for truth. The new intellectual climate disables the conventional attacks against Christianity and offers new possibilities for a Christian apologetic.

Rejecting the currently fashionable philosophical assumptions of Marx, Freud, and Nietzsche, Christians can formulate a "hermeneutics of suspicion" of their own. Christians believe that there is something lurking beneath human consciousness that is even more all-determining and more sinister than money, sex, and power. It is called sin. Christians believe that fallen human beings are motivated and disabled by a primal rebellion against God.

Christians can agree that people do construct meanings for themselves—philosophies, religions, ideologies, and rationalizations—all in a vain attempt to evade the truth of God. Constructing one's own meanings and one's own gods rather than acknowledging the one living God is called idolatry. "You shall not *make for yourself* an idol in the form of anything in heaven above or on the earth beneath or in the waters below" (Exodus 20:4). Idolatry is rejection of truth and an attempt to replace God. "They exchanged the truth of God for a lie, and worshiped and served created things rather than the Creator" (Romans 1:25; see also Isaiah 44:9-19).

Idols must be cast down. This is true not only of graven images but of intellectual constructions. As Paul says, "We demolish arguments and every pretension that sets itself up against the knowledge of God" (2 Corinthians 10:5). This calls for a sort of deconstruction.

The modern age has subjected Christianity to withering critiques, all in the name of Enlightened rationalism and scientific objectivity. In the postmodern intellectual climate, many of these objections have lost their force. Postmodern analysis uncovers the assumptions and worldviews that lie behind even ostensibly objective statements. Christians can play this game too.

For example, is Darwin's theory of evolution a scientific fact, or is it a construction? Darwin's theory can be deconstructed by putting it in the context of his time and by paying close attention to his figures of speech. His theory of evolution argues that progress comes from free competition and the survival of the fittest. Is this biology, or is it a description of nineteenth-century *laissez faire* capitalism? Is this objective science, or is it also an assertion of power—an attempt to rationalize British imperialism, the rich oppressing the poor, and other predatory social behavior by turning it into a law of nature? Thus contemporary postmodernists might deconstruct Darwin (although I am not aware of their doing so). Christians may well agree with this line of attack.

Christians would go deeper, though, focusing upon Darwin's theological and moral evasions. Darwin's theory of evolution is another of the human attempts to evade God. Darwin is seeking to account for the creation without a Creator. In doing so, he inverts the Biblical morality of love and kindness with a counter-ethic of selfishness and violence. It all comes down to sin.

Francis Schaeffer's "worldview criticism"—his practice of uncovering the worldviews implicit in culture, philosophy, and the arts—is a very postmodern approach. The attention to worldviews, popularized by Schaeffer and appropriated by other Christian scholars, is similar to the postmodernists' attention to the succession of "metanarratives" and "paradigms." Schaeffer's way of showing how secular statements of truth actually mask complex philosophical and religious assumptions is eminently postmodern. So is his evangelistic method of probing for the contradictions in the unbeliever's life and beliefs, "taking the roof off," bringing the sinner to the edge of despair, but broken and open to the grace of God. Schaeffer did not deconstruct texts; he deconstructed sinners.[34] Schaeffer is by no means a postmoder*nist*, but he is something of a postmodern theologian.

HUMAN LANGUAGE AND GOD'S LANGUAGE

Christians can agree with postmodern theorists that meaning is made up of language. But whereas the secular theorists assume that language is only a human phenomenon, Christians go much, much further.

> In the beginning was the Word, and the Word was with God, and the Word was God. He was with God in the beginning. Through him all things were made; without him nothing was made that has been made. In him was life, and that life was the light of men. The light shines in the darkness, but the darkness has not understood it. . . . The Word became flesh and made his dwelling among us. We have seen his glory, the glory of the One and Only, who came from the Father, full of grace and truth. (John 1:1-5, 14)

Language—*God's* language—existed before human beings and before the physical universe. Language is indeed intrinsic to thought and to personality itself. God's Word is an intrinsic part of His unfathomable being.

Furthermore, God's language made the world. The universe was created, according to Genesis, by a series of speech-acts. ("God *said*, 'Let there be light,' and there was light," and so on [Genesis 1:3].) The Word of God brings into existence whatever He declares. "By the word of the LORD were the heavens made. . . . For he spoke, and it came to be" (Psalm 33:6, 9). Before God spoke, "the earth was formless and empty" (Genesis 1:2); God's Word gave form and fullness to existence. The order of the universe, the reality of scientific laws, the languagelike codes of DNA, and the mathematical consistency of physics all have their origin in the Word of God.

Like God, human beings have language. God is personal, capable of thought and of relationships, which are mediated through language. Adam and Eve could speak because they were created in God's image. The source of their personality, including their capacity for language, was the personality and language of God. Genesis, however, makes clear that there is a difference between God's language and human language, even before the Fall.

> Now the LORD God had formed out of the ground all the beasts of the field and all the birds of the air. He brought them to the man to see what he would name them; and whatever the

man called each living creature, that was its name. So the man
gave names to all the livestock, the birds of the air and all the
beasts of the field. (Genesis 2:19-20)

Significantly, God gave human beings a certain autonomy of language. Adam was allowed to make up his own words for what God
had made. "Whatever the man called each living creature, that was
its name."

This distinction between God's almighty words and human
words, which are transient and arbitrary, means that human language is not sacred as such. It is likely to be changeable, limited,
and somewhat clumsy. Just as there must be a vast difference
between the infinite God and the limited though sinless creature,
there is an innate gap between human language and God's language. This gap and the limits of human language became even
more profound and complicated with the Fall.

The devil used words to seduce Adam and Eve into sin. He
invented lies, severing language from truth. The devil, or serpent,
cast doubt on God's Word ("Did God really say, 'You must not eat
from any tree in the garden'?" [Genesis 3:1]). Eve sinned; then she
talked Adam into sinning. They then used language to rationalize
what they did and to berate each other. They hid from God's voice
("Then the man and his wife *heard the sound* of the LORD God
. . . and they hid" [Genesis 3:8]).

The sinfulness of human language built through history until
God executed a special judgment against language itself. "Now the
whole world had one language and a common speech" (Genesis
11:1). The unity of the human race and the ability of everyone to
understand each other seem a utopian ideal, but these noble-sounding goals forget the reality of human sin. Human unity meant that
the potential for tyranny, idolatry, and every kind of evil was only
magnified. As these unified people began to build themselves a great
city with a tower that reached the heavens, God intervened.

If as one people speaking the same language they have begun
to do this, then nothing they plan to do will be impossible for
them. Come, let us go down and confuse their language so they
will not understand each other. (Genesis 11:6-7)

After Babel, human language is confused. We can no longer fully understand each other. Although our language presumes to erect structures that reach the heavens, in reality we are using our words to rebel against God's Word.

God's Word creates and condemns, but it also redeems. God *called* to Adam and Eve, and gave His Word as a promise to all of the patriarchs. God reveals Himself in human language in the words of the prophets and in the inspired text of the Bible. God's Word is not only far above human language, but it is of a different order completely. God's Word is Jesus Christ, the Second Person of the Trinity. God's language is not merely meaningful sounds or marks on a page, but God's mind, His self, His only begotten Son who became incarnate in the world that He Himself had spoken into existence: "The Word became flesh and made his dwelling among us" (John 1:14). The Incarnate Word died on the cross to atone for all of human sin. Pentecost undid the curse of Babel when the gift of the Holy Spirit enabled the apostles to preach in a way intelligible to speakers of many languages (Acts 2:1-12).

God continues to work in a powerful way by means of His Word. Whenever we read the Bible, whenever a pastor preaches a sermon on a text of Scripture, whenever we explain the gospel to someone, the Holy Spirit is at work. "For the word of God is living and active. Sharper than any double-edged sword, it penetrates even to dividing soul and spirit, joints and marrow; it judges the thoughts and attitudes of the heart" (Hebrews 4:12). Just as God's Word called the universe into existence from nothingness, so God's Word can create faith in the formless void of a sinner's heart. "Faith comes from hearing the message, and the message is heard through the word of Christ" (Romans 10:17).

Postmodern theorists are right when they focus upon the centrality of language. For them, however, language is a prison house, a cultural creation. They say that there is no transcendent *logos*, no meaning outside of language. They assume that there is no God. For those who do believe in God and in the transcendent *logos* who is Jesus Christ, the case is more complicated.

Yes, human language has gaps, limits, and slippage. Our language is clumsy; using words to express what we mean is sometimes like trying to thread a needle while wearing gloves. But human language is a sign, a trace, of a divine language. Language may get in the way sometimes, but it is also revelatory. Meaning is not only subjective; the external world is itself grounded in the Word of God, which established its form and gave it an objective meaning. When we study science, we are not merely making up mental models, but we are, in a sense, reading the divine language inscribed into the universe. Language is not merely a prison house; God's language can break in from the outside and give us freedom.

THE LIMITS OF REASON

Christian theologians have always stressed the limitations of human reason. Augustine, Aquinas, Luther, Calvin—all agree that our intellects are fallen. This does not mean that Christians reject reason altogether. Reason is valid in its sphere. Aquinas even believed that reason can prove the existence of God; he stressed, however, that reason can tell us nothing about what God is like or what He has done for our salvation. To know that God is a Trinity, that He was incarnate in Christ, that He loves us, we must rely on revelation. Luther and Calvin questioned whether reason could lead us to God at all. The only things we can know about God or other spiritual realities are what He chooses to tell us. We are utterly dependent upon God's Word.

The postmodernists are right to question the arrogance of the Enlightenment, the assumption that human reason can answer every question and solve every problem. They are wrong, though, to deny reason altogether. They are right to question the certainty of modern truths; they are wrong to reject the very concept of truth in favor of intellectual relativism.

Without a belief in God, however, it would be difficult to avoid the postmodernist conclusions. If there is no transcendental *logos*, then there can be no absolutes, no meaning apart from human culture, no way out of the prison house of language. Such postmodern theories may represent the ultimate development of secular thought—skepticism turning upon itself, human autonomy discovering its own impotence. Postmodernism may represent the dead-end—the implosion, the deconstruction—of human attempts to do without God.

Truth exists, though it often eludes us, and we may fail to grasp it perfectly. Christians have always known this. What God reveals in His Word is absolutely true. These truths can be reasoned upon, fit together with other truths, and applied. Moreover, the revelation that God created the universe gives us a basis for believing in other kinds of objective truths.

This does not mean that human beings can intellectually comprehend the vastness and complexity of God's revelation. There is an old story about a theologian attempting to comprehend the doctrine of the Trinity while walking along the beach. He noticed a boy who had dug a hole in the sand and was filling it with water from the ocean. The theologian realized that he had been trying to do the same thing—attempting to fit the limitless ocean of God's being into the tiny hole of a human mind.

As Francis Schaeffer has pointed out, what the Bible reveals is true, but it is not exhaustive.[35] It does not reveal *every* truth about God or the world. Scripture is inexhaustibly rich, setting forth the complexities of spiritual reality. The paradoxes of God's election and human responsibility, the mysteries of the Trinity and God's incarnation in Jesus Christ, the way Jesus took into His own innocent body the sins of the whole world and atoned for them all in the cross—such truths boggle the finite human mind. Those who contemplate such mysteries cannot expect to fully grasp them intellectually; rather, those who contemplate the mysteries of salvation can only melt in praise (Romans 11:33-36).

Furthermore, the facts about God and about history revealed in the Bible call for interpretation. As a result, different theologies exist, even among those who agree on the full inerrancy and authority of Scripture.

Postmodern scholars have been studying "hermeneutics," the process of interpretation, showing the difficulties and complexities involved in interpreting the meaning of a text.[36] This sort of study is valuable, testifying again to the clumsiness of human reason, showing the incursion of bias and subjectivity into our simplest attempts at understanding. Many specialists in hermeneutics argue that understanding a text requires an "interpretive community," whose shared assumptions and shared language make interpretation possible.

The Bible itself makes clear that understanding of the Word of God comes only through the illumination of the Holy Spirit, who works through the Word and indwells the members of Christ's

Church (1 Corinthians 2:9-16). This does not open the door to subjectivity nor to private interpretation (2 Peter 1:20). The Holy Spirit employs the Spirit-inspired words of the Bible to convict its readers of sin and to testify to the work of Jesus Christ (John 16:8-15). The church becomes a sort of interpretive community.[37]

It is easy, however, to make too much of the difficulty of interpreting Scripture. In most cases, its meaning is all too clear. The main problem is not interpreting the Bible, but acknowledging its authority—particularly when it conflicts with our own desires—and obeying what it teaches.

Now that we are fallen, our intellectual capacity is not only limited but deceptive (Romans 1:21-28). Because of our sinful nature, we tend to rebel against the the source of all truth. We question God and establish ourselves as the highest authority. We use our reason, pathetically clumsy as it is, to rationalize our sins and to construct systems that allow us to do without God.

In this sense, Christians are right to "doubt the instrument." Christians must depend utterly on the revelation of God as given, in human language, in the "text" of Scripture. Postmodernists point to the innate ambiguity of language, and much of what they say about the imprecision and volatility of human language is valid. And yet Christians must insist that language is also revelatory. Truth may not be totally accessible to the human mind, but there is absolute truth nonetheless.

Christians can agree that the modernist and Enlightenment pretensions to having captured truth by a reductionistic science are futile. But Christians can go beyond postmodernism to discover a core of meaning that remains once all human constructions are cleared away. Although human beings and all of their works are unstable and fragile, condemned, as postmodernist scholars demonstrate, to ceaseless change, there is a transcendent truth and a transcendent language.

> For all men are like grass, and all their glory is like the flowers of the field; the grass withers and the flowers fall, but the word of the Lord stands forever. (1 Peter 1:24-25; Isaiah 40:6-8)

THE CRITIQUE OF THE HUMAN

*F*or the last two centuries, modern thought has assaulted Christianity in the name of reason and in the name of humanism. Christian theology was dismissed as superstition, unworthy of rational, educated human beings. Christian morality was also dismissed as repressive, built around fear and guilt. Just as religious dogmas would be replaced by the dogmas of human reason, religious values would be replaced with *human* values. According to these humanistic assumptions, the human being, not God, is the measure of all things. The good is not what some abstract God dictates, but what contributes to the liberation, growth, and progress of human beings. Instead of being God-centered, we should be human-centered. This impulse to humanism—which can be traced from the Greeks through the Renaissance and into its apotheosis by modern secular humanists—has been a formidable rival to Biblical Christianity.

Just as postmodernist thought dismantles the reason of the Enlightenment, it also dismantles humanism. Christians can take heart that humanism is falling out of favor. And yet, just as the postmodern critique of reason goes on to undermine all claims to absolute truth, including those of Biblical doctrine, postmodern anti-humanism goes on to diminish human beings, attacking personality and the very concept of the individual. Christians—who believe in the immortality of the soul and in the value of each human being as someone who bears God's image and is loved by Him—must object.

Once again Christians can enjoy the spectacle of the latest secular ideology destroying their old enemy—until the new victor turns on them as well. For two centuries, Christianity has been attacked in the name of rationality and humanism. Now that the rational and the human are being assaulted, Christians are in the ironic position of having to champion the value of reason and the value of human beings. While Christians might employ the postmodern critiques of humanism to mop up the remnants of modernism, the new enemy may prove even more dangerous.

The contemporary human condition is summarized by a young woman, a punk-rocker:

> I belong to the Blank Generation. I have no beliefs. I belong to no community, tradition, or anything like that. I'm lost in this vast, vast world. I belong nowhere. I have absolutely no identity.[1]

What she is expressing is taken as a positive creed by many postmodernists, who find this free-floating lack of fixed identity to be the ultimate liberation. Her words, however, must seem poignant and tragic to a Christian. Without beliefs, community, tradition, and identity, she is not only blank but, by her own admission, lost.

The postmodern mind-set can have a devastating impact on the human personality. If there are no absolutes, if truth is relative, then there can be no stability, no meaning in life. If reality is socially constructed, then moral guidelines are only masks for oppressive power and individual identity is an illusion.

Postmodern ideas are mirrored in the pressures of contemporary society. Both the ideas and the pressures are amplified by electronic technology, as television and computers and other high technology threaten to alter what it means to be human. New modes of thinking opened up by the new technology threaten to tear apart sequential thinking and with it any kind of unified consciousness. As the mass culture becomes more and more impersonal, individuals lose themselves in the mass mind or in highly segmented groups. The human is lost. While many postmodernists think that this loss of personality is a very good thing, Christians are in a position to pick up the pieces of the human condition.

THE CRITIQUES OF THE HUMAN

"The most startling fact about postmodernism," says David Harvey, is "its total acceptance of the ephemerality, fragmentation, discontinuity, and the chaotic."[2] Modernism also recognized fragmentation and chaos, but it fought disorder and meaninglessness, seeking to impose order on the chaos. Postmodernism, on the other hand, accepts, affirms, and embraces the chaos. Postmodernism, as Harvey says, "does not try to transcend it, counteract it, or even to define the 'eternal and immutable' elements that might lie within it. Postmodernism swims, even wallows, in the fragmentary and the chaotic currents of change as if that is all there is."[3]

Sabina in *The Unbearable Lightness of Being*; Andy Warhol with his cultivated shallowness, blandly surfing the waves of fashion; the cyberpunks who live inside their computers and their video worlds; those of the homeless who reject offers of shelter, preferring to live in the wide-open, dangerous streets of the city—these are the role models for postmodern humanity.

The contemporary academic world is busily deconstructing the human. Modernism took as its project the death of God. David Levin shows how postmodernism takes the next step. Keeping the idea that God is dead, postmodernism has as its project the death of the self.[4]

German existentialist Martin Heidegger has made key contributions to the new thinking about human beings. "That period we call modern," said Heidegger, "is defined by the fact that man becomes the center and measure of all things."[5] Heidegger rightly stresses the relationship between humanism and modernism. Because of this connection, postmodernist critiques of modernism will also target humanism.

From Heidegger's complex philosophy flows much of postmodernist theory. Heidegger sought to construct a new humanism, which, as his commentators have noted, is actually a kind of antihumanism. As David Levin explains it, "Heidegger's 'humanism' is radically open: it places, it situates, it releases us, as human beings, in an openness-to-Being which is radically decentering."[6] Whereas modernist existentialists stressed the active *creation* of meaning, Heidegger advocated simply remaining "open" to existence, accepting the lack of objective meaning and cultivating a more passive "openness" to experience as it comes. Authentic experience of "Being" comes not from constructing some purpose in life, but from "decentering" experiences—that is, experiences that unsettle our stable beliefs.

Furthermore, Heidegger attacked the notion of a universal humanity, which exalts "mankind" over against nature and against particular human beings and cultures. "Nor can 'Man' remain standing as the sole measure and ground," in Levin's words, "in a sense which tolerates false pride, intolerance of difference, neglect of the ecology of the earth, and totalitarianism."[7] Human beings, according to Heidegger, are no longer at the center. There is no center.

According to Patricia Waugh, the term postmodernism was first used in literary criticism in the 1950s to describe the American poet Charles Olson's "new non-anthropocentric poetry whose Heideggerian anti-humanism was directed at seeing 'man' as a being in the world, as radically situated as any other object."[8] The assumption that a human being is largely like "any other object" ties in with two major ideological movements of postmodern thought: environmentalism and political radicalism.

Whereas modernism sought human control over nature, postmodernism exalts nature at the expense of human beings. While a love of nature and a concern for the environment are laudable, many environmentalists go to anti-human extremes. David Brown, former head of the Sierra Club, sees the destruction of human life as being no more tragic than the destruction of the wilderness. "While the death of young men in war is unfortunate," he says, "it is no more serious than [the] touching of mountains and wilderness areas by humankind."[9] The Finnish Green Party activist Pentti Linkola argues that human beings are an evolutionary mistake, a cancer of the earth. Linkola goes so far as to say that he has more sympathy for threatened insect species than for children dying of hunger in Africa.[10]

Environmental extremism has also spawned the Animal Rights movement. In a world without absolutes, there is no basis for saying that human beings are any better than any other species.

To think one's own species is somehow superior to other species is branded "speciesism," the moral equivalent to racism. According to Ingrid Newkirk, president of People for the Ethical Treatment of Animals, "A rat is a pig is a dog is a boy."[11] Her point is that a human child is not innately better and should have no higher privileges than a dog, a pig, or a rat.

No wonder human children have become a special target of postmodern policies. Environmental arguments have fueled efforts to limit the world's population by restricting the number of children born. The new anti-humanism is inevitably anti-child, assuming as it does that new human life is a problem, a drain on the earth and on the parents' resources. We scarcely hear the classic view that a child is itself a resource, a valuable addition to the human race.[12]

Thus, we have "the right to an abortion," a way to eliminate children that has become a rallying political cause. Belief in "the right to an abortion" may be the defining mark of the postmodernist sensibility. The new anti-humanism finds expression in the new radical politics.

For postmodernist thinkers, humanism and modernism resulted in oppression. "We have seen enough of the modern epoch to see how the humanism of reason, [while] emancipatory, nevertheless produces, reproduces, and even legitimates, conditions of alienation and oppression," says David Levin. "In the postmodern situation, which is partly a question of awareness, it is not possible to trust in the old vision of reason—and in the 'Man' of its humanism."[13]

Perversely, postmodern theorists see the oppressiveness of humanism in Western capitalism and democracy rather than in Marxism, to which the criticisms could reasonably apply. Many Western academics, remember, are social constructivists, believing that *societies* create the perceived reality. This fits well with the collectivist theories of Marx, to whom the social constructivists are indebted. If classical Marxism is discredited as a modernist economic and social theory, Western intellectuals are not deterred. The postmodernists consider themselves to be "post-Marxist."

David Horowitz explains:

No one believes any longer in the revolutionary myth of the proletarian international, but Marx's discredited paradigm has been resurrected by his epigones in the American academy. The fulcrum of this revival has been the development of post-Marxist theories that substitute other "oppressed" groups—blacks, women, and homosexuals—for the missing revolutionary term. Behind each of these theories lies a version of the constructivist idea: the social construction of a race, class, or gender creates the premise that it is socially "oppressed." Thus women have been historically excluded from certain roles not as a result of biological realities—for example, the hazards of childbirth before the development of modern medical techniques—but because "patriarchal society" has *defined* their roles in order that men can oppress them.

It should be obvious that radical theory is, in fact, a radical depreciation of the humanity and dignity of ordinary people. . . . In the radical view, society reflects neither nature nor history, and individual human beings have no complicity in their historical fates. They are mere social creations.[14]

The Marxists who ruled the Soviet Union considered individuality to be a bourgeois concept, a manifestation of the middle-class desire for independence, private property, and a free economy. Communism set out to liquidate all expressions of individual identity in favor of a collective, communal consciousness. Schools encouraged group competition, rather than individual competition. Socialist realism in the arts portrayed people in terms of their social class, not as distinct individuals. Everywhere conformity and group solidarity were encouraged and individuality crushed.

Post-Marxists likewise seek to deconstruct the concept of individual identity. N. P. Ricci sums up the critique of individual identity as carried out by Roland Barthes, Michel Foucault, and Jacques Derrida: "In current theory, identity—individuality, subject-hood—is held to be a construct. . . . constituted by a web of forces of which consciousness is the effect rather than the point of origin."[15] We experience ourselves as being distinct individuals with our own thoughts and experiences. And yet because our lives are culturally determined and because our very thoughts are shaped by our language, this individuality is only an illusion.

Such concepts as moral responsibility and individual freedom are thus also illusions, shaped by our own Western bourgeois culture. Foucault went so far as to argue that "the concept of liberty is an invention of the ruling classes."[16] Democracies train their citizens to police themselves; those who think they are free are actually being more efficiently controlled than those who live in police states.

Remember that postmodernist theorists, following the "hermeneutics of suspicion," believe that all social relationships are only masks for power. Thus, oppression is intrinsic to all social institutions and to the language that gives them utterance. Individual identity must therefore be deconstructed.

"To become subject," says N. P. Ricci, "also means to subject, to give priority to identity, to authorship, to ownership, to situate consciousness at the origin of truth while excluding everything that is different and 'other.'"[17] Much of deconstruction proceeds by wordplay—here, Ricci equates the word *subject,* as in subjectivity, with the active verb *to subject,* meaning to oppress. Ricci relates identity (in psychology) to other concepts that are anathema to postmodernists—to ownership (in capitalist economics) and authorship (in literary criticism). (Postmodernist literary criticism tends to minimize the "*author*ity of the author." Shakespeare's intentions have nothing to do with the meaning of his work. Shakespeare, in fact, is not some creative genius with a unified personality; rather, he is the vehicle for a wide range of social forces that found voice in his work. In Shakespeare's works, the culture's values—including those that subjugate women and legitimate economic exploitation—find supreme expression, which is why the West has "canonized" his works and holds them in such high esteem.)

The postmodernists attack humanism on two fronts. Not only do they seek to deconstruct the concept of individual identity; they also deconstruct the concept of universal humanity. Thus, one deconstructionist argues that the word *we* is "a form of grammatical violence,"

which aims to deny and obliterate the specificity of the "you" and the "she" of other cultures through the false promise of incorporation within a universal humanity. We must therefore wean ourselves away from the "we," that grammatico-political category that can never exist except as legitimating myth operating in the service of appropriative and oppressive cultures. Instead we must embrace and promote every form of cultural diversity, without recourse to universal principles.[18]

Notice how this very argument against using the word *we* uses the word *we*! One wonders about the grammatico-political violence being inflicted upon the reader—who is the "we" who "must therefore wean ourselves away from the 'we'"? Who is the "we" who "must embrace and promote every form of cultural diversity"? This critic, by his own admission, must be trying to coerce readers into his own oppressive culture.

However incoherent the logic, his point is that there is no universal humanity. We must not assume that human beings have *anything* in common. To do so is innately oppressive, forcing others into our own molds. There are no universal principles. Yet he says that "we must embrace and promote every form of cultural diversity." Of course, he ignores the question of how there can be a culture without a "we." He also ignores how, by eliminating the concept of universal humanity, he has eliminated any basis for empathy, common understanding, or moral action.

When an American meets a New Guinea tribesman, there are great cultural barriers, but because both are human beings, they also have a great deal in common. Both are likely to love their families, to know pain and pleasure, to experience gratitude and a sense of moral obligation. On the basis of their common humanness, they can become friends. They can even learn each other's language (which would seem impossible if language is such a cultural prison house). Postmodernists laud cultural diversity, but if there is no universal humanness, why respect people from other cultures? The tribesman would be wholly different from the Westerner, alien and completely "other." The tribesman would be like "any other object." If there are no universal principles, why act morally toward him, or, as we used to say, why treat him *humanely*? Why not treat him like a rat or a pig or a dog? If he is utterly different from me and if the key to our relationship is how much power I have over him, why should I not turn him into my slave? The Christian opponents of slavery, on the other hand, fought slavery on the grounds that human beings of all races are equal before God because they share a common humanity.

The anti-humanism of the postmodernists cannot sustain any of the so-called "human values." Freedom, individuality, self-worth, dignity—these are social constructions. Empathy, kindness, altruism, love—these are masks for oppression. The individual human being is swallowed up by culture; cultures are swallowed up by nature.

Postmodern scholars stress the importance of "contextualizing," putting an author or an idea in the context of the times and showing its connections to all of the other "texts" that constituted the culture. It is revealing to contextualize Heidegger, who originated the anti-humanism of both the academic theorists and the environmental movement. Earlier we quoted David Levin who said that Heidegger criticized humanism for tolerating totalitarianism. Levin was being disingenuous. The fact is, Heidegger was a Nazi.[19]

Heidegger's active involvement in the Nazi party and his zealous promotion of its ideology puts a different light on his rejection of the individual, his repudiation of traditional human values, and his glorification of nature and culture. All of these postmodernist concepts were tenets of fascism. It should not have been so surprising that the deconstructionist critic Paul de Man had also been an apologist for Nazism.

Postmodernists and the fascist intellectuals of the 1930s both embrace a radicalism based not so much on economics but on culture. They both reject individual identity in favor of cultural determinism. They reject moral absolutes in favor of the will to power. They reject reason in favor of irrational emotional release. They reject a transcendent God in favor of an impersonal, mystical nature.

In my book, *Modern Fascism: Liquidating the Judeo-Christian Worldview*, I discuss in more detail fascist ideology, its intrinsic opposition to the Bible, and its survival in contemporary culture and postmodernist thought.[20] For now, it is enough to stress that the irrationalism, the cultural reductionism, and the anti-human values of the postmodernists have already been tried once, and the result was catastrophic. Fascism is coming back. Communism has fallen, but throughout the former Soviet Empire democracy is opposed by a new alliance of ex-Marxists and nationalists, who are trying to forge a National Socialism. American academics think of themselves as post-Marxists, but their desire for a government-controlled economy, their cultivated irrationalism, and their reduction of social issues to questions of culture and race are more similar to Mussolini than to Marx. If Marxism is modern, fascism is postmodern.

For all of their earnest championing of the oppressed and their politically correct sensitivities, postmodernist intellectuals, no doubt without realizing it, are actually resurrecting ways of thinking that gave us world war and the Holocaust. Perhaps the post-modernists think their good intentions will mitigate the implications of what they are saying. But, as David Hirsch has warned, "Purveyors of postmodern ideologies must consider whether it is possible to diminish human beings in theory, without, at the same time, making individual human lives worthless in the real world."[21]

LIVING WITHOUT IDENTITY

The postmodernist attacks on individual identity and universal human values are not merely academic exercises. How the intellectual establishment thinks about human beings reflects how ordinary people are affected by the contemporary condition.

Postmodern society, like the postmodernist ideologies, grows out of the failures of modernism. The allure of the modern has discredited the wisdom and the traditions of the past, which have always lent stability to human life. It is little wonder that those who have experienced no tradition, who have no roots in a community, and who never knew a stable family would have difficulty believing in absolute, unchanging ideas.

Modernist values have atomized the family. The exaggerated individualism that characterizes modernism has split families, with each parent seeking his or her own private identity with no regard for the children, who likewise are left on their own. Ironically, such extreme individual autonomy does not allow for the formation of a strong sense of identity, which is generally formed by nurturing solid families. It is little wonder that a generation left to fend for itself rebels against the concept of individuality.

A major force in the shaping of the postmodern mind is the impact of contemporary technology. The product of modernist rationalism, the electronic media may well make rationalism impossible.

Neil Postman has shown how a society's information media affect the very way its people think. Reading a 300-page book demands sequential thinking, active mental engagement, and a sustained attention span. Reading also encourages a particular sense of self—one reads in private, alone with oneself and with one's thoughts. Watching television, on the other hand, presents information rapidly and with minimal effort on the part of the viewer, who becomes part of a communal mass mind. Visual images are presented, rapid-fire, with little sense of context or connection.[22]

To find examples, just turn on the TV. I did. In five minutes on CNN, I watched segments on whaling, a political election, a sex scandal, and a royal wedding. Then followed commercials for a theme park, deodorant, shampoo, and yeast infection medicine. On news programs, coverage of major political events will be juxtaposed with hype for the latest movie. Images of starving children in Africa will be followed by Madonna's latest video. Television undercuts any sense of coherence, consistency, and unity for its viewers.

Cable television has produced a new way to watch the tube, further fragmenting our perceptions. Since there are so many channels and so many choices, cable viewers avoid having to commit themselves to any one of them. Instead of watching a complete program, most viewers use their remote controls to "channel-surf" through their fifty-three channels, sampling interesting images from CNN and MTV, old Westerns and the Sci-Fi channel, watching a few seconds from a black-and-white Fred Astaire movie, catching a joke from an *Andy Griffith* rerun, and then flashing over to watch cars blow up on the movie of the week.

An individual television drama will usually have the coherence of a traditional plot line, though the story will be constantly interrupted by commercials. But the way television presents *facts* in the news, talk shows, or docudramas exemplifies the tenets of postmodernism.

Television blurs the line between truth and entertainment.[23] Film and video can now render the wildest fantasies and make them seem realistic. Real events, by the same token, are fictionalized. It is little wonder that the TV generation has a hard time distinguishing between truth and fiction and that intellectuals raised on TV argue that there is essentially no difference between the two.

Neil Postman worries that our current electronic environment subjects us to information overload, that we are being bombarded with so much information that none of it has any meaning.[24] David Harvey points out how television presents a collage of unrelated images and equal events.[25] As a result of the dominance of television, one idea seems as good as another. Entertainment, gratification, and sensory stimulation displace reason, morality, and truth.

The video screen has in fact become the new metaphor to describe human beings. The human mind, says Jean Baudrillard, is "a pure screen, a switching center for all the networks of influence."[26]

An even more precise metaphor might be the computer screen, with the individual computers hooked into a vast network of "cyberspace." Already a subculture of computer aficionados known as "cyberpunks" has emerged. Their goal is to exist in their own electronic world of virtual reality, virtual sex, and virtual communities. They seek to achieve, in the words of one observer, "the fusion of humans and machines."[27] There will be no distinctly human identity—just flickering electronic impulses on the neurons.

Arthur Kroker, himself a postmodernist, says that the key psychological mood of this postmodern culture is *panic*, a "free fall" that comes from "the disappearance of *external* standards of public conduct . . . and the dissolution of the *internal* foundations of identity." People no longer acknowledge the authority of social institutions or their own obligations to society "when the social itself becomes the transparent field of a cynical power." This cynicism towards external social standards is accompanied by a loss of internal personal standards. "The disappearing ego," says Kroker, is "the victory sign of postmodernism." Postmodernists see themselves as passive vessels for their culture. "The self is transformed into an empty screen [notice the metaphor] of an exhausted, but hyper-technical culture."[28] Without external standards and without internal standards, there is only cynicism, panic, and "free fall."

"The most problematic facet of postmodernism," confesses another postmodernist, is "its psychological presuppositions with respect to personality, motivation, and behavior." The fragmentation of language breeds schizophrenia. When there are no external frames of reference, experience is reduced to "a series of pure and unrelated presents in time." There is no centered self-identity.[29]

If there are no absolutes in the objective realm, neither can there be absolutes in the subjective realm. There can be no fixed identity, no sense of self, no unified human soul. Modernism was activist, optimistic, and self-confident. Postmodernism is passive, cynical, and insecure.

David Harvey honestly faces the consequences of living without absolutes. If there is no unified representation of the world, he asks, how are we to act coherently?

> The simple postmodernist answer is that since coherent representation and action are either repressive or illusionary (and therefore doomed to be self-dissolving and self-defeating), we should not even try to engage in some global project. Pragmatism (of the Dewey sort) then becomes the only possible philosophy of action.[30]

Today people have little patience for systematic thinking and abstract ideals. Pragmatic questions (what works? what's practical?) dominate contemporary discussions, from Congress to church boards. But even pragmatism will be stymied without some kind of "coherent representation." Pragmatic considerations themselves need goals (what are we trying to do?) and values (is this working the way it should?) to plan and evaluate the action. These take us back to the need for absolutes. The postmodernists try to find in their philosophy some basis for positive moral and political action, but they cannot. When it comes to improving the world, by their own presuppositions, "we should not even try."

The only other alternative is to play the same games as the rest of society. If social issues are nothing more than "the transparent field of a cynical power," it is possible to exercise cynical power. Those who believe that all social relationships are masks for power might become very efficient wielders of power. Disabused of the traditional ideals that limit power—such as belief in truth, individual integrity, and objective morality—postmodernists could play a ruthless brand of politics.

Postmodernist politicians, given their philosophical assumptions, may well play fast and loose with the truth (since there is no truth); alter what they say according to their audiences (since each group has its own reality); and do everything they can to advance their group's agenda and crush their opponents (since there are no ideals beyond a Machiavellian pragmatism and no values beyond power). This may already be evident in the viciousness of university politics, the "Borking" of conservative nominees, and the tactics of national political campaigns. The connection of such a political philosophy to fascism again should be obvious and a cause for concern.

Ordinary citizens in the meantime are easily victimized because with the new mind-sets, they are easily manipulated and distracted. Because they lack a sense of identity, postmodern folks tend to be highly oriented to playing roles. The postmodernist artist Cindy Sherman has a series of photographs depicting women from different walks of life; the teenager looks completely different from the housewife and the bag lady. It turns out that all of the pictures are of the artist. She is dressing up, acting a variety of parts. The self-portraits do not depict a single Cindy Sherman; she has no identity apart from the roles she plays.

It is true that we tend to act in different ways when we are at church, at home, and at work. With one set of friends, we might present ourselves as being intellectual; with another, as "down home." Postmodernist theorists point out how each of us is engaged in diverse "language games" and "interpretive communities." We use the language of our profession to impress our colleagues and superiors. We use religious language to seem pious at church.[31]

Classical, Christian, and modernist thought has always recognized this sort of role-playing, but has insisted that the different games we play all mask a single authentic identity. Moralists from the classical, Christian, and modernist camps, for all of their differences, have commended honesty and condemned hypocrisy. They have all stressed the importance of being consistent in the different dimensions of life and of being true to oneself. Postmodernists, on the other hand, insist that there is no identity apart from our social roles. We really *are* different people at home, at work, and at church.

Postmodernists stress *style* over substance. Since there are no absolutes, any kind of objective meaning is problematic, including the notion of an absolute identity. The *surface* is more significant than the interior. This is true not only in the arts, as we shall see, but in social life. Life in the city, says Jonathan Raban, consists solely of role-playing.[32] Everyone is *acting*. Everyone is affecting *style*. The office worker dons his power suit and plays the part of the corporate bureaucrat. After work, he plays another part with his friends. Whether he goes to a fern bar or a leather bar, whether he tries to impress women by being sensitive or macho, whether he projects himself as a free spirit or a world-weary cynic, it is all an act. And in the course of a day, he plays many parts.

Since style, surfaces, and group identity are so important in contemporary life, postmodern society is highly geared towards fashion. The postmodern social scene is preoccupied with what's "in" and what's "out." Being on the cutting edge becomes an obsession. Fashion, of course, must be in a state of constant change. Otherwise it cannot serve its function of sorting out the high-status trendsetters from those who are backward and *déclassé*. Whereas the classical era defined status by position (ruler, head of the family, office of the ministry), and the modern era defined status by achievement (property owner, self-made millionaire, star athlete), postmodern society defines status in terms of style (wearing the right clothes, striking the right attitude).

Thus, contemporary teenagers define themselves by the music they listen to and the clothes they wear, which in turn makes them part of a group. One teenager told me that in her high school, people are identified and sorted out into cliques according to the radio station they listen to. Head-bangers listen to heavy metal; blacks and "wanna be's" listen to rap; the popular crowd listens to pop; the FFA subculture listens to country. Teenagers, whose personal identity is still forming, naturally crave a sense of belonging. Lacking a strong identity of their own, they conform to a group identity.

Adults, no less than teenagers, are subject to peer pressure. Yuppies are careful to own the right name brands, to eat the trendiest cuisine, to affect the latest beliefs. Keeping up with fashion is a sign of status, a way to identify themselves with the group that sets the trends. In the postmodern world, people are increasingly defining themselves in terms of race, ethnicity, gender, or "sexual preference." Others define themselves by associating with a cause or "interest group"—environmentalism, physical fitness, animal rights, natural foods. In another ominous parallel to fascism, individuals find their identity by submerging themselves in a group.

There is no stability, however, even in group identity. Whereas traditional communities—families, villages, churches—gave a sense of both belonging and permanence, the contemporary social scene is characterized by impermanence. Fashions continually change. In-groups become out-groups. Friends drop each other; causes change; even families are disposable. It is little wonder that those caught in the contemporary social scene are in a continual state of panic. Will people like me? Can I find someone to love? Even if they find someone to love, because they tend to lack a stable, interior identity of their own and because they have become so oriented to change, it is hard for postmodern lovers to make permanent commitments. In time, they abandon each other.

This studied rootlessness and rejection of permanence results in a wide range of contradictory impulses. As Arthur Kroker points out, "the postmodern condition is fully ambiguous, charged with opposing tendencies towards domination and freedom, radical pessimism and wild optimism."[33] For all of its talk about the death of the self, postmodernism actually isolates the self. Everyone becomes locked into mutually inaccessible worlds.[34] Postmodernism encourages selfishness without individuality; subjectivity without identity; license without freedom. For all of its talk about culture, postmodernism lacks culture, since the traditions and beliefs and moral values that define culture are all disabled. Postmodernism stresses tolerance, pluralism, and multiculturalism, but in its dismissal of *all* beliefs, it trivializes all cultures and tolerates none. The contradictions of postmodernism are the contradictions of attempting to live without God, who alone can redeem our humanness.

THE TWO SELVES OF CHRISTIANITY

Christians can be glad that the confident humanism of the modern age has been deflated. But the postmodernists go to the other extreme, to the anti-human. The modernist trust in the self was certainly misplaced. The postmodernists are right to undermine the self, but as they did with their rejection of reason, they go too far.

The Bible teaches that the unregenerated self is sinful. Those without faith are described as unstable and "double-minded" (James 1:8). Although we are inclined to be selfish, our identity is so confused that we are also inclined to hypocrisy. The word *hypocrisy* literally means "playing a part"; a hypocrite, to the Greeks, was an actor on the stage. According to postmodernism, we are all hypocrites, acting various parts and following various scripts without any real identity of our own.

Jesus, however, excoriates hypocrisy (Matthew 23). He makes it clear that we hypocrites are inconsistent in our beliefs and actions; like the postmodernists, we are overly concerned with surfaces and insufficiently concerned with our inner lives. "You are like whitewashed tombs," Jesus says, "which look beautiful on the outside but on the inside are full of dead men's bones. . . . In the same way, on the outside you appear to people as righteous but on the inside you are full of hypocrisy and wickedness" (Matthew 23:27-28). Despite what the postmodernists say, Jesus insists that human beings do have an "inside."

According to Christianity, human identity does not rest on culture, groups, nature, or individual autonomy. Every human being has an immortal soul. There is a human identity that survives even death, that exists eternally in damnation or beatitude. Your soul makes you a unified person, so that you are the same person you were ten years ago, even though every atom of your body has been replaced. Having a soul means that while you might play many roles and have a succession of different thoughts and feelings, you are still one person.

And yet our souls are fallen, corrupted, lost. The sinful self must be put to death. The Bible, like the postmodernists, advocates the death of the self. But unlike the postmodernists, the Bible promises a redemption and resurrection of the self:

> For we know that our old self was crucified with him so that the body of sin might be done away with, that we should no longer be slaves to sin. . . . Now if we died with Christ, we believe that we will also live with him. (Romans 6:6, 8)

In our baptism, Paul writes, we have been united with Christ's death and His resurrection (Romans 6:3-5). On the cross our

Savior bore our sins in His body, and thus He put to death our "old self." As Jesus rose from the dead, we too rise from death. We have a new resurrected self.

By the death and resurrection of Christ, which we receive by faith, the self is regenerated by the Holy Spirit—this is described in the doctrine of justification. The relationship between the old self and the new self is also explored in the doctrine of sanctification. Although the victory was won once and for all on the cross, Christians must still struggle with the old self, which remains in conflict with the regenerated self (Romans 6-8). Sanctification, like justification, is essentially God's work. It is complete only when we die, whereupon our sinful nature turns to dust, leaving the new self victorious before God forever.

Notice how the apostle Paul speaks of these two selves: "You have taken off your old self with its practices and have put on the new self, which is being renewed in knowledge in the image of its Creator" (Colossians 3:9-10). The new self is continually "being renewed" as it grows in knowledge, fed by God's Word, whereby the Holy Spirit brings the new self into greater conformity with the image of God. Significantly, the next verse sharply distinguishes this new self from any sort of *cultural* identity: "Here there is no Greek or Jew, circumcised or uncircumcised, barbarian, Scythian, slave or free, but Christ is all, and is in all" (Colossians 3:11). The old self, to be sure, may have thought of itself in these cultural terms. The new self, however, finds its identity wholly in Christ. Paul amplifies the point: "All of you who were baptized into Christ have clothed yourselves with Christ. There is neither Jew nor Greek, slave nor free, male nor female, for you are all one in Christ Jesus" (Galatians 3:27-28).

This means that Christians are not to define themselves primarily by their social position, their culture, their race, or their gender. As part of the Christian's life in the world, such social realities must be dealt with, but the Christian's true self-identity is to be found in Christ. Furthermore, Christians "are all one in Christ Jesus." In the Church, people of all cultures and stations are unified with each other because of their common relationship to Christ. For all the postmodernists say about multiculturalism, the universal Church, spread through history and throughout the globe, is the one true multicultural institution.

The unity of the Church, however, does not efface the diversity of its individual members. On the contrary, the members of the Church are as different from each other as the different organs in a body. In the Church, unity and diversity, community and individuality find their balance. Notice how Paul in his great exposition of the Church as Christ's body begins once more with the way baptism brings us beyond cultural identity:

> The body is a unit, though it is made up of many parts; and though all its parts are many, they form one body. So it is with Christ. For we were all baptized by one Spirit into one body—whether Jews or Greeks, slave or free—and we were all given the one Spirit to drink. Now the body is not made up of one part but of many. If the foot should say, "Because I am not a hand, I do not belong to the body," it would not for that reason cease to be part of the body. . . . But in fact God has arranged the parts in the body, every one of them, just as he wanted them to be. If they were all one part, where would the body be? As it is, there are many parts, but one body. . . . Now you are the body of Christ, and each one of you is a part of it. (1 Corinthians 12: 12-15, 18-20, 27)

Unlike monolithic cultures that demand conformity and exercise worldly control, the Church is a unity of distinct and different personalities.

From a Christian perspective, the desire for solidarity with a group is no reason to efface individuality. Nor should a desire for individuality mean destruction of the community. Even on the secular level, the ideal should be neither conformity to a mass society nor anarchic individualism, but a unity *of* individuals. *E Pluribus Unum*. On an even more profound level, the ideal of an absolute unity of distinct persons is grounded in the very being of the Triune God Himself, in whom the separate Persons of the Father, the Son, and the Holy Spirit co-inhere into a perfect unity, while still maintaining their distinct personalities.[35]

Christians can agree with the postmodernists on the weaknesses and instability of the self, which is full of contradictions and contending impulses. Christians can also agree with the postmodernists on the futility of humanism.

And yet, Christians, for all of their severity, believe that human beings are more than video screens. The value of human life comes not from culture, nor from individual choices, but from God's image that inheres in every person's immortal soul. The problem of the self is the problem of sin.*Postmodernism unmasks problems that modernism tried to hide, but postmodernism can by no means solve them. For the Blank Generation, the gospel of Jesus Christ can be very good news indeed.

PART TWO

POSTMODERN ART

PLAYING WITH CONVENTIONS:
Art and Performance

*A*rt always brings abstract philosophies down to earth. Artists express their beliefs in concrete forms, thus making clear the implications of their worldview and dramatizing what it means for human life. Postmodernist art vividly demonstrates the consequences of postmodern thinking.

More important, it is chiefly the arts that communicate worldviews throughout the culture. This is especially true of postmodern art, which seeks to break out of the "high culture" of the art world into the "popular culture" of the mass mind. Not many people read Jacques Derrida; but practically everyone today watches television, goes to movies, and listens to rock 'n' roll.

Not all postmodern art reflects postmodern*ism*. Again "postmodern" refers to the time in which we live; "postmodern*ism*" refers to the ideology emerging in reaction to both modern and Christian ways of looking at reality. Postmodern artists often struggle *against* the strictures of contemporary thought and culture. Many postmodern artists react against modernist art by bringing past styles back to life, returning to representational art, recovering beauty and human values. This sets them against the postmodern*ists*.

As we keep seeing, the reaction against modernism has many features that Christians can share in and applaud. Postmodern ideas are revitalizing the arts, opening them up to the past and to ordinary human life. These ideas have had a particularly bracing effect on literature and architecture. And yet the "isms" of contemporary thought are too often the fly in the ointment.

MODERNISM AND POSTMODERNISM IN THE ARTS

Many of us have not yet digested modern art, let alone postmodern art. Throughout the twentieth century, artists have turned away from traditional renditions of the external world, creating works solely from their own private imaginations—abstract paintings that reorder the objective world into strange new shapes, novels that find their realism by plunging into depths of human psychology, buildings that approach pure form. Classicists lamented the demise of representational art with its assumption that the external world reflects ideal beauty and objective meaning.

Postmodern art's reaction against modernism is long overdue. The reaction, though, goes in different directions. Modernism, for all its rebellion against the past, did not reject absolutes; rather, it attempted to arrive at absolutes—pure form, disembodied beauty, the "truth" of human experience—through art. Modernism, with its humanistic attempts to do without God, failed. This failure perhaps opens up a window of opportunity for a genuinely Christian aesthetic. For the most part, however, postmodernism has responded to the failure of modernism by rejecting absolutes altogether.

The intellectual and spiritual climate described in the preceding chapters finds its full expression in the arts. Since the fine arts of the "high culture" tend to be ahead of their time, they provide important clues to where our culture is heading. The entertainment industry spreads postmodernist ideology into every home with a TV set.

Terry Eagleton gives a succinct description of the postmodernist aesthetic:

> There is, perhaps, a degree of consensus that the typical post-modernist artifact is playful, self-ironizing and even schizoid; and that it reacts to the austere autonomy of high modernism by impudently embracing the language of commerce and the commodity. Its stance towards cultural tradition is one of irrev-

erent pastiche, and its contrived depthlessness undermines all metaphysical solemnities, sometimes by a brutal aesthetics of squalor and shock.[1]

In other words, postmodernist art does not take itself too seriously. Whereas the modernists affected high purpose, the integrity of the artist and the work of art, and sought their own visions of truth, postmodernists play with their art, are blatantly commercial, and make no pretense of truth.

A modern novel might achieve the highest levels of historical and psychological realism. Postmodernists, though, point out that the truth of the story is only an illusion, an effect created by manipulating certain techniques and conventions that make the story seem real. However realistic it might seem, the novel is still fiction. In fact, according to postmodernist ideology, *everything* is fiction; all truth is an illusion created by social conventions. Postmodernist artists attempt to heighten awareness of these conventions by blurring the boundaries between truth and fiction. They do so by playing with the conventions of art.

Fredric Jameson has contrasted the modern and the postmodern sensibilities. Whereas modern artists assume that the artist, like all human beings, is a unified personality, postmodernists work from the assumption that self-identity is itself an illusion. Modernists, believing the artist is a unique individual, strive for a unique style. Postmodernists work with a collage of different and often recycled and mass-produced styles. Modernists are "deep," concerned with inner realities and complex truths. Postmodernists are "flat," obsessed with surfaces and superficial appearances.[2]

Modernists idealized the individual artist laboring to create a unique work of art. Their values, as Steven Connor says, were "uniqueness, permanence, and transcendence." The work of art stands alone, valuable in itself, set apart from the world. Postmodernists, on the other hand, undercut both the uniqueness of the artist and the exalted status of the work of art. Their values are "multiplicity, transience, and anonymity."[3]

Modernists exalted the work of art as a self-contained, almost sacred object. They purposefully removed the work of art from any connections to the external world, to nature, to history, to human life. Art that reflected natural beauty or that expressed human emotions was dismissed as "less than pure." Art existed for the sake of art. The meaning of the work of art referred primarily to itself, not to the world outside. Art was concerned only with *aesthetic* meaning—not moral, political, philosophical, or religious meaning. In abstract art, fields of color and geometrical shapes were manipulated to reduce art to pure aesthetic form.

Modernist scholarship fostered the "New Criticism," which analyzed works solely in terms of their internal structure as self-contained artifacts. Religious poems were dissected for their imagery and irony, instead of for the religious experience they dramatized. Christian paintings were discussed as masses of color and light, with no reference to their theological significance.

Postmodern scholarship, to its credit, attempts to restore art to its external references. Believing that texts have no meaning apart from their *context*, postmodern critics reject the idea that the work of art is some isolated, privileged object. Instead, they emphasize the work's relationship to society, nature, and human life. Relating art to the rest of reality is promising, opening up possibilities for art that fully engages moral and spiritual issues. Postmodern aesthetic theories can in many ways vindicate Christian artists and Christian critics.

Postmodern*ists*, however, reject moral and religious absolutes just as they reject aesthetic absolutes. They seek to tie the work of art to life, but the way they do so is shaped by their view of life. Representational art is back, but it tends to be critical rather than celebratory, stressing bleak and shocking images rather than the beauty of nature or intimations of divine order. Because postmodernists believe that reality is socially constructed, their art will tend to be *political* rather than moral or philosophical.

Some contemporary artists relate their art to the outside world by making the work's surroundings part of the art. They seek to bring art out of the museums into the streets or into the natural environment. Thus we have artists who devise King Kong balloons and install them on the Empire State Building, artists like Christo who wraps civic landmarks in cloth, earth artists who pile up dirt in a desert with a bulldozer, and artists who stage elaborate "happenings" such as running into an elegant restaurant to play the accordion.

Another way postmodernists reject the privileged status of the work of art is to collapse the distinction between what is artistic and what is not.[4] Ordinary objects—such as coke bottles, sleds, or toilets—are displayed as if they were art. Conversely, artists might make meticulously realistic paintings of a coke bottle, a sled, or a toilet. One artist displays his bowel movements. Instead of making art that is beautiful and pleasing, some artists experiment with art that is purposefully ugly and infuriating.

Modernists assumed that the artist has creative control of the work and that the artist's intention is the key to its meaning. The postmodernists downplay the artist. In line with the new ideology's critique of the individual self, postmodernists reduce what the modernists assumed to be creative genius to mechanical processes, social role-playing, and cultivated impersonality. Artists purposely efface themselves by depending on machines, by submitting themselves to random forces, and by self-consciously surrendering to commercialism and the mass mind.

Minimizing the role of the artist places a greater emphasis on the audience. According to the new ideology, a work has no single authoritative meaning determined by the artist or by anyone else. Since "there are no absolutes," meaning is subjective and relative. The reader determines the meaning of a book; the viewer decides the significance of a painting. Both traditional criticism, which seeks what the work means objectively, and the New Criticism, which seeks what the work means in itself, are replaced by "reader response criticism," which reduces the meaning of a work to its subjective impact. Attention to the audience does not mean subservience to viewer judgment, as in traditional evaluative criticism where critics judge whether the work is good or bad. Since there are no absolutes, there are no aesthetic standards. "Postmodernism can judge the spectacle," says one critic, "only in terms of how spectacular it is."[5]

Modernists exalted art above the reach of ordinary people. Artists were an elite priesthood. Only highly trained specialists or others "in the know" had any idea what they were trying to do. Postmodernists, on the other hand, in line with their radical political ideas, reject the institutional elitism of the high culture. While they still in practice scorn ordinary people, they affect a sort of populism. They mock the conventions of the art world and openly (though sometimes ironically) embrace pop culture, consumerism, and kitsch.[6] Today postmodernists love to flout the high-toned galleries where they exhibit their paintings of Elvis, collages of gum wrappers, and intentionally gaudy, tacky images.

Whereas modernism emphasized unity, postmodernism favors diversity. Postmodernism embraces "multiculturalism" and continually invokes "pluralism." The principle of diversity as a governing value also manifests itself stylistically.

Postmodernist art typically does not employ a single unified style, but is a collage of many styles. Television presents not only a collage of images, but also a collage of styles and ideas, with nostalgic "Leave It to Beaver" reruns juxtaposed with "Star Trek" futurism, images of warm family values interspersed with images of salacious sex and horrific violence. By the same token, a postmodernist painting might be a pastiche of the Mona Lisa (in the Renaissance style), a Greek god (the classical style), and Donald Duck (pop art) all cavorting in a super-realistic landscape. A postmodern office building might feature modernist glass and steel decorated by medieval gargoyles and Victorian gingerbread.

Jacques Derrida has said that the primary form of postmodernist discourse is the collage. Contemporary art tends to assemble disparate images and incompatible meanings, producing, he says, "a signification which could be neither univocal nor stable."[7] In other words, postmodernist art refuses to speak with one voice; it is designed in its very style to be unstable, to resist a single meaning.

Jameson says that the multiplicity of styles in postmodern art imitates contemporary social life.[8] Today unified frames of reference no longer exist. Each group has its own values, language, and style. In a pluralistic society, many styles hold sway at the same time. One is as good as another. Multiple styles also promote a particular view of history. Connor summarizes Jameson's argument:

> The key that connects the leading features of postmodern society—among others, the acceleration of cycles of style and fashion, the increased power of advertising and the electronic media, the advent of universal standardization, neocolonialism, the Green revolution—to the schizoid pastiche of postmodernist culture is the fading of a sense of history. Our contemporary social system has lost its capacity to know its own past,

Major Point!

has begun to live in "a perpetual present" without depth, definition, or secure identity.[9]

This "perpetual present," ironically, includes the past.

Whereas the modernists dismissed the past as irrelevant to the present, postmodernists freely appropriate the past. The brand-new office building with gargoyles and gingerbread brings the Middle Ages and the Victorian age into the present day. Television juxtaposes diverse periods of history—a western evoking nineteenth-century America, a cartoon version of medieval fairy tales, a "Masterpiece Theatre" recreation of Edwardian England.

New television technology, ironically, has *preserved* television history. Broadcast TV packaged a new season of programming every year so that viewers were always watching new shows (corresponding to the modernist phase of the industry). Cable TV, on the other hand, depends for much of its programming on rerunning shows from previous decades. A channel-surfer can watch Jackie Gleason reruns from the 1950s, Jack Webb on *Dragnet* refighting the culture wars of the 1960s, Bob Newhart with his wide ties of the 1970s.

This postmodern openness to the past is good and holds promise. In general, however, the leveling of history ends up as a "schizoid pastiche." Television reduces all of history to a perpetual present, occurring simultaneously on our TV screens, empty of context and meaning. History is not something we can learn from or interpret our own times by. Rather, history becomes a "style." Whereas modernist culture kept trying to come up with brand-new fashions, postmodernist culture—though equally fashion obsessed—keeps recycling the old, with nostalgic revivals of the '40s, the '60s, and even (heaven help us) the '70s, all expressed in up-to-date "retro" fashions.

This approach to history also works to contemporize the past. Revisionist historians reinterpret past events according to contemporary concerns, seeing history through the lens of feminism, multiculturalism, and post-Marxist politics. Instead of recreating the mind-set of the time, contemporary renditions present the past as a mirror of our own times. The movie *Robin Hood, Prince of Thieves* presents the medieval outlaw as suffering posttraumatic stress syndrome from the Crusades. Accompanied by his merry band of multicultural homeless victims, he and the feminist Maid Marian oppose the Sheriff of Nottingham's multinational corporation and save Sherwood Forest's environment. Postmodernism thus has history, but not a "sense of history," since all historical moments are reduced, swallowed up by the contemporary, and relativized.

Jameson's comment that postmodern culture is "without depth" points to another stylistic feature of the arts. In contrast to modernism, postmodernism has, according to Harvey, a "fixation with appearances, surfaces, and instant impacts that have no sustaining power over time."[10] A society devoted to instant gratification, conditioned by the immediacy of its information media and by its lack of moral restraints on immediate pleasure, will demand instant gratification in its arts and entertainment. While books encourage inner reflection, video images present only surface appearances. People who have no beliefs lack a sense of personal identity and an inner life. They are thus, in every sense of the term, superficial.

This superficiality manifests itself in the arts as what Jameson terms "contrived depthlessness."[11] Portraits show blank faces, void of an inner life. Landscapes become cartoons. Contemporary novels depict, in the words of one critic, "the flattest possible characters in the flattest possible landscapes rendered in the flattest possible diction."[12] This depthlessness is sometimes used ironically, as a way to satirize what contemporary society has become; sometimes flatness is celebrated as a positive aesthetic value.

PERFORMANCE

"The unifying mode of the post-modern," says Michel Benamon, is *performance*.[13] Just as contemporary society is made up of people performing various roles, contemporary art can be understood as various kinds of performances.

Whereas the modernists saw the work of art as transcending time, postmodernists see the work of art as existing only in time. The modernists, as well as the traditionalists, valued permanence. Postmodernists value transience. Thus, postmodernist art is unabashedly fashion-conscious, fully aware that nothing in art (or anywhere else) is permanent.

Instead of trying to create timeless artifacts, postmodernists create ephemeral art, existing only in the moment. Some artists construct an object only to dismantle it, leaving behind historical documentation to show that it once existed. Other contemporary artists eliminate the object of art altogether and simply perform what they consider to be some imaginative act.

In New York City, an artist devised a work of art that put itself together and then destroyed itself. Christo, exploring in the postmodernist way the boundary between art and nonart, wraps historical buildings in fabric and erects cloth fences across fields. He stages a well-publicized event, then takes down his fabric, and the work of art is gone.

Often a visitor to a gallery today sees on the walls not a painting but typed pages and Polaroid photographs. This is a sign of "conceptual art." The artist displays the "documentation," the written description of his idea and possibly photographs of his artistic event. Sometimes the work of art no longer exists. One artist spelled out the word *SEA* in pebbles along the shore. He took a series of photographs as the waves washed the pebbles away, destroying his work of art. Sometimes there is not even a work of art to begin with. The artist simply describes his "concept."

The significance of the work of art often inheres not in the work itself, but in the *chutzpah* of the artist. Sherrie Levine took pictures of famous photographs and presented them as her own. They looked, of course, exactly like the photos made by famous photographers. Her purpose, in the words of one critic, was "to assault the cult of authorial personality." Not only was she carrying out the postmodernist distaste for humanness and personality, she was also attacking "the capitalist conceptions of ownership and property." She tempered this Marxism with a post-Marxist feminism, associating "the patriarchal identification of authorship with the assertion of self-sufficient maleness."[14] Others might call it plagiarism.

Perhaps the most characteristic expression of postmodernism in the art world is the development of "performance art." The pioneer of this art form was the German artist Joseph Beuys. Here a critic solemnly describes one of Beuys's typical works:

In one of Beuys's rituals, known as *Fat Corner*, a lump of fat, usually margarine, is packed in the shape of an inverted cone in a corner. The ritual involves simply leaving the fat to spread and stink over the course of days. The piece consists of the fat, its slow spreading, and the viewer's response.[15]

Notice that part of the work of art is *the viewer's response.* Any reaction of outrage, disgust, or puzzlement *becomes part of the work of art!*

Beuys also pioneered "throw-away" art and "reproducibles" by signing ordinary objects and pieces of paper. Such gestures undercut traditional artistic institutions, the museums and collectors that traffic in one-of-a-kind and thus valuable *objets d'art.* Beuys signed (and sold) manufactured objects to signify the postmodernist dictum that "everything is art." This also signified the postmodernist assault on the individual self and the status of the artist. Beuys abandoned all artistic conventions governing subject, style, technique, labor, creativity; he retained one and only one artistic convention—the artist signing (and selling) his work. In signing objects that he did not make, Beuys was deconstructing the role of the artist.

Beuys later injected himself even more directly into the artistic event. "In another ritual, Beuys smeared his face with honey and gold and had himself locked into a museum in which he walked around, carrying a dead hare in his arms while explaining his pictures to it."[16] In another work, entitled "I Love America, and America Loves Me," Beuys had himself wrapped in felt and put onto an airplane. Upon arriving in New York, he was picked up at the airport, still wrapped in felt, and taken directly to the museum. He was put into a room with a live coyote, said to represent Native Americans and other "victims of American oppression." The artist, shrouded in felt, would bow to the coyote. Periodically, he would pace around the animal and touch it with a stick, and then lie down in a bed of straw. The coyote would look puzzled.[17]

Performance art is the latest vogue in the art world. Sometimes aided by video monitors, rock music, and laser lights, artists dispense with the necessity of actually making an object of art and now simply put themselves on center stage. In Milwaukee a performance artist screamed abuse at the audience. He then stuck fishhooks into his skin and cut himself with razor blades. He was dramatizing how artists make themselves suffer to entertain their wealthy audiences.

Karen Finley expresses her feminism by taking off her dress, pouring gelatin down her bra, slathering her body with chocolate, and sticking bean sprouts (representing sperm) all over herself. Taxpayer money through the National Endowment for the Arts funded this performance, causing considerable controversy. But Finley's performances are nothing compared to those of Annie Sprinkle, former porn star and now performance artist. Calling herself a "post-porn modernist," Sprinkle masturbates on stage and invites members of the audience to come up and inspect her genitalia with a flashlight.

The role these artists really play is that of the artist as a cultural guerrilla.[18] Stirring up shock and outrage, making their audiences uncomfortable and the general public furious, is part of their art. They imagine these performances and the controversy they raise as politically subversive acts. *Avant garde* artists not only play with conventions—they fly in the face of conventions.

DEHUMANIZING THE ARTS

Despite the apparent self-aggrandizement of the performance artists, postmodernist art engages in a purposeful assault on humanness. Postmodernists favor art created by technology. Mass-produced art has the virtue of dehumanizing both the artist and the work. Andy Warhol christened his studio "The Factory" and hired workers to churn out prints of Marilyn Monroe and other icons of pop culture. "Did it matter that the works were not unique?" asked one critic. "And did it matter that Warhol himself had not actually made them?"[19] Not to the postmodernist art world.

Mass reproductions supposedly liberate art from wealthy institutions and open up the artistic process to the people. Warhol mass-produced art that depicted the mass culture—movie stars, advertisements, consumer goods—furthering his populist statement. (Of course, ordinary people were the last to appreciate Warhol's Brillo boxes and Campbell soup cans. If this is art, they reasoned, they can get it from the grocery store. But his work was eagerly purchased by the museums and collectors he mocked.)

Warhol also had a way of leveling the trivial and the profound. His prints of celebrities—Elvis, Liz Taylor, Jackie Kennedy—were, in effect, icons of our secular saints. Intermixed with his prints of movie stars and consumer goods, Warhol's Factory started churning out prints depicting electric chairs and car crashes. Warhol silk-screened photographs of gruesome accidents—mangled bodies in car wrecks, a man impaled on a telephone pole. He rendered these horrific images in the same bland, bright-colored style as his pop culture prints. The tragic and the trivial are reduced to the same level of banality. Warhol observed that reproducing these gruesome images over and over again makes them lose their impact. Just as the brutality of television and movies desensitizes us to violence, Warhol was intentionally trying to deaden human sensibilities. For Warhol and other postmodernists, personality was something to get away from; the human, with its pain and imperfections, was something to avoid. "Andy wanted to keep the human out of his art," reported one of his friends, "and to avoid it he had to resort to silkscreens, stencils, and other kinds of automatic reproduction. But still the Art would always manage to find a way of creeping in. A smudge here, a bad silkscreening there, an unintended cropping. Andy was always antismudge. To smudge is human."[20]

Warhol carried out this rejection of individual personality in his own life by projecting an air of cultivated blandness. In doing so, ironically, he became a celebrity. "His nature," says one admirer, "was that of a vacuum, a void. He never made the earnest statements about his work that most artists are prone to, and apparently conversed entirely on trivialities. He condemned nothing and seemed to find any odd manifestation of human behaviour fascinating."[21] As Warhol himself said, "The reason I'm painting this way is that I want to be a machine."[22]

Mass reproduction has another result: the commercialization of art. Warhol became wealthy beyond the dreams of the typical *avant garde* artist toiling away in his garret possessing only his artistic integrity. By repudiating the very concept of artistic integrity, artists could both make a politically correct statement and make lots of money. There are only seventeen paintings by Leonardo Da Vinci in all the world, but nearly every art museum has an "original" Andy Warhol.

The ideal of technological reproduction and its resulting dehumanization goes far beyond the eccentricities of the art world. Warhol could make his color prints because of new printing technology. He later abandoned painting for film. The new technological environment does have profound implications for the arts. Reproducible media such as photography, film, recordings, and television are becoming the dominant art forms.

Rock music, for example, is lauded by the postmodernists for its "unifying global reach and influence on the one hand combined with its tolerance and engendering of pluralities of styles, media, and ethnic identities on the other."[23] Rock music is multicultural, with its African-American roots and its popularity around the globe. Not only tolerant, it promotes moral permissiveness and has an edge of rebellion against authority. New styles continually emerge, but the old styles are kept alive on the "oldies" stations. Electronic art forms, says one critic, are intrinsically contemporary, so they are more postmodern than older art forms.[24]

Rock music also fits the canons of postmodernist art by depending on technological reproduction and on performance. A truly multimedia art form, rock music blares from stereos, radios, and MTV. But there is also the rock concert. As one critic pointed out, concerts are usually not successful unless the group has made some hit records. Part of the thrill of a live concert is to hear songs, in the actual presence of the singers, that one has already heard on the mass media. Ironically, concerts today usually feature giant video screens so that fans can see the live performance up close by means of TV! Reality and the reproduction are thus, in the postmodernist way, hopelessly confused. (The confusion is compounded when performers "lip sync" their act, or when the concert is itself turned into an album, producing the strange paradox of a "live recording.")[25]

The new technology undercuts traditional ideas about authorship—a movie is a collaboration of many artists, from the writer to the director to the actors to the cinematographer and more. Photocopiers wreak havoc with copyright laws. Videotape recorders, tape players, and programmable compact discs enable consumers to reproduce films, TV shows, and music for their own use. As a result of both legal reproduction and illegal pirating, artists scarcely hold title to their own work. This mass production of the arts is dehumanizing—for the artist, the work, and the culture as a whole.

Some people decry the dehumanization; others embrace it. Some postmodernists, like Warhol, affect a pose of blank openness to the mass society. They hold to no beliefs, and, as was said of Warhol, "condemn nothing." Other postmodernists are fiercely political. They seek to undermine existing power structures. Both camps, however, minimize the role of the artist and ridicule the notion that art exists to elevate society.

THE POLITICS OF ART

It is odd that artists, of all people, should be so anti-art. One reason is the "hermeneutics of suspicion," the belief that all expressions of cultural value only mask power and oppression. Postmodernist criticism speaks of "the myth of the artist," assuming as a matter of course that artists, especially those considered by society to be the greatest artists, only passively transmit values designed to justify the ruling elite. Shakespeare is a tool of his patriarchal society; Michelangelo is a public-relations man for the Medicis and for the Catholic church; the impressionists offer soft-toned insulation for the leisured middle class. This is a formula for artists' self-loathing.

While Warhol and his followers blithely embrace commercialism, many post-Marxists in the arts worry about "commodification," art being turned into simply another commodity by the forces of capitalism. They feel guilty that their works are subsidized by "multinational corporations" who fund museums and create wealth for collectors to buy art.[26] Artists definitely want the money, but at the same time they want to feel politically correct.

One way of doing so is by irony. Artists can self-consciously play the culture game while ridiculing it at the same time. As a postmodernist critic explains, "If art must always seem to protect itself from the threat of this commodification by art galleries, theatres, TV networks and universities, then the logical extreme of this attitude is to refuse to be art at all."[27] Many of the strangest examples of contemporary art—random daubs of paint, empty frames, brutal scenes of violence and depravity, displays of the artist's bowel movements—can be understood by this in-your-face refusal. The deconstruction of the arts takes place when art repudiates art—the art world rebels against itself.

Post-Marxist critics do respect subversive art, works that come out of an oppressed class. Many postmodernist artists thus find their identity as members of some oppressed group (women, racial minorities, homosexuals, child-abuse victims; some consider artists to be an oppressed minority). These artists use these groups' agendas to shape their work. Abandoning traditional artistic values such as beauty and form, this approach to art reduces aesthetics to politics. Art becomes propaganda. (The 1993 Biennial Exhibition at New York's Whitney Museum of American Art featured the video of Rodney King's beating, "sleazy cartoonish paintings [that] skewer male domination," and various images celebrating homosexuality and lamenting AIDS. Visitors to the show had to wear admission buttons that read, "I can't imagine ever wanting to be white.")[28]

Postmodernists are thus concerned for extra-aesthetic issues, but their focus is not moral (which would seek reform based on objective ethical principles), nor is it philosophical (which would seek to understand the underlying causes of these issues). Rather, their focus is political. Moral and philosophical issues are reduced to questions of power and oppression, which artists typically respond to, not in a spirit of rational inquiry but with undiluted rage.

Postmodernist political art consists largely of satire and indignation. Subjects are flattened, in accord with the assumptions of social constructivism and group identity, into social stereotypes. These are aligned according to the postmodernist mythologies with secularized demons (wealthy white males; multinational corporations; the tacky middle class) and saints (women, homosexuals, the poor, racial minorities, and every other victim, including the suffering artist). The artists respond to power with power games of their own, attempting to shock and humiliate their bourgeois audiences.

Artists, with their audience-centered critical theories, work hard to provoke their audiences. Many artists today are concerned not so much with aesthetics, creating works of beauty, but with rhetoric, manipulating an audience to provoke a desired response.

When Andres Serrano submerged a crucifix in his own urine, the shock and public outcry was exactly what he wanted.

Postmodernists tend on principle to rebel against authority. This includes not only objective authorities (such as God, parents, the state), but also the authority of the text (which has no innate meaning) and the authority of the artist (the word *author*ity being based on the word *author*). This stifling of the artist's traditional role is justified for political reasons. "Minimizing the authority of the cultural producer," observes David Harvey, "creates the opportunity for popular participation and democratic determinations of cultural values, but at the price of a certain incoherence or, more problematic, vulnerability to mass-market manipulation."[29] The "cultural producer," that is, the artist or the author, must decrease so that the masses may increase. The role of the artist, according to this theory, is to offer raw material for consumers to recombine and interpret as they wish.

This liberation movement in the arts is exemplified in Bernard Dort's rabble-rousing theories about drama. The director, he believes, is an agent of repressive power, who "has not only gained authority over all the other workers in the theatre, but left them helpless and impotent, and in some cases reduced them almost to slavery."[30] Most people do not think of Broadway and Hollywood as being sweat shops, much less cotton plantations in the old South. To compare the *angst* of well-paid, pampered actors and movie stars complaining because they have to obey a director to the genuine suffering of black slaves is, of course, appallingly shallow. Notice too the Marxist rhetoric implicit in the whole analysis: the actors are "workers"; they are wage slaves; the artists are all cultural "producers." The director exercises authority over others, and all authority is assumed to be intrinsically oppressive.

Postmodernist dramatists even rebel against the authority of the author (what right does the playwright have to tell me what to do?). Instead, plays should be put together by group authorship. Everyone collaborates. Dramatists also rebel against the authority of the text (why should I follow the script?). Instead of memorizing lines, actors improvise.[31]

Ultimately, the play should be turned over to the audience. Dramatists have experimented with various ways to include the audience in the collaborative experience. A particularly obnoxious example has been adopted in dinner theaters across the country—resolving a mystery plot by allowing the audience to *vote* during the intermission on who they think "did it." The play then ends the way the audience wants it to. This, of course, makes nonsense of the plot, rendering any clues meaningless and totally ruining the intellectual puzzle provided by a good mystery. Still, the audience is "empowered." Another example is the newly developed technology of "interactive" entertainment, in which movies are interrupted at various points for the audience to make a decision by pushing a button, which determines what will happen next.

"Where the [modernist] ideal of the unified work of art concentrated upon the figure of the author-director," observes Connor, "postmodern theatre dissolves this unity; and with the surpassing of the authority of the single director goes the notion of the unified production."[32] What is true for drama is true for all of the arts. The New Criticism of modernism assumed the unity of the work of art and demonstrated how all of the parts cohere into a whole. Postmodernist criticism assumes *disunity*, focusing on the multiplicity of styles and themes, uncovering the work's linguistic and ideological contradictions. Postmodernist artists, with this in mind, are turning out works that purposely achieve disunity—novels that contain diverse and incompatible points of view, paintings that incorporate incompatible styles, nonfiction argumentation that self-consciously contradicts itself.

Art that surrenders its meaning; artists that surrender their creativity—such is the artistic self-abnegation of postmodernist culture. At its root is a profound repudiation of the human.

TOWERS OF BABEL:
The Example of Architecture

Not confined to elite galleries and *avant garde* salons, post-modern art has spilled over into television and movies, rock music and computer games. Postmodernism is a major force not only in literature but in architecture—the office buildings where people work, the malls where they shop, and the homes where they live.

Even more than the art of the museums, the places where we live and work testify to the climate of the times. Since architecture must appeal to the people who pay for the design and who must live in the building, it tends to reflect popular tastes and values more accurately than the "fine arts."

Contemporary architecture, in reacting against modernism, can in some ways serve as a model for a positive postmodern aesthetic. Although postmodern*ism* manifests itself in architecture too, contemporary building design has made stylistic breakthroughs that Christians can applaud.

MODERN ARCHITECTURE

The glass-and-steel skyscraper best represents modernist architecture. Looming over the old-fashioned buildings of the city, with their low stone walls and their Victorian bric-a-brac, the monumental glass towers dwarfed the past and made history seem irrelevant. The new structures were awe-inspiring in their sheer size and in the marvel of their construction, suggesting no limits to what "modern man" could do. In this respect the new constructions called to mind an earlier skyscraper, the Tower of Babel.

Employing new materials and new technology, modernist architects also advocated a new aesthetic for the twentieth century. Modernist architects rejected the ornamentation of the previous century as old-fashioned. Formerly, buildings were designed so as to refer to the past or to some meaning outside themselves. Government buildings might be built with Greek columns and Roman domes, associating American democracy with its origins in the classical republics. Churches would have steeples and stained-glass windows, as did the Gothic cathedrals of the great age of faith. Modernist architects rejected this sort of "referentiality." A building should be self-contained, referring only to itself.[1]

The modernist aesthetic was based on the principle of "form follows function." Instead of designing a structure around some pre-existing meaning or form, the *function* of the building should have priority.

Churches, for example, were traditionally designed in the shape of a cross. The church building would feature a long "nave" (the main hall) crossed at some point by a hall at right angles known as a "transept." From above, the building would look like a cross. Worshipers would literally join together in the cross—a profound theological statement. Traditional church design was governed by other theological principles (with the structure of narthex, sanctuary, and altar alluding to the three-part division of the Biblical Temple). In such an approach to design, the form and the meaning of the building—its theology—come first.

The modernist approach to church design would first ascertain the practical functions the building needs to fulfill. A church, for example, would have to accommodate a certain number of worshipers so that everyone could see and hear the pastor. An auditorium would be designed accordingly. If needed, classrooms for Sunday school, a kitchen, a fellowship hall would be tacked on. In this approach, practical matters and the convenience of those who will use the building have priority.

I do not mean to criticize modern church buildings. Styles to a large extent are *adiaphora*, indifferent matters unregulated by Scripture. Obviously, Christians can worship very well in modern buildings, just as they can make use of other modern styles and conveniences. But the shift away from a theologically informed style to a sheerly functional, and thus human-centered style, is significant.

"Form follows function" did not mean that modernists were indifferent to form. They believed that attention to function would result in a pleasing form. By attending only to the laws of physics, mathematical precision, and technological requirements, architects found that beauty could be a by-product of a scientific fidelity to the natural order. To a large degree, they were right. The office buildings that dominate Chicago's skyline are enormous, but they are also slim and graceful, models of unity and simplicity. That beauty can result from attention to objective natural law is a testimony to the marvelous ordering of God's creation.[2] The modernist architects, however, were working out of the Enlightenment confidence in human reason, the orderliness of nature, and a utilitarian value system.

Modernism in architecture manifested itself not only in skyscrapers but in mass-produced housing. Builders constructed vast tracts of suburban housing in which each house looked exactly the same as its neighbors. While it is fashionable now to criticize these "cookie-cutter" houses, these tract homes, since they followed standardized designs, could be built economically, opening home ownership to ordinary Americans in a way never before possible.

Such standardized housing, to be sure, is impersonal, just as the skyscrapers overwhelm any kind of human scale. Human beings need more than just functional efficiency. The monotonous drabness of the glass and steel towers, void of bright colors or other decorative touches, the conformity of block after block of identical little boxes, the exaltation of function and technology over the human, soon grew stifling. Despite the utopianism of the urban planners, human beings could not live for long in a totally modernist environment.

Instead of solving the problems of the cities, modernism actually made them worse. Urban Renewal programs bulldozed close-knit neighborhoods. The middle class migrated along the new interstate highway system to suburban housing developments. Regional differences and the individual character of communities dissolved in the prefab construction and fast-food franchises. Small towns covered over their old-fashioned Victorian buildings with fiberglass facades.

Those who built the Pruitt-Igoe housing project in St. Louis designed a form to follow the function of solving the housing problems of the urban poor. Unfortunately, like the other social engineering schemes of the Great Society, it did not work. Designed according to every modernist principle, the project proved unlivable. In 1972 the city dynamited Pruitt-Igoe, marking the end of modernism in architecture.[3]

POSTMODERN ARCHITECTURE

Disillusioned with the modernist dogma that the present is always the best, architects and the public they serve rediscovered the value and beauty of the past. They started restoring old buildings. When they needed a new building, they incorporated styles from the past. New housing developments started requiring that every house have a distinct design. Office buildings began to be designed on a more human scale. A new regionalism sought to restore the unique character and culture of communities.

Whereas modern architecture is abstract, postmodern architecture is referential. Modern buildings were self-contained; postmodern buildings tie in to their surroundings. The modern worships the present; the postmodern is open to the past. Modern design works to achieve unity; postmodern design is historically and stylistically pluralistic.[4]

Modern buildings look typically drab in their concrete and steel. Postmodern high-rises often flaunt bright colors and rich decorative detail. The ornamentation is flagrantly nonfunctional and often draws from past styles. A contemporary building may include Art Deco touches from the 1920s or updated classical columns or simplified Victorian bric-a-brac.

Postmodern architects took as their key text a book titled *Learning from Las Vegas*.[5] Against the elitism of modernist architecture, its author, Robert Venturi, champions the glitzy, but populist and human-centered architecture of the Las Vegas strip and other commercial buildings. Instead of the concrete slabs of modernist architecture, Venturi celebrates buildings that frankly cater to the whims and fantasies of ordinary people (such as the gaudy luxury of Vegas hotels). Contrary to what the modernists said, a building does not refer only to itself, but is a "text," a type of language. Buildings, therefore, *should be* referential. Venturi is fascinated with buildings that incorporate language into their design (such as the gargantuan neon signs of the Las Vegas strip) and with buildings that openly declare their meaning in their very structure (such as hot dog stands shaped like giant hot dogs). Venturi sees nothing wrong with buildings that are playful, funny, or in conventionally bad taste.

Recovering historical styles, respecting sheerly aesthetic touches, designing buildings that people enjoy instead of creating structures that intimidate them, returning form to function—the postmodern movement in architecture has been a refreshing change.

DECONSTRUCTIVE ARCHITECTURE

Other architects, however, go much further, applying the tenets of postmodern*ism* to architectural design. They reject the modernist ideal of unity and have devised a new aesthetic based on disunity. Instead of merely constructing buildings, some architects are deconstructing them. As it has on nearly every level, the postmodern age has made possible both a new conservatism and a new radicalism. Key

Philip Johnson designed and built the AT&T building in New York City in 1978, a thirty-seven-story skyscraper with a baroque-style arched entryway. Whereas the neighboring modernist skyscrapers usually have flat roofs, the AT&T building is topped by a classical pediment with a hole in it, a design modeled after Chippendale furniture. The result is a hybrid of modernistic highrise and grandfather clock.[6]

Much postmodern architecture has been genuinely trying to recover the past, restoring historical buildings and constructing new buildings that draw on the old aesthetics. Yet much postmodernist architecture is like the AT&T building. It pilfers various historical styles and works them into a pastiche (the characteristic postmodernist form), void of coherence or meaning. The combination of discordant styles (modernism, baroque, classicism) and discordant scales (a skyscraper turned into a piece of furniture) is a sort of joke. By lifting these incompatible styles out of history and tacking them together, the styles lose their significance. History is reduced to a smorgasbord of styles, to be sampled according to one's taste. The effect is to deconstruct style and to relativize history.

The AT&T exhibits pluralism for pluralism's sake. Postmodernists have pointed out that in the urban sprawl of a city, different styles really do coexist side by side.[7] A modernist skyscraper may stand next to a Gothic cathedral, which adjoins McDonald's golden arches. Across the street a restored Victorian opera house may abut a boarded-up, burned-out, graffiti-scarred tenement. Postmodernists in all of the arts see such diversity as a virtue, employing diverse styles even within a single work.

The postmodernists' obsession with surfaces and role-playing manifests itself in the manipulation of facades. The Red Lion Row development in Washington, D.C. appears to consist of a block of historically restored row houses. Actually, these quaint relics of the nineteenth century are only a facade—a stage set. Behind them in plain sight looms the real building they are attached to, a huge, impersonal structure of glass and steel.[8]

Some postmodernist architects have set about overtly deconstructing their own designs. Parodying architectural conventions, they make buildings that contradict themselves and mock both their forms and their functions. James Wines designed a series of Best stores that made people driving by the shopping strips do a double take.[9] He decorated parking lots with cars half-buried, fins up, in the asphalt or impaled on giant spikes. One of his stores in Milwaukee looked as if it were falling apart. The front wall was apparently peeled away in a pile of bricks, revealing shelves holding plaster replicas of lamps, toasters, and Barbie dolls. A customer would walk past this facade, past the plaster replicas, through the glass doors, and into the store with its shelves of real lamps, toasters, and Barbies. The store was designed as a parody of itself, employing the conventions of strip-mall department stores, only to make fun of them. The store, with its fake rubble and gaping hole in its structure, was not so much a construction as a deconstruction. (When another corporation bought the store, it tore away Wines's distinctive touches. Now the structure looks just like all of the other featureless, boring buildings on the strip.)

MALLS AND THEME PARKS

Contemporary architecture has a curious feature, the confusion of interiors and exteriors.[10] If you walk from the street into a new office building, the first thing you see inside may well be trees! Many buildings today include atriums complete with trees, nature paths, and bright sunlight. The outdoors is brought indoors. Idealizing nature in an environmentally correct sort of way but unwilling to do without technological conveniences such as air conditioning, postmodernists prefer parks indoors.

Just as the atrium brings the outside inside, many postmodernist buildings bring the inside outside. Structural framework such as beams and ventilation ducts may appear on the surface for everyone to see. An extreme example is the Pompideau Center in Paris, built in 1977. Support beams, tie rods, and the plumbing appear to be on the *outside* of the building, painted in bright, garish colors. The inner workings of the building are visible behind a thin skin of transparent glass. An escalator snakes along the *exterior* of the building. It is as if the building were turned inside out. The effect is unsettling, like looking at a man but seeing only his insides—his lungs, blood vessels, and red guts.

Perhaps the most characteristic and widespread example of postmodern architecture and its relationship to contemporary society is the shopping mall. On the outside one sees a featureless, windowless concrete bunker sprawling over acres and surrounded by a sea of free parking. Inside, though, the shopper encounters something like the old-time village squares, complete with trees, fountains, plazas, and sidewalk cafes. Each shop has its own decor, with display windows but no doors. Music is piped in. The air is cooled or heated. The whole space is attractively decorated and designed around the desires and whims of the customer. Every detail proclaims the message: Spend money! The mall stands as a temple to consumerism and all of its values—comfort, affluence, convenience, and fashion. The Middle Ages had its cathedrals; the modern age had its factories; the postmodern age has its shopping malls.

Another contender for the representative postmodern construction is the theme park. Different sections of the park are typically modeled after various historical periods and cultural milieus. The shops, restaurants, and rides in each section depict a "theme"—the Old West, Pirates of the Caribbean, European Village, Main Street U.S.A. Characteristic styles of the period or culture (as they exist in the popular imagination, with little effort to be historically accurate) carry out the theme. These parks offer a sort of "virtual reality," a fantasy world of stage-set facades and vicarious experiences. Everything exists to indulge the fantasies of the customer. The real theme of a theme park is total entertainment.

The ultimate postmodernist structure may be Minnesota's Mall of America, a mall and a theme park rolled into one. As someone who occasionally goes to both malls and theme parks, I do not want to put them down. That would be both snobbish and modernist. They are wonders of free enterprise and American culture. Trips to a mall or to Disneyland are essentially innocent activities. Malls and theme parks do, however, exalt consumerism and entertainment as the prime values, an attitude that, if allowed to run out of control, could be deeply problematic from a Christian perspective.

Sometimes today *churches* resemble malls or theme parks, not only in their architecture, but in the way people think about them. Megachurches sometimes resemble malls—with the parking lots, atriums, information booths, and shops featuring Christian merchandise. Employing marketing research and addressing people accustomed to the variety of choices offered at the local mall, these megachurches offer a range of activities and interest groups catering to every taste. Robert Schuller's Crystal Cathedral is something like a religious theme park, featuring babbling brooks and luxuriant plant life (*inside* the building) and multimedia sensory overload.

Just as the gospel can be proclaimed in a modernist auditorium as well as in a traditional sanctuary, Christ can certainly be preached in a postmodernist architectural setting. The problem comes when the *mind-set* of the malls and the theme parks becomes confused with Christianity.

Christians, like everyone else in today's economy, are consumers, but they dare not apply consumer values to God. Notice the implications of the phrase "church shopping." Surely, shopping for a church in the same way we shop for a major appliance is dangerous. Instead of looking for a church that teaches the Word of

God, we sometimes look for a church that "fills our needs." The church does not exist to provide its members "services"; rather, it should challenge its members to engage in "service" to God and to their fellow human beings. When we think like consumers, we put ourselves first, picking and choosing what best corresponds to our desires. Christianity is a matter of truth, of submission to a Holy, righteous God whose authority over us is absolute and who in no way is subject to our consumer preferences. Christianity must not be tainted with consumerism.

Nor is the church a theme park. Our tendency in the postmodern age is to evaluate everything in terms of its entertainment value. Judging a worship service according to how entertaining it is misses the point. Choosing a church because we like the music or because the preacher tells funny jokes is dangerous. Worship is not entertainment, but coming into the presence of a holy God. A relationship with Christ is not contingent upon how good we feel. Rather, as those who worshiped in traditional churches were always reminded, it is a matter of being gathered into His cross.

BABEL REVISITED

What has been happening in architecture illustrates what is happening throughout the arts and the culture after the collapse of modernism. Christians will applaud some trends and question others. The sheer diversity of postmodern expressions gives a new opening for the church. The temptation, however, is to capitulate to the new mind-set rather than work to redeem it.

If modernism in its pride and pretension recalls the Tower of Babel, postmodernism in its pluralism and confusion represents the curse of Babel. Yet, just as the confusion of tongues was an appropriate judgment on those who erected the Tower, postmodernism is in many ways a salutary correction to modernism.

The postmodern age has room for Christianity in ways that modernism did not. Its openness to the past, its rejection of narrow rationalism, its insistence that art refers to meanings and contexts beyond itself—these insights are all useful to the recovery of a Christian worldview.

But the postmodernist rejection of absolutes, its triviality and relativism, and its penchant for self-gratification undercut

Christianity. To get past the dead end of modernism and to resolve the chaos of postmodernism, the contemporary world stands in need of a Pentecost, the gift of a language that communicates to all, and the Holy Spirit, who alone can undo the curse of Babel.

METAFICTIONS:
TV, Movies, and Literature

Some say that the age of literacy is over. Reading has become obsolete. The written word is giving way to the electronic image. Reading demands abstract thought, the connection of sequential ideas, and an inner life. Once reading goes, the anti-intellectualism, relativism, and shallowness that already characterize postmodern society will accelerate out of control.[1] To a degree, this is happening. The electronic media is the supreme postmodernist art form, both aesthetically and in its all-pervasive influence.

On the other hand, even television scripts have to be written. Those who still read and write will remain the cultural producers of the postliterate age. Just as literature underlies drama, it underlies the electronic media. People still read and write, and literature both questions and pushes the envelope of postmodern culture. Christians need to recognize the developments in these fields, not only to be alert for negative influences but to participate in a positive way in contemporary thought. After all, Christians, being "people of the Book," can never abandon reading and writing. Thus, Christians may be in a unique position to be cultural producers themselves.

TELEVISION

It has been said that television *is* the real world of postmodernist culture. Nothing counts unless it gets on TV.[2] Only what is televised can enter the national consciousness—the political issues deemed worthy of attention, the events that will seem significant, the fashions and new products that will sweep the country, even (ironically) the books that will become bestsellers.

In accord with the tenets of postmodernism, the TV culture includes a diversity of styles and a jumble of histories.[3] The postmodernist rejection of words in favor of images, the replacement of reason with emotional gratification, the abdication of meaning in favor of entertainment are all inherent in the genre. The TV watcher submits to a collage of unconnected images, to appearances, to surfaces—in short, to all of the characteristics of postmodernism.

Postmodernist philosophers argue that all truth is a kind of fiction; postmodernist artists attempt to blur the distinction between art and reality. Such theories may seem esoteric, but they are the bread and butter of television.

The boundary between fiction and reality blurs every day on the news, which shapes actual occurrences into "media events." Again, "something isn't real until it's on TV"—an event does not get the attention of the country unless it shows up on the network news and CNN. Conversely, an event, no matter how trivial, becomes magnified out of all proportion when broadcast on television. The criterion for newsworthiness is essentially whether the audience will find the story stimulating. On television life is transfigured into entertainment.

The lines between truth and fiction further blur in docudramas, which take actual events and fictionalize them for the camera. These typically do more than dramatize history. The stories will be twisted to give them more entertainment value. Viewers are left with the impression that they have seen the truth. A docudrama on the last days of Marilyn Monroe (of which there have been many, each with new lovers and conspiracies), showed her having an affair with Robert Kennedy, of which there was no evidence whatsoever. Docudramas favor sensational crimes and lurid sex scandals, projecting the impression that this is the real world.

Another favorite genre is the "disease of the week" made-for-TV movie, showing a loving family, one of whose members gets a horrifying disease. We might also define another subgenre as the "moral dilemma of the week." The protagonist faces an agonizing decision, usually involving medical ethics. A loving family has a baby with a dreadful deformity; in their loving way they decide to remove the feeding tube, but right-wing religious extremists go to court to interfere with the family's decision and prolong the baby's pain. TV shows that treat such topics are—for all their pretense to honesty and sensitivity—completely predictable. They always favor abortion, "pulling the plug," euthanasia, and suicide—presenting them with tears and violin music as unimpeachable acts of heroic compassion.

We also have "reality-based" TV. Talk shows interview interesting people, such as "self-mutilators" and "adopted people who are sexually attracted to their natural siblings" (actual listings for one week's Maury Povich show). On TV these people are warmly accepted by the host and the studio audience, except for a few who are unattractively "judgmental." The guests all seem so, so normal.[4]

In another kind of "reality-based" TV program, a camera follows police officers or paramedics on their nightly rounds. This more directly turns truth into a TV show. Footage of police patrols are, of course, edited. We do not see the hours in the squad car, the tasks of writing up reports, the gathering of evidence, and the footwork that make up the real substance of a police officer's job. All we see are the raids, the arrests, and (if the TV producers are really lucky) the suspects getting roughed up. The "reality," in other words, is edited so that it follows the format of television crime shows!

With "reality-based" television splicing scenes of actors into actual footage, truth and fiction become hopelessly mixed up. What is real? What is just a special effect? It is becoming increasingly difficult to tell the difference. When NBC filmed an exposé of alleged safety problems in GM trucks, they installed ignitors on the trucks so they would blow up. While championing truth-in-advertising and supporting the rights of consumers against the sinister multinational corporations, they staged the very safety problem they claimed to be exposing.

Viewers will tend to accept what they see on TV as truth. After all, they saw the truck blow up with their own eyes. They saw the crime being committed, despite the printed subtitle "dramatic reenactment." That actress did look like Marilyn Monroe, and you know about those Kennedys (from other docudramas). Watching the CIA plan her death makes it plausible to think that maybe they did have something to do with it. After all, "seeing is believing." But not on TV. Television, in the postmodernist way, gives us only appearances.

As if it were not postmodern enough, contemporary TV is now self-consciously imitating some of the cutting-edge experiments of postmodern writers. In fact, television provides some of the clearest and most accessible examples of distinctly postmodernist literature.

You are watching a made-for-TV movie about a young man dying of AIDS. The tears of his family fade out for a commercial break. To upbeat music, a woman wrapped in a towel gets ready to step into the shower. The images register in your mind: *soap commercial*. Suddenly, into the bathroom comes a toy rabbit beating a drum. A voice-over says, "Still going!"

You are caught up short—you *thought* it was a soap commercial because it followed all of the conventions of soap commercials. But you realize that what you were watching was nothing but a joke, a parody of a soap commercial. And yet it *is* a commercial after all, but for a different product. It promotes Eveready batteries by showing this toy rabbit "still going" from commercial to commercial, interrupting pitches for other products, powered by a battery that just never runs down.

This playing with conventions, the creation of levels of fictionality, the blurring of the barriers between what is real and what is not, are characteristic of postmodern styles. While the Eveready rabbit may be wearing thin, expect to see more of this kind of postmodernist commercial. For example, some magazine ads follow the conventions of magazine ads, only to negate them. A sumptuous and alluring photograph will be marked with the company logo, but the photograph will have nothing to do with the product, which will not even be shown. Some postmodern ads are particularly entertaining, such as the Snapple commercial in which an actual consumer is strapped to a lie detector to see if he really likes the product.

Just as these commercials tend to be more clever than the ones we are used to, some elements of postmodernism offer a breath of fresh air from the arid modernism that has been stifling the arts. Because it tends to trivialize what it portrays, postmodernism works best as parody or as a mindless but amusing game. When it trivializes what should be taken seriously and when it becomes nothing more than a convention of its own, void of content and emotion, it wears thin. In a recent movie, when Martin Sheen's Rambo parody was interrupted by the Eveready rabbit, he took his machine gun and blasted it to smithereens; everybody cheered.

Modern situation comedies present their characters as if the people were in a self-contained world; viewers eavesdrop into Jackie Gleason's flat or Rob and Laura's living room. In postmodern situation comedies, Garry Shandling steps out of his role and addresses the camera and us as viewers directly, interrupting the action to tell us how great it is to work with his guest star or putting shaving cream on the camera lens and giving us a shave. In Shandling's new program, he plays a fictional talk show host; what we see is a talk show, pretty much like every other talk show. ("The Garry Shandling Show" has since influenced other situation comedies such as "Seinfeld," in which the comedian Jerry Seinfeld plays a comedian named Jerry Seinfeld who is working on a TV show about a comedian named Jerry Seinfeld.) The multi-layered teenage world of "Parker Lewis Can't Lose," the reality-bending humor of David Letterman, the short-lived mystery series in which the viewer, through the camera, took the role of the detective's sidekick—these are all self-conscious experiments in postmodern TV.

FILM

A good example of a modernist movie would be *Citizen Kane*. The film explores the life of its central character, trying to solve the mystery of his personality by investigating a question: What is the meaning of the last word he uttered on his death bed—*Rosebud?* The film delves deeply into his past and into his psyche. It does so by approaching Kane from various points of view, presenting him through the eyes of his guardian, his best friend, his estranged wife, all in an attempt to fix objectively what this man was like. This is the same method employed in the paintings of Picasso and the novels of Faulkner, presenting reality from a number of different points of view as a way of fixing its meaning. Modernism, as Harvey observes, uses multiple perspectives as a way to capture an objective reality.[5]

Postmodernist films, on the other hand, as Harvey explains

them, set up different worlds, all occupying the same space. Characters must try to discover what world they are in. In David Lynch's *Blue Velvet*, a small-town 1950s world coexists with an underworld of nightmarish perversion. One is a mask for the other, and the characters inhabit both of them simultaneously.[6] Connor points out how *Blue Velvet* combines the style of Frank Capra's small town film with that of the pornographic cult film, juxtaposing the commonplace (white picket fences and bright manicured lawns) with the unpresentable (a rotting ear lying in the grass).[7]

Other postmodernist films would include, on a lighter note, *Roger Rabbit*, with its interplay between the cartoon world and the "real" world (both of which are integrated into the larger fictional world of the film itself). *Blade Runner* sets up a futuristic world of high-tech space platforms orbiting a world of urban squalor; the hero must track down renegade androids, but in a world where humans act like machines and machines act like humans, it is never clear which is which. *Brazil,* another example of postmodern science fiction, has a futuristic setting, but the characters wear clothes from the 1930s; this brave new world is both a utopia and a dystopia; the story is a montage of satire and adventure, comedy and tragedy.[8]

In *The Purple Rose of Cairo*, a woman falls in love with a character in a movie, who eventually steps out of the screen into her life. Similarly, in *The Last Action Hero*, a boy watches a movie and enters the screen to share adventures with his hero; then the hero enters his world where smashing your fist through a window actually hurts and where bad guys sometimes win. Oliver Stone's *JFK* intercuts actual footage of the assassination with fictional dramatizations of his daft leftist conspiracy theory, confusing truth and fiction so egregiously that his movie persuaded Congress to call for new investigations!

What they all have in common is playing with the conventions of movie making and movie watching. In setting up fictionalized worlds and then confusing the boundaries between them, these films call into question the barriers we set up between what we think is real and what we think is made up. Are not our romantic dreams and our imaginative fantasies, shaped as they are by Hollywood, an important part of our "real" lives? Beneath the facade of ordinary small town life, is it not true that demons often lurk? Which is "real"? Is not reality itself an imaginative construction?

METAFICTION

Much of this pop postmodernism is a type of "metafiction." The term, from postmodernist literary criticism, refers to fiction about fiction. Garry Shandling sets up situation comedies about situation comedies, talk shows about talk shows. *The Purple Rose of Cairo* is a romance movie about romance movies. As Umberto Eco has observed, we now have television programs about television programs, TV whose only content is TV, such as the awards shows and talk shows (in which celebrities are interviewed whose only claim to fame is that they are on TV).[9]

In literature metafiction is defined as the "exploration by literary texts of their own nature and status as fiction."[10] Critics have long noticed how a work of fiction can create and sustain a world of its own,[11] an illusory sense of reality that is almost palpable to the imagination as we read. Postmodern authors push the boundaries of these imaginary worlds, probing them for their limits and experimenting with ways of drawing in the external world without breaking the spell—and sometimes breaking the spell on purpose.

John Barth's "Life-Story" is about a writer writing a story, which in fact is the story that we are reading. "Without discarding what he'd already written, he began his story afresh in a somewhat different manner," it begins. "He being by vocation an author of novels and stories it was perhaps inevitable that one afternoon the possibility would occur to the writer of these lines that his own life might be a fiction, in which he was the leading or an accessory character." He goes on, developing this idea and sometimes interrupting himself with commentary on what he has written. ("What a dreary way to begin a story he said to himself upon reviewing his long introduction.")

Towards the end, he addresses "you," the reader of his story:

> The reader! You, dogged, uninsultable, print-oriented [expletive], it's you I'm addressing, who else, from inside this monstrous fiction. You've read me this far, then? . . . How is it you don't go to a movie, watch TV, stare at the wall. . . . For why

do you suppose—you! you!—he's gone on so, so relentlessly refusing to entertain you . . .? Why has he as it were ruthlessly set about not to win you over but to turn you away? Because your own author bless and damn you his life is in your hands! He writes and reads himself; don't you think he knows who gives his creatures their lives and deaths? Do they exist except as he or others read their words?

The fictional world exists only as it is being imagined by readers. Fictional characters—and himself as a character—are utterly dependent upon those of us who read these words.

In the story, it turns out that the author/character yearns to die:

But as he longs to die and can't without your help you force him on, force him on. Will you deny you've read this sentence? This? . . . As if he'd know you'd killed him! Come on. He dares you.

He begs the reader to stop reading and thus let him die. This, he says, is the real reason why he has refused to entertain us by writing such an unconventional story. If we do stop reading, of course (or haven't made it this far), we do what he requests. If we keep going, we sustain his life against his will.

At the end of the story, the author realizes that he *must* be real because he can recall no other story in which a character suspects that he might be a work of fiction. (Until, one supposes, this story is published.) He realizes that his whole premise must be false (thus contradicting and deconstructing everything he has written thus far). His wife comes into his study and interrupts him by kissing him. "He did at last as did his fictional character end his ending story endless by interruption, cap his pen."[12]

I have to admit, I enjoy this sort of thing. Nor is this self-reflexive fiction exactly new. Chaucer makes himself one of the characters in *Canterbury Tales*; when it is his turn to tell a story, this giant among authors makes an effort, but it is so bad that the other characters won't let him finish. The very first novels used such devices. Don Quixote reads a book about his adventures, presumably "Part I," which we have just read, and comments on its inaccuracies. In Richardson's *Pamela*, the villain reads the heroine's writings, which is what the rest of us have been reading. When this character reads the novel in which he is the villain, he is so ashamed that he becomes converted and asks Pamela to marry him. The levels upon levels of fictionality are also explored in ancient tales such as *The Arabian Nights*, with their stories within stories, and in Renaissance drama, with its plays within plays. The effect of these fictional games is to tease the reader into making distinctions between levels of reality and unreality, blurring the boundary between the story-world and "real life."

A Christian would have no problem with the concept that life is a story. Christians believe that God created, sustains, and sovereignly controls all of existence by His Word, much as human authors create and control their fictional worlds. In fact, English translations of the Bible often describe Christ as "the author" of faith and salvation (Hebrews 2:10, 12:2), "the author of life" (Acts 3:15). There is, though, a crucial difference between the Christian imagination and that of the postmodernists who believe that there is no author of life. John Barth says as much in the story we have just discussed:

> Inasmuch as the old analogy between Author and God, novel and world, can no longer be employed unless deliberately as a false analogy, certain things follow: 1) fiction must acknowledge its fictitiousness and metaphoric invalidity or, 2) choose to ignore the question or deny its relevance or, 3) establish some other, acceptable relation between itself, its author, its reader.[13]

In his story, Barth reverses the traditional metaphor. Instead of the author being God, in his formulation the *reader* is God, responsible for sustaining the imaginary world in the process of reading. This aligns well with the postmodernist dictum that the meaning of a work of art is determined by the audience, that meaning as a whole is primarily subjective and relative. But in raising the issue of God, Barth cuts to the heart of the matter.

When Christian authors (such as Chaucer, Cervantes, Shakespeare, Richardson) play with metafiction and the metaphor of life as a story, they do so with the assumption that there is in fact an "author of life." (Barth himself suggests as much when he says to his readers, "your own author bless and damn you.") To say that life is a story implies for Christians two things: First, life has a meaning, a plot complete with conflicts (the battle with sin), a turning point (rejecting or accepting Christ), and a final resolution with either a tragic ending (namely, Hell) or a comic ending (with the sinner redeemed to live "happily ever after" in Heaven). Second, a fictional story, in reflecting the narrative of life, can be in some sense true.

Postmodernists, as we have seen, begin by rejecting the notion that life has an objective meaning. They agree with the existentialist notion that "there is no meaning in life," that there is no rhyme or reason, no plot or resolution to human existence. Postmodernists explicitly reject the idea that existence makes up a coherent story when they deny the ultimate truth of any "metanarrative." When postmodernists say that life is a story, they do not mean, as the Christians did, that a story can be true; they mean that *truth is only a story.*

In Barth's terms, "fiction must acknowledge its fictitiousness and metaphoric invalidity." Postmodernists exult in the fact that fiction is not real and does not have to be, opening up limitless possibilities for the writer. The real world too, they believe, is organized by "fictions," paradigms and "metanarratives" that are equally the product of human imagination. Postmodernists employ techniques of literary criticism to dissect laws, institutions, and moral traditions just as they dissect the structures and conventions of a novel. They might value some of these institutions, just as they value a good book, but any illusion of objective reality these might project is ultimately fictional. While postmodernist authors are busy writing "fiction that acknowledges its fictitiousness," postmodernist critics are busy acknowledging the "invalidity" of fiction, deconstructing both artistic narratives and the other narratives that give order to life.

Barth faces the issue honestly, given his assumption that "the old analogy between Author and God can no longer be employed." (But why not? Isn't the assumption that God can no longer be a factor because of the time period we live in a *modernist* sort of statement?) Barth is left with either fiction that acknowledges its invalidity, ignoring the problem, or the possibility of working out some other relationship between the text, the author, and the reader. As postmodernists struggle with the dilemmas posed by their own theories, they might experiment with the possibility that life really is a story, which really does have an author.

MAGICAL REALISM

In addition to writing metafiction, postmodernist authors play in other ways with the boundaries between the real and the unreal, putting both into question.

Modernist fiction tended to be highly realistic. Steinbeck, Hemingway, and Faulkner tried to convey the "truth" of experience, rendering not only the natural order with great fidelity, but capturing social conditions and the psychological dimension of their characters. Postmodernists call into question this modernist obsession with truth.

For all of its apparent realism, Steinbeck's *Grapes of Wrath* is still a work of fiction. In fact, Steinbeck's portrait of the Okies is rife with historical, geographical, and economic inaccuracies. Far from being an objective account of the Dust Bowl, the novel projects Steinbeck's own political and philosophical ideas, rendered in highly charged symbolism (much of which is drawn from the book of Exodus). The sense of realism that we experience when we read this book is an illusion created by Steinbeck's mastery of literary conventions. His descriptions, his selection of detail, his ear for dialogue, the way he organizes his narrative are all techniques for achieving verisimilitude, the impression that what is unfolding in our imaginations as we read is lifelike, enabling us to "suspend our disbelief" and imaginatively accept this fictional world.

Postmodernists find that these same techniques for achieving verisimilitude can also create the illusion of reality for things that are definitely *not* real. Postmodernist authors revel in the fictionality of their work. No longer under the constraint of having to imitate the external world, contemporary authors are creating sheerly from their imaginations. No longer is fantasy seen as an inferior genre, but as perhaps the purest form of fiction (a view that has helped the critical reputation of Christian fantastists such as J. R. R. Tolkien and George MacDonald).

Some postmodernists work in a style called "magical realism." Pioneered by Latin American authors such as Gabriel García Márquez, this style is a hybrid of fantasy and realism. Márquez writes about ordinary village life suddenly interrupted by the crash landing of an angel, who takes the form of a decrepit old man with enormous wings and lice in his feathers. Another of his characters unexpectedly ascends into Heaven while doing her laundry. Pieces of paper turn into butterflies. A whole village loses its memory overnight. Though marvels abound in Márquez's fiction, his characters pay little attention, going about their lives in a matter-of-fact way, oblivious to the wonderful things happening all around them.

This style, heavily indebted to the popular spirituality of Latin American Catholicism, can be exhilarating in the hands of a master storyteller such as Márquez. It may well be a method of raising spiritual issues. Its effect, though, is to blur the distinction between truth and fictionality. For this reason, it has become a signature style of postmodernism, even in popular culture. Think of the beer commercials that show a woman in a hot, gritty desert. She looks up and a man appears, though we never see his face. He opens a bottle of beer, and it begins to snow. He then either pours water from his boot to mark off a circle that turns into a tropical island, or they disappear into an empty well, or some other variation on the theme. This is magical realism, and it can be found in commercial after commercial, as well as in the programs they sponsor, from "The Simpsons" to MTV.

Think of how many popular movies today turn on inexplicable fantasies, which are then played out with deadpan realism. In *Groundhog Day*, a man keeps reliving the same day over and over. While a modernist movie would give some sort of reason, however far-fetched, for this dilemma (some sort of time machine or magical amulet gone awry), this movie gives not even a hint of explanation. The fantastic premise is accepted at face value by the audience, and it is then worked out in ingenious detail. Movies such as *Batman* combine sordid images of urban decay with comic book whimsy. In *L. A. Story*, Steve Martin gets advice from a wise and sensitive billboard. In *Field of Dreams* (based on a novel by the postmodern novelist W. P. Kinsella), Kevin Costner builds a baseball diamond in a cornfield for the late Shoeless Joe Jackson.

This is all magical realism. It is not conventional fantasy—no flights into other worlds, no medievalism, no ethereal dreaming. This fantasy is earthbound, grounded in a hard-edged, even depressing landscape in which wild, absurd, or wonderful things nevertheless take place.

BEING POPULAR

The Postmodernists' fascination with the conventions of fiction has revived "formula" fiction—genres such as mysteries, romances, medieval fantasies, science fiction, westerns. High-minded modernists have generally looked down on such works, but these have always been popular among ordinary readers. These genres do tend to have predictable patterns. In a mystery, a group of people are assembled (at a country estate, a workplace, a dinner party); one of them is murdered. A detective gathers clues, leading to the revelation of the killer's identity.

This structure is predictable, yet capable of infinite variation. To a mystery fan, the conventions of the genre are part of what makes it so delightful. These are not restrictive, any more than the structure of a sonnet limits a poet or the rules of the game get in the way of an athlete. Romances have conventions (a woman must choose between two suitors); as do medieval fantasies (knights rescue princesses and embark on quests). Science fiction has its predictable space voyages and alternative worlds. Westerns have their strangers coming to town to clean out the corrupt politicians and bring civilization to the frontier (whereupon the hero, himself a product of the frontier, has to move on, leaving behind the civilization he helped to create).

There are reasons why these forms are so popular, despite the disdain of academic critics. They embody primal themes—the conflict between good and evil, how to tell one from the other, choosing between the two. They engage the imagination and the intellect in complex ways. It is time to treat these genres with respect and bring them into the literary mainstream.

Postmodernists, remember, are reacting against the elitism of modernist high culture by embracing in a self-conscious way the popular culture. Distinguished literary artists now write mysteries, science fiction, historical romances, and they play with other popular formulas. This has had the salutary effect of making "serious" fiction entertaining again. Modernist fiction, with its earnest realism and aesthetic purity, had become somewhat dull. One would read the latest modernist masterpiece more out of a sense of duty than pleasure. Now talented writers are turning to popular forms, which benefits both serious literature (by making it more entertaining) and popular literature (by enlivening it with good writing).

Thus, the postmodernist theorist Umberto Eco turns out a medieval mystery, *The Name of the Rose*. Larry McMurtry outdoes the pulp westerns with *Lonesome Dove*. W. P. Kinsella writes baseball novels. Walker Percy, the much-respected Catholic novelist, writes the pro-life thriller *Thanatos Syndrome*.

These genres are sometimes played straight. Other times, they are played with in "metafictional" ways. For example, I have just finished a mystery novel by the Italians Carlo Fruttero and Franco Lucentini.[14] It is built around a historical fact. Charles Dickens's last work was a mystery novel, *The Mystery of Edwin Drood*. He died before finishing the manuscript, leaving a well-constructed mystery without an ending, without the final revelation of "who did it." Dickens scholars and mystery fans have tried to piece together the clues for themselves and have proposed a wide range of solutions. This Italian novel assembles a convention of the world's greatest detectives—Sherlock Holmes, Mrs. Marple, Philip Marlowe, Father Brown, and many more—to solve the mystery. The novel actually prints Dickens's manuscript, chapter by chapter, interspersed by chapters in which the great detectives analyze what is going on. The interplay between narrative levels (Dickens's manuscript; the commentary by characters who are also *fictional*) gets more and more complicated. A detective from one of Dickens's other novels slips into *Edwin Drood* to talk to some witnesses; clues are drawn from Dickens's *actual* life; another mystery plot emerges among the world's greatest detectives. Finally—well, you get the idea.

The swing of the pendulum away from stuffy modernism to a more entertaining brand of literature is healthy. There are, however, problems with this trend when seen in the context of postmodernist ideology.

Reducing literature to its conventions is part of the postmodernist project of dehumanizing culture. As we have seen, postmodernists reject the idea of the artist as a distinct individual creating original works out of a unique creative imagination. This view of the artist is too individualistic, giving too much credit to the powers of the human being. Postmodernist critics, dismissing the "myth of the author," reduce literature to the cultural forces and paradigms of power that it represents.

Postmodernist authors, while often avoiding the political interrogations that critics—like KGB agents—would like to put them through, are similarly abdicating the traditional role of the artist. By following well-established formulas, these authors do not pretend to be creating anything new. The conventions they follow do not even seem to be the creation of some previous author; rather, they seem to have simply emerged out of the culture, like myths and legends. However ingeniously contemporary authors play with the conventions, they are merely working variations on pre-existing themes. They are turning writing into a process that is, in accord with postmodernist orthodoxy, essentially impersonal.

This approach to writing, in accord with postmodernist theory, is also audience-centered. Following popular formulas is a way of giving the audience what it wants. Artists used to struggle to express themselves, refusing to compromise their integrity in conveying their unique insights to an often uncomprehending world. Today the artist might do market research to find out what the world wants to hear and then create the work of art accordingly. Whereas Milton wrote for a "fit audience, though few," contemporary authors seek a mass audience. This means that the audience, not the artist, determines, shapes, and is actually responsible for what is written.

The postmodernists' way of minimizing the artist does have its compensations. Instead of the poverty-stricken genius laboring in a garret to produce a classic, contemporary authors enjoy the celebrity and multimillion dollar advances of the best-seller list. Artistic integrity has its price.

It also has its cost. When writers give their readers exactly what they want, the readers are seldom enriched. They hear only what they already know; their prejudices are confirmed, their weaknesses pandered to. The audience is entertained, but not challenged or instructed. This is the weakness of so much postmodernist fiction. It may be scintillating, but it is ultimately trivial.

Few writers today, however talented, even attempt to take up the sort of serious themes that writers of the past explored as a matter of course. Milton asserted eternal providence and justified the ways of God to men. Keats probed the relationship between truth and beauty. Whitman celebrated democracy. Today such themes could only be treated with self-conscious irony, as parodies or hip jokes. Most contemporary authors have problems asserting anything. To be sure, many postmodernist writers *are* passionately engaged with important issues, often construed as social or political issues, but the force of their work is disabled by the philosophical poverty of contemporary thought. In the absence of the traditional absolutes (the true, the good, the beautiful), the great subjects for art evaporate. Authors are left with the hollow shell—the conventions without the substance.

NEW JOURNALISM

Reducing literature to conventions and blurring the distinctions between fiction and truth has another corollary: that reality is also merely a matter of conventions. This tenet of postmodernist orthodoxy manifests itself not only in metafiction and the new fantasy, but in the postmodernist styles known as "new journalism" and "super realism."

Postmodern literature is open to history and to the external world. Thus, historical novels are back in vogue. This is a refreshing change from modernist literature, which tended to minimize the work's historical context and to favor twentieth-century settings. Unfortunately, instead of using fiction to illuminate truth, many postmodernist writers are using fiction as a substitute for truth.

Consider one of the most popular forms of writing today, the "new journalism." Notice how many bestsellers today deal with "actual" events—lurid crimes, exposés of scandals, sensationalistic biographies, investigative journalism. These are often "nonfiction novels."

The "new journalists" write about actual events but use the techniques of fiction. They present events from the point of view of one of the "characters" involved, presenting the events as they unfold. They give descriptions, dialogue, even the thoughts of the different people they write about. The books usually have a clearly defined plot, complete with heroes and villains. Of course, no writer can know exactly what two people said to each other, much less what they were thinking. Nor does real life have the clear-cut plots that we are used to in fiction with its melodrama, suspense, and intrigue. New journalists feel free to shape their material according to their own purposes in the same way that novelists do.

Although this new technique makes historical events "come alive," it inevitably distorts the truth in the process. Truth is fictionalized. Like television's docudramas and Oliver Stone's pseudo-documentaries, fact and fiction become inextricably mixed up. Readers and viewers have the impression that this is all true, since they have experienced it vicariously while reading. In the case of a movie or television show, they have seen it with their own eyes. They will often change their opinions based on the work of art. And yet the work is mostly an imaginative construction.

Postmodernists justify the distortion by saying that our perceptions of truth are always imaginative constructions, always "fictions" of one kind or another. New journalists know exactly what they are doing and make no bones about their biases and lack of objectivity. Because postmodernists do not recognize the boundary between truth and fiction, even when they are being "realistic," they reject objectivity and maintain their position that truth is relative. Marvin Olasky has shown how mainline journalism has gone from a modernist attempt at objectivity (first giving "just the facts," then a Faulknerian rendering of multiple points of view) to a postmodernist denial of objectivity and the subsequent bias of today's journalism.[15] The illusion of reality entertains readers, but it also lies to them.

SUPER REALISM

Modernism promoted abstract art. The work of art was to be a self-contained aesthetic artifact, uncontaminated by references or meanings outside itself. The most characteristic paintings were nonrepresentational, not pictures "of" anything; rather, they depicted colors and forms arranged into some aesthetic design.

Today representational art is back, but not usually the beautiful landscapes or portraits of traditional art. If you go into an art museum, you might notice in one of the galleries a janitor sweeping up. After awhile, you realize that the janitor never moves. Looking closer, you see that this figure in overalls and a cap is not an actual human being at all, but a work of art. You are astounded with how *real* it looks. The clothing, the colors, the posture, the hair, the face—everything is exact, down to the pores in the skin. The effect is unsettling. This is the exact image of a human being, but there is no life. It is like looking at a corpse. And yet the effect is also strangely funny. When they see this sort of art, most people laugh.

This sort of sculpture has become popular in art galleries across the country. After going through the galleries of abstract art, people enjoy seeing something they can recognize. Yet these hyper-realistic wax figures exude an air of condescension and parody. They tend to be on the ugly side and usually portray bag ladies, blue-collar workers, or tackily dressed tourists. The laughter comes because the artist is making fun of them. The figures are stereotypes—portrayed not only without life but also without dignity. To be sure, they are realistic, but something is missing.

Compare one of these physically correct mannequins to a portrait by Rembrandt, who viewed human beings as created in the image of God. The portrait will not be so realistic, so obsessed with hard-edged detail, but it will shine with life. A Rembrandt portrait evokes the depths of the human soul endowed with value and spiritual significance. Contemporary realism presents the *surface* in obsessive detail, but there is nothing inside.

In the postmodernist style known as "super realism," artists often work from photographs, projecting the image on a canvas with an opaque projector and then painting it in. This results in an image that is intensely realistic while being completely flat and expressionless. The subjects are typically *cultural* artifacts, usually scenes of urban or suburban squalor—automobiles (either rusted hulks or muscle cars), neon signs, fast-food restaurants, highway pavement, linoleum, overweight women wearing tacky clothes.

In contemporary literature, super realism manifests itself in detached narratives about working-class people in low-rent settings. Because these writers continually recite brand names, the style has been called "K-Mart realism." This passage from Bobbie Ann Mason gives a good sense of both the style and the tone that characterizes super realism throughout the arts:

> They go to Penney's perfume counter. There, she usually hits a sample bottle of cologne—Chantilly or Charlie or something

strong. Today she hits two or three and comes out of Penney's smelling like a flower garden. . . . With her paycheck, Jeannette buys Rodney a present, a miniature trampoline they have seen advertised on television. It is called Mr. Bouncer. Rodney is thrilled about the trampoline, and he jumps on it until his face is red. Jeannette discovers that she enjoys it, too. She puts it out on the grass, and they take turns jumping. . . . That night, she has a nightmare about the trampoline. In her dream, she is jumping on soft moss, and then it turns into a springy pile of dead bodies.[16]

Note the short monotonous sentences, the bored tone, the emotional and spiritual emptiness, the implied disdain for ordinary people. "The flattest possible characters in the flattest possible landscapes rendered in the flattest possible diction."[17]

Obsessively imitating the external world is another way of dehumanizing the arts. The artist no longer "creates" or "expresses" some vision of an autonomous self. Rather, he or she slavishly imitates external images, generally bland products of a commercial culture. Artistic skill is subordinated to an impersonal process. Both the artist and the subject are drained of personality. Super realism replaces a "humanistic" view of the arts in accord with postmodernist ideology.

Traditional art is representational, but its concern goes beyond external appearances. Artists consider the *meaning* of what they depict. A Greek statue may depict an athlete with muscular accuracy, but it also tries to convey an image of perfection. No actual Greek athlete probably looked as good as the statue. The Greeks expressed their fascination with the *ideal* in their art. Classical landscapes attempt to convey the formal perfection of nature. Romantic landscapes, on the other hand, depict the wildness and sublimity of nature. A portrait reveals not only what the subject looks like, but something about the person's character. In each case, the artist would also be concerned with the formal composition of the painting, its balance of color and form. The point is, traditional art has always hinged on the interplay between the external world and the artist's expression, a synthesis of appearance and meaning.

With the loss of a comprehensive worldview, such as

Christianity, art split. Modernist art promoted meaning apart from the external world; postmodernist art promotes the external world apart from meaning. Art becomes a matter *either* of expression or representation, meaning or appearance, reality or illusion, truth or convention. Both modernists and postmodernists have forgotten that art can be both.

PART THREE

POSTMODERN SOCIETY

THE NEW TRIBALISM

*I*n a typical evening, an American family might drive their
Japanese car to a Mexican restaurant, return to their Tudor
home to watch a western on TV and listen to some reggae music.
Contemporary culture, like postmodernist art, is definitely eclectic.[1]
Surrounded by diverse styles and cultures, we pick and choose from
a global smorgasbord. We are told that we live in a pluralistic society, that we work in a global economy, that we must develop multicultural awareness.

One effect of this multicultural awareness is more relativism.
Since different cultures have different ways of thinking and of living, who is to say which is right? To imply that our Western mind-
set is the only truth and that all other cultures are wrong seems the
height of arrogance. In a pluralistic age, no one point of view can
have a monopoly on truth. To think otherwise labels one as eth-
nocentric, blind out of ignorance or bigotry to the world's diversity. Since today it is harder to ignore the presence of other cultures,
cultural relativism becomes for many people inescapable.

On the other hand, while postmodernism promotes stylistic
diversity, it also reduces style to *surfaces*. Is eating a burrito at Taco
Bell really equivalent to entering into the experience, history, and
values of the Mexican people? Is listening to reggae music on a
Japanese CD player really a multicultural encounter with the West
Indies and Japan? Contemporary westerners' understanding of
other cultures often only skims the surface, like tourists sampling
cultural stereotypes instead of genuinely engaging another civilization. If all cultural values are relative, then none need be taken seri-

ously. Postmodernist multiculturalism might affirm all cultures, but in doing so it may destroy them all.

The fact is, real cultures promote strict ethical guidelines. From Mexico to Africa, family ties are strong and sexual promiscuity is strictly forbidden. No culture (other than our own) would teach that there are no absolutes. Contemporary Western culture with its pornography, consumerism, and all-encompassing skepticism toward authority and moral traditions is ravaging traditional cultures.

Postmodernism has the effect of both leveling cultures and exaggerating the differences between them. Postmodernism fragments society into contending and mutually unintelligible cultures and subcultures. Even within a single society, people are segmenting into self-contained communities and contending interest groups. Christianity itself is ghettoized. From Bosnia to American universities, we see the emergence of a new tribalism.

SEGMENTATION

"Society is splintering into hundreds of subcultures and designer cults," a journalist observes, "each with its own language, code and life-style."[2] The combination of social changes, technological developments, and postmodernist ideology has undermined the very principle of a unified national culture and has driven individuals to find their identities in subcultures.

This loss of an overarching cultural identity can be partially explained in sociological and technological terms. The breakdown of the family has had catastrophic effects at every level. It is difficult for children to develop any sense of continuity and permanence when the most basic institution of their lives has no stability. It is little wonder that children whose parents have divorced and who have to adjust to a completely different family (or families) when parents remarry grow up to be relativists. (Such children, however, often grow up to form very strong families because they know how miserable unstable families can be. This seems especially evident within the church.)

Automobiles, interstate highways, and air travel have also damaged our sense of place. Few adults these days live in the same place where they grew up. Generation after generation used to live in the same neighborhoods or small towns. Extended families provided closeness and support. Living in such a stable environment and in a network of close personal relationships brought a sense of rootedness and community. That is gone now.

To be sure, many individuals found such close-knit communities stifling. So apparently did the early settlers of America, who left their ancestral villages and extended families in the old country for the freedom of the American wilderness. So did the pioneers whose wanderlust settled the frontier. (The Laura Ingalls Wilder books are wonderful models of American culture and family values, but did you ever notice how often that family—without benefit of cars or interstate highways—*moved*?)

Nevertheless, the pioneers worked together and depended on strong nuclear families. American culture found a way of balancing community and family spirit with rugged individualism. Today as we lurch to the extremes of either group conformity or self-centered isolationism, we often lose that delicate balance.

Modernism, in its social applications, homogenized society. Unity was achieved by obliterating past traditions in the name of progress. Technological standardization eroded the sense of place and the sense of local identity. National chain stores pushed out local businesses, and the cafés with their EAT and Home-Cooked Meals signs were torn down to make room for the ever-identical McDonald's. As a result of modernization, the commercial strips in just about every small town, suburb, and big city look pretty much the same. Radio disk jockeys from Charleston to Brooklyn, Des Moines to Bakersfield, speak with the same accent. In modern America, the whole nation watched the same television programs, listened to the same music, and wore the same fashions.

While modern innovations have created a certain unity at the expense of local identity, postmodern innovations are reversing the process. Technology once promoted unity, but now technology is being pushed so far that it promotes diversity. Network television homogenized society by making the whole country depend upon three centrally controlled networks for their information and entertainment. *Cable* television, on the other hand, allows the viewer to choose among an enormous number of channels. Broadcasting is giving way to narrowcasting in which channels are aimed at particular interests and particular *segments* of the audience.

Now we have a science fiction channel and a western channel, and channels for sports, comedy, health, and news. In the works is an all-golf channel so golf fanatics (and insomniacs) can enjoy the thrill of watching other people play golf twenty-four hours a day. Some channels appeal primarily to women, blacks, or Hispanics; others to Christians. Thus far the full potential of narrowcasting has not been realized. Most cable stations fill their time with reruns of old programming from the networks, endlessly repeating episodes of "Andy Griffith" and "Gilligan's Island" (thus in the postmodernist way preserving the past). But new fiber-optic technology will soon allow *hundreds* of new channels, creating an ever-more segmented audience.

Local communities, awakened by the postmodern historical preservation movement, are tearing off the plastic facades of downtown buildings and restoring them to their former splendor. Billboards, neon signs, and fast-food franchises are being zoned into control, and some communities are trying to restore a sense of regional and local personality. Such attempts, in the postmodern way, often deal with the surface rather than substance. (Developers often painstakingly restore historically rich nineteenth-century buildings on the outside and then install a shopping mall on the inside.) Still, this is an improvement over the technological standardization that bulldozed history and personality in the name of progress.

Segmentation, however, is more than diversity and more than a marketing device. People are finding their identities, not so much in themselves, nor in their families, nor in their communities or nation, but in the groups that they belong to.

The Civil Rights movement drew attention to the plight of racial minorities in this country, did much good in ensuring constitutional rights for black Americans, and taught other groups to assert their own special claims. American Indians, Hispanics, and Asian-Americans also began to organize to ensure their civil rights. Then the feminist movement claimed that women too are an oppressed group in need of civil-rights protection. Next homosexuals presented themselves as a persecuted minority. Soon a plethora of other minorities emerged—the handicapped, Vietnam veterans, AIDS victims—each claiming to be victims of discrimination and demanding federal redress.

In the meantime, American politics was becoming segmented in other ways. With the clout of the two traditional political parties fading, politics has become a battle of special interest groups. Environmental activists fight with Chambers of Commerce; anti-nuclear groups, black activists, gay rights coalitions, feminist organizations, and other special interest groups exercise, through their lobbyists and demonstrations, an influence far beyond their number.

I am not criticizing special interest groups. This is the way politics has to be conducted in the postmodern age, and Christians have had to learn to play this same game. The anti-abortion movement has demonstrated, lobbied, and exerted political pressure. Christian pro-lifers have done much to counter the much more powerful pro-abortion faction.

There is a problem, however, with this segmentation of politics. It destroys a common ground for argument or persuasion. Environmentalists and loggers, the American Civil Liberties Union and anti-pornographers have almost no common frames of reference. Pro-lifers know how difficult it is to discuss abortion with a militant pro-choicer. Appeals to Biblical morality, to the constitutional right to life, to scientific facts about the development of life in the womb, to the brutality of abortion techniques—these objective issues carry no weight with people whose worldview allows for no external absolutes, who accept no moral criteria beyond a woman's arbitrary choice, or who uncritically accept the orthodox feminist party line.

Because they lack a common philosophy and a common language, these special interest groups cannot persuade each other or even forge a compromise. They can only exert power over each other. One wins, the other loses, and the battles are often ugly and ruthless. The segmentation of society turns the different groups into hostile camps—pitting the old against the young, blacks against Koreans and Hispanics. In a return of class warfare the poor, the middle class, and the rich all blame each other for their economic problems.

Debate over moral values has erupted into a "culture war" that splits political parties, school boards, and even churches. As Leith Anderson has pointed out, "the culture and the church are entering an extended era of greater diversity, increased segmentation, polarization, division, even hostility." Anderson believes that "the church of the twenty-first century may be less divided over mode of baptism and more divided over race, money, abortion, homosexuality, and gender roles."[3] People will continue to hold strong opinions about moral issues, even though they will be less and less able to ground them in a common truth.

The fact is, Christians too have become a segment of society rather than an integral part of the culture. The church is on its way to becoming a subculture. Christians have their own bookstores, their own contemporary music, their own television networks, and their own schools. In many ways, Christians have formed a parallel culture to that of the secular world.[4] Christians have not so much withdrawn from secular arenas as they have been excluded from them. The ghettoization of Christianity, however, must be seen as part of the larger trend of the segmentation of postmodern culture.

Dominant ideologies have often dealt with religious minorities by sealing them off into self-contained ghettos. Reducing religion to just another subculture is a way to marginalize Christianity, to silence its arguments. ("You pro-lifers are just trying to force your religion onto other people.") On the other hand, religious segregation can have unintended results. The Jews were forced into ghettos as a means of persecution, but this had the secondary effect of building a vital, close-knit Jewish community. Something similar may be in store for Christianity.

Many people had assumed that Christianity was not believable to "the modern mind" and that all supernatural ideas would simply fade away. That idea is another of modernism's many failed prophecies. Postmodern society allows at least some room for Christianity. In their own cultural space, Christians may well develop a stronger identity and a richer sense of community, leading to a more faithful church.

MULTICULTURALISM

The doctrine of multiculturalism intensifies the segmentation of society. Academics focus on our pluralism and promote the postmodernist premise that diversity is good. They also indict Western civilization for its assertion of absolutes and universal principles, which have allegedly resulted in racism, imperialism, sexism, homophobia, and the whole litany of post-Marxist evils. Today universities and their spheres of influence—including public schools, the media, and policy makers at almost every level—are dismantling the concept of a unitary American culture in an attempt to establish a "multicultural" state.

Premodern nations promoted their own cultures—what else did they have? Modernism undercut the importance of culture in favor of objective scientific knowledge that applies universally to every culture. The modern technology and advanced education challenged and disrupted "nondeveloped nations," the traditional cultures of Africa and Asia. Yet most tribal peoples eagerly embraced the improved health care and higher standard of living made possible by modernization. Both the premoderns and the moderns assumed that education involved teaching objective information.

In fact, neither premoderns nor moderns had much consciousness of "culture." A group of people had its heritage and its customs. No one thought of "culture" in the postmodern sense of defining our entire identity and determining everything that we think and do. People instead spoke of "civilizations," connoting the active accomplishments of a particular society, rather than its passive social forces. The word *culture* in the sense of some organic, all-encompassing social force and identity is in fact a new term,[5] a concept from the social sciences (the ruling discipline of postmodernism just as the physical sciences are the ruling discipline of modernism).

America has always been a "multicultural" society composed of people from all over the world. The very motto of the United States is "*e pluribus unum*," out of many, one. Just as many states joined into one republic, people of many nationalities and ethnic groups have joined into one nation. Immigrants have always been free to have whatever culture they want, but to attain citizenship they would have to undergo intensive training in the ideals of democracy. The American principles of freedom, equality, and self-government were considered universal. This distinctly American heritage was not so much a culture as a "meta-culture," a framework which could allow diverse peoples to form a single nation. People from Ireland, Poland, and China, Catholics and Jews, black people and white people could all be patriotic Americans. Being

American was a matter of belief—of embracing the principles of the Constitution—not ethnic identity.

To be sure, as immigrants learned English, they assimilated the ways of their neighbors. They often abandoned the language and customs of the "old country." The differences between people of various backgrounds became less and less noticeable. Few people considered this sort of assimilation to be a loss. Parts of the old heritage would still be retained in family customs and ethnic festivals. Other parts of the old heritage would be gratefully accepted into the larger tapestry of American life. Witness the proliferation and popularity of "ethnic restaurants." The immigrants, however much they valued their ancestral heritage, also cultivated an identity as Americans.

The American "melting pot" was the ideal, though the reality often fell short. Certain groups have encountered prejudice and exclusion from the mainstream of American life. Most groups came to the United States seeking freedom from the oppression of their native cultures. Those brought over from Africa, on the other hand, found not freedom but slavery. That a nation dedicated to freedom and equality would countenance slavery and racism is the tragic flaw of American history. Slavery based on race ignited the Civil War, which almost dissolved the nation. Racial problems continue to thwart the American dream.

The modern Civil Rights movement, as exemplified by Martin Luther King, Jr., stressed the *unity* of society. Black Americans should have the same right to vote, the same access to education, and the same economic opportunities as every other American. They had the same goal as every other immigrant group—full assimilation into American life.[6]

The postmodern Civil Rights movement, on the other hand, as exemplified by Malcolm X, stresses the *disunity* of society. In the 1960s, frustrated by the slow pace of reform, many blacks began to repudiate the dominant "white" society altogether. They adopted a black nationalism, an identity centered in race and in the recovery of African culture. Other ideologies, such as Islam and post-Marxism, leavened Black Nationalism. Whereas premodern separatism was a way to discriminate against blacks, postmodern separatism was embraced as something good.

The movement that had begun by attacking the very concept

of racial tests now *demanded* racial quotas. Those who had once demonstrated for integrated schools now demanded separate "African immersion schools" for black children. Martin Luther King's appeal for equal opportunity and a "color-blind" society mutated into demands for entitlement programs and affirmative action.

To be on the cutting edge, the academic world embraced this separatism in the name of diversity. As other groups claimed their "civil rights" (now understood as the right to be separate rather than as the right to be included), their demands began to influence scholarship and curricula. Since blacks had been excluded and "marginalized," universities instituted intellectual affirmative action programs. Literature classes studied black authors, textbooks highlighted the achievements of black Americans, and schools organized Black Studies Departments. When feminists protested, schools added female writers to the "canon" of literary classics, and Women's Studies became a new academic discipline. Now other groups clamor for the same treatment. Some universities have departments of Hispanic Studies, Asian Studies, Gay Studies, and Men's Studies.

Besides creating whole new academic disciplines, schools have revised existing disciplines to reflect this "multicultural awareness." Individual courses must reflect multicultural diversity. No longer can "dead white European males" dominate the curriculum. Textbooks must reflect a balance of genders and include "minority voices." In many universities, courses in "multicultural sensitivity" are required for graduation. The segmentation and cultural demarcation of knowledge is changing the very nature of the intellectual establishment.

Unfortunately, instead of looking at other cultures in their own terms, professors often present these through the distorting lens of post-Marxist ideology. Classes in Western civilization emphasize its legacy of "oppression" rather than its legacy of freedom and democracy. They vilify the West and romanticize other cultures—distorting both legacies. At the very time that less-developed cultures are trying to learn from the West, Western universities are repudiating their own intellectual heritage.

Across academia what had been relegated to the "margin" is placed at the "center." It has been observed that postmodernists cultivate "the romance of the marginal," claiming moral authority by championing groups that have been excluded from power.[7] By identifying with groups outside the boundaries of official culture, postmodernist intellectuals step out of that culture themselves.[8] Such scholars strike a blow for the dispossessed by inverting the conventional distributions of power.[9] If previous scholarship was "Euro-centric," presenting knowledge from a West European vantage point, new scholarship will be "Afro-centric," correcting the former bias by promoting a different bias. "Patriarchy" will be countered by "matriarchy."

Eager to accommodate all oppressed minorities, many college campuses today segment them all the more. After all the hard-fought battles to integrate higher education, today we see a re-segregation of the university. Racial minorities often have separate dormitories, separate dining areas, separate student unions, separate yearbooks, and separate graduation ceremonies. Affirmative action programs base admissions and scholarships on race, unfairly stigmatizing qualified minority students by implying that they could not succeed on their merits alone. Though all this multiculturalism aims at promoting tolerance, more racial tension and animosity exists on campuses today than ever.[10]

After meeting such success on college campuses, multicultural education now finds its way into high schools and elementary schools. The flag salutes, essays on Americanism, lessons in free-enterprise economics, and patriotic assemblies that many of us remember from our school days are things of the past. Textbook writers purge history texts of "American mythology" and emphasize the darker side of American history (slavery, massacres of Indians, the "robber barons" of capitalism, unjust wars), with special emphasis on the contributions of blacks, women, and various ethnic groups. School children celebrate the Chinese New Year and Cinco de Mayo (*Mexico*'s independence day!).[11]

Nations have always passed on their own culture; it seems both eccentric and futile to attempt to pass on other nations' cultures instead. While it is good to study other cultures, to *be* multicultural would be to have no culture of one's own.

Certainly, learning about other civilizations, studying other languages, and appreciating other customs is valuable. The postmodern approach, however, goes no deeper than the *surfaces* of these other cultures. Few postmodernists study these cultures' actual history or do anthropological analyses of their customs and value systems. (Otherwise students would learn about the strict moral standards and the nonfeminist roles of women in African ethnic groups and Guatemalan villages.) There is little foreign language study, even though by the postmodernists' own admission language is the key to culture. Genuine study of other cultures would be valuable. As it is, multicultural education tends to promote idealized cultural stereotypes, some condescending version of the *Western* ideal of the "noble savage."

Multiculturalism, of course, leads to relativism, the impression that since all cultures think differently, then no one culture (particularly my own) can have a monopoly on truth. But if instead of studying their surfaces, schools would study these cultures in a rigorous way, it would be evident that cultures *do not all* think differently. Actually there is a great deal of cross-cultural agreement, especially in areas unfashionable to postmodernists, such as moral responsibility.

Furthermore, the very definition of "culture" is unclear. Do women constitute a different *culture* from men? In raising children, women probably have done more than men to shape and pass down the received culture. The differences between men and women, first denied, then exaggerated by feminists, are surely not cultural as such since both genders exist in the same culture. It is also questionable whether homosexuals, usually affluent and influential, constitute an actual culture. Black Americans have some cultural distinctives due to being segregated from white society for generations. However, as those who have gone to Africa know, these African-Americans are in every sense of the word *Americans* rather than Africans.

The larger American culture is sometimes divided up into "subcultures." Teenagers, ethnic groups, homosexuals, computer hackers, *Star Trek* fans, and other interest groups might be seen as distinct communities with their own customs and idiosyncrasies. But interest groups and people who share a "lifestyle" (another postmodernist term) surely do not constitute a culture in the broad, all-determining sense of the term. To be sure, teenagers and *Star Trek* fans have their own distinct languages, but teenage slang and sci-fi jargon is an *ad hoc* micro-language, not something distinct from their native tongue. Computer hackers may be a distinct breed, but they are hardly determined by their love of computers; rather, their distinct personalities led them to an interest in computers and to their kindred spirits. The fact that a single individual nearly always belongs to many so-called subcultures proves that postmodernists exaggerate the differences between subcultures. A black teenager may be homosexual, be interested in computers, and go to *Star Trek* conventions.

Still, the mind-set that sorts everyone out into groups helps to segment and polarize society. Justice Clarence Thomas, a black man, is criticized for his conservatism—he does not "think black." What is that supposed to mean? Is he any less black because he is not a liberal? Do black people have to think in a certain way? Under the canons of postmodernism, those who act as individuals and dissent from the way their group is supposed to think often face intense criticism for violating group solidarity. Conversely, group members often surrender their individuality and their true opinions in order to conform to their group.

Although designed to promote tolerance (perhaps the only absolute moral value insisted upon by postmodernists), the sorting of human beings into mutually exclusive cultures tends to produce intolerance. "Group-think," to use Orwell's term, can have catastrophic results when it takes root in a society, as we are seeing throughout the world.

The postmodern segmentation of society is not confined to the United States. The Soviet Empire, like the United States, was a pluralistic nation held together by an overarching ideology. Once that ideology was overthrown, its constituent ethnic groups turned against each other in hatred and bloodshed. Yugoslavia was a multicultural nation, but tension among its ethnic groups exploded into the genocidal dismemberment of Bosnia.

Benjamin Barber has observed that "the planet is falling precipitantly apart *and* coming reluctantly together at the very same moment."[12] At the very time that the mass culture and the global economy are uniting the world, a phenomenon he describes as "McWorld," we are seeing the retribalization of the world, a phenomenon he describes as "Jihad," a term borrowed from the Islamic doctrine of holy war.

McWorld, he says, is essentially indifferent to democracy,

Understand [margin annotation]

Will the Beast of Rev. 13 provide the world with a salvatory "overarching ideology? [handwritten note at bottom] thriving under dictatorships as well, keeping the populace happy by bringing them consumer goods and prosperity, even at the expense of "independence, community, and identity."[13] Jihad, on the other hand, is antithetical to democracy, a mind-set wholly geared to group identity, community, and solidarity. This is not mere nationalism—the nation is a modern invention. Rather, the contending tribes of Jihad "are cultures, not countries; parts, not wholes; sects, not religions; rebellious factions and dissenting minorities at war not just with globalism but with the traditional nation-state."[14] The dangers of Jihad are already evident in the Middle East, in Bosnia, and across the length and breadth of the former Soviet Union. Modern warfare is a means to an end; Jihad sees "war not as an instrument of policy but as an emblem of identity, an expression of community, an end in itself."[15]

Before the advent of the modern nation-state, most people of the world organized themselves into tribes. The segmentation of society into multiple competing cultures is a formula for tribalism. Today from Africa to India, from Serbian nationalism to the neotribal structures of American street gangs, once-unified societies are fracturing into tribes at war with each other. Going beyond the modern, being postmodern, sometimes is nothing more than the rebirth of the primitive.

As one critic has pointed out, "Bad multiculturalism promotes tribalism, the root of much of the world's meanness. Good multiculturalism underscores commonality, the footing for respect and understanding."[16] The concept of "commonality," of a universal humanity that people of all cultures share, is exactly the point under attack by postmodernist ideology. If we are wholly determined by our cultures, as the postmodernists say, if we are locked away from each other in a "prison house of language" so that people of different cultures are mutually inaccessible to each other, we have no alternative but to pull back with people like ourselves into our own tribes. To have "respect and understanding, on the other hand, assumes the existence of values that go beyond culture, a set of trans-cultural moral absolutes and a vision of a common humanity.

Christianity thus has a stronger basis than postmodernism for "good multiculturalism." Christians affirm the innate kinship of all human beings. We are all related through our creation in the image of God, through Adam's Fall, and through the redemption of Jesus Christ. The Church is in fact one of the world's most "multicultural" institutions, extending throughout time and throughout the world, both unified and diverse, "a great multitude that no one could count, from every nation, tribe, people and language, standing before the throne and in front of the Lamb" (Revelation 7:9).

THE POLITICS
OF POWER

*A*merican democracy arose from a long-held intellectual and spiritual tradition. Its balance of individual rights and majority rule and its heritage of economic and ideological freedom have been among the greatest achievements of Western civilization. The question is, can American democracy survive in a postmodern society?

What will happen to America's freedoms once the "self-evident" truths upon which they were founded are no longer self-evident? Currently, nearly every assumption that gave rise to democracy is under attack, from the freedom of the individual to the existence of a transcendent God whose Law is above all cultures and who endows human beings with inalienable rights. Not only do postmodernist theories undermine the notion of a free, self-governing society; the practice of contemporary politics seems to be following their lead in moving governmental structures in a sinister, anti-democratic direction.

On the other hand, if the truly defining event of the postmodern age is the fall of the Berlin Wall, perhaps democracy can rejuvenate itself. While the old democracies of the West seem to be jettisoning democratic principles, the rest of the world is just discovering them. Whether the freedoms America has enjoyed for generations will blossom throughout the postmodern world, or whether these freedoms will deconstruct and be replaced by totalitarian structures of absolute power remains to be seen.

THE POLITICAL IMPLICATIONS OF POSTMODERNISM

Let us recall the tenets of postmodernist ideology, as we have seen them emerge in the previous chapters:

(1) *Social Constructivism.* Meaning, morality, and truth do not exist objectively; rather, they are *constructed* by the society.

(2) *Cultural Determinism.* Individuals are wholly shaped by cultural forces. Language in particular determines what we can think, trapping us in a "prison house of language."

(3) *The Rejection of Individual Identity.* People exist primarily as members of groups. The phenomenon of American individualism is itself a construction of American culture with its middle-class values of independence and introspection, but it remains an illusion. Identity is primarily collective.

(4) *The Rejection of Humanism.* Values that emphasize the creativity, autonomy, and priority of human beings are misplaced. There is no universal humanity since every culture constitutes its own reality. Traditional humanistic values are canons of exclusion, oppression, and crimes against the natural environment. Groups must empower themselves to assert their own values and to take their place with other planetary species.

(5) *The Denial of the Transcendent.* There are no absolutes. Even if there were, we would have no access to them since we are bound to our culture and imprisoned in our language.

(6) *Power Reductionism.* All institutions, all human relationships, all moral values, and all human creations—from works of art to religious ideologies—are all expressions and masks of the primal will to power.

(7) *The Rejection of Reason.* Reason and the impulse to objectify truth are illusory masks for cultural power. Authenticity and fulfillment come from submerging the self into a larger group, releasing one's natural impulses such as honest emotions and sexuality, cultivating subjectivity, and developing a radical openness to existence by refusing to impose order on one's life.

(8) *Revolutionary Critique of the Existing Order.* Modern society with its rationalism, order, and unitary view of truth needs to be replaced by a new world order. Scientific knowledge reflects an outdated modernism, though the new electronic technology holds

great promise. Segmentation of society into its constituent groups will allow for a true cultural pluralism. The old order must be swept away, to be replaced by a new, as yet unclearly defined, mode of communal existence.

What are the political implications of these ideas? → *providing they have the right spiritual tradition!*

The belief that reality is socially constructed, as David Horowitz has pointed out, can only be a formula for totalitarianism.[1] Democracy assumes that individuals are free and self-directed. They can govern themselves. Postmodernism holds that individuals are not free and are directed by their society. If the members of the society are passive and are wholly controlled by social forces, then self-governance is impossible. If reality is socially constructed, then the power of society and those who lead it is unlimited. Whereas Christianity teaches that *God* constructs reality, to see *society* as the creator is to divinize culture. With these assumptions, every problem must have a societal solution, and nothing will escape the scope of those who direct the society. "Totalitarian" means that the state controls every sphere of life, which is exactly what postmodernism assumes.

Postmodernism minimizes the individual in favor of the group. This can only result in a collectivist mentality in which the claims of the individual are lost in the demands of the group. An ideology that believes that personal liberty is an illusion can hardly be expected to uphold or allow individual freedom.

Moreover, excluding transcendent values places societies beyond the constraint of moral limits. Society is not subject to the moral law; it makes the moral law. If there are no absolutes, the society can presumably construct any values that it pleases and is itself subject to none. All such issues are only matters of power. Without moral absolutes, power becomes arbitrary. Since there is no basis for moral persuasion or rational argument, the side with the most power will win. Government becomes nothing more than the sheer exercise of unlimited power, restrained neither by law nor by reason. On the personal level, the rejection of all external absolutes in favor of subjectivity can mean the triumph of irrationalism, the eruption of madness, and the imposition of terror.

To be sure, most postmodernists today do not explicitly advocate totalitarianism. On the contrary, they intend their positions to be liberating, freeing oppressed groups from the "one truth" proclaimed by oppressive cultural forces. And yet it is difficult to see how their premises could in any way support a free society. Clearly, democracy rests on the *opposite* of postmodernist tenets—on the freedom and dignity of the individual, on humane values, on the validity of reason, on God rather than the state as the source of all values, on a transcendent moral law that constrains both the tyranny of the state and the tyranny of individual passions.

Significantly, thoughtful postmodernists are themselves recognizing the dangerous political implications of their ideology. Steven Connor recognizes that rejecting universal values leads either to

> the adoption by default of the universal principle that might is right; or to the sunny complacency of pragmatism, in which it is assumed that we can never ground our activities in ethical principles which have more force than just saying "this is the sort of thing we do, because it suits us." (In the end, in fact, the pragmatic option will always turn into the agonistic, since it will only work satisfactorily until somebody refuses to agree with you, or refuses to allow you to disagree with them.)[2]

By "agonistic" he means *struggle*. The only alternative to transcendent, absolute values is a power struggle in which might makes right. Many postmodernists do claim to be pragmatists—they will work to solve particular problems and adjust to life in a flexible way, without any kind of overarching moral code. Connor realizes that pragmatism alone must turn into a power struggle whenever it confronts opposition. (Notice how the pro-abortion and pro-gay factions consistently steer away from objective argumentation about their positions, justifying their actions simply by saying "it suits us." Then they employ crushing political and legal power in an attempt to destroy their opponents.)

Connor notices too "the apocalyptic inheritance from Nietzsche . . . which suggests that the only form of value is to be found in the embrace of theoretical extremity."[3] This is to say, postmodernists tend to be extremists.

While classical Marxism has been discredited in former Communist countries, it still appeals to Western intellectuals, partly no doubt out of sheer rebellion against their own societies. But

[margin handwritten note: No longer will it be "right makes might," but "might makes right."]

theirs is a slightly different Marxism from that of Engels and Lenin. Classical Marxism believes that economic change, culminating in socialism, will transform the culture. The new Marxists, following the teachings of the Italian Communist Antonio Gramsci, teach that cultural change must *precede* socialism. Today's left wing shows little concern for the labor movement and economic theory, unlike the Marxists of the last generation. Instead, the Left emphasizes *cultural change*. Changing America's values is seen as the best means for ushering in the socialist utopia. This is why the Left today champions any cause that undermines traditional moral and cultural values and why leftists gravitate to culture-shaping institutions—education, the arts, and the media.[4]

Post-Marxist radicalism constructs new revolutionary ideologies by replacing Marx's concern for the oppressed working class with other oppressed groups (blacks, women, gays). Status and moral legitimacy come from being "excluded from power." The victim has the favored role.[5] Because of the "romance of the marginal," even affluent university professors cast themselves in the role of the victim of oppressive power. Scholarly papers quiver with outrage, self-pity, and "theoretical extremity." To be black, female, or gay is to enjoy a sort of secular sainthood. But even these categories are segmenting into ever-smaller sects of victimhood.

John Leo describes an academic conference on "Rage!" at a California university.[6] He tells about a paper titled "The Politics of Teaching Victimhood in Asian-American Literature East of California," about an Asian-American professor's frustration that East Coast students are insensitive to the plight of Asians in California. Another professor agonized over her working-class background—how she is victimized by her middle-class colleagues—and her knowledge that teaching Shakespeare "institutionalizes subordination" because of his racism and classism. A controversy broke out when a white scholar gave a paper on the rage expressed in movies by black directors. That a *white* scholar presumed to speak for blacks violated the postmodernist principle that a person from one culture (especially that of the oppressor) can never understand or fully enter into the world of another culture.

A transsexual (a man who had a sex-change operation) gave a paper on her (or his) rage at not being accepted by lesbians as a woman. She (or he) went on to analyze the "transphobia" that infects American culture. Another scholar gave a paper titled "Why I Support Gay Bashing." His paper expresses his rage at gays who want to enter the mainstream of American society by getting married or joining the army. He attacks "self-centered white gays and smug white lesbians" (calling someone "white" is an unanswerable postmodernist put-down), accusing them of endorsing "liberal pluralism, free speech, the American dream and other such B.S." (The anti-democratic implications of postmodernism are evident in the explicit rejection of "free speech" and presumably other human rights.) Despite participants' general hostility not only to society but to their fellow victims, they did have a lot in common. "There was general agreement," Leo reports, "that America is inherently oppressive and that the only correct response is to organize around group victimization and rage."

To be sure, the participants of the "Rage!" conference do not seem much of a political threat. Their hysteria and the triviality of their grievances make it hard to take them seriously. Such extremism, fueled by self-righteous indignation and recognizing no moral constraints beyond the interests of their groups, might at most result in terrorism (the postmodern mode of warfare). We already see this in the tree-spikings and lab bombings of the Animal Rights activists (an exemplary postmodernist movement). But surely such hyper-segmented groups, by their very nature, are too small to have political impact.

This is true and it gives hope. But for all their protestations of powerlessness, these groups and especially the mind-set they represent do have power. Their presence and moral authority in academia is real. The academic world is not the ivory tower that it sometimes seems, detached from the "real world." That ivory tower indoctrinates the nation's teachers, lawyers, journalists, and government officials.

Already free speech (condemned as "B.S." by the gay activist at the "Rage!" conference) is being restricted on campuses, both by informal pressure and by statute, in the name of sensitivity to aggrieved groups. Stanley Fish, a literary theorist and administrator at Duke University who is at the center of the "politically correct" controversies, wrote an article entitled "There's No Such Thing as Free Speech and It's a Good Thing, Too."[7] He argues that universities should censor offensive speech. Fish admits that he has no objective standards by which to judge. Roger Lundin summarizes his thinking:

> Since all principles are preferences—and only preferences—they are nothing but masks for the will to power, which is the ultimate source of what we call "values." Instead of appealing to authority outside ourselves, we can only seek to marshall our rhetorical abilities to wage the political battles necessary to protect our own preferences and to prohibit expressions of preference that threaten or annoy us. Fish is candid about the groundlessness of his own beliefs and about his willingness to wage political battles to silence those of whom he disapproves.[8]

"Someone is always going to be restricted next," says Fish, "and it is your job to make sure that the someone is not you."[9]

Arthur Pontynen summarizes the connection between postmodernism and "political correctness" policies on the university campus:

> Because there is no wisdom, we are told, there is no such thing as free speech (and policies are put into place to limit free speech on campuses). We are told that there is no such thing as individual responsibility and dignity (and policies are advocated which promote the treatment of persons not on the basis of individual merit but on the basis of such restrictive categories as race, gender, and class . . .). We are even told that there is no such thing as science, only meaningful fictions; that there is no such thing as culture, only paradigms of oppression.[10]

Might similar restrictions to individual freedom spill over from the campuses to the society as a whole?

Bureaucracies, legislatures, and the courts are exhibiting similar "sensitivity" in their zeal to fight "harassment" and in their ever-widening application of civil rights laws. If we ever come to the point of "affirmative action laws" forcing churches to ordain women against church teachings, or "anti-discrimination" laws requiring Christian organizations to hire homosexuals, or "political-lobbying laws" forcing churches to remain silent on social issues such as abortion, then religious freedom will have been extinguished. Already some postmodernist sects advocate such measures; all they lack is power. Militant feminists already have power enough to institute abortion on demand, leading to the slaughter of millions of human beings; next on their agenda is to silence and imprison those who protest.

Connor recognizes "a strange dialectic which pushes renunciation of authority and of unified form to a point of absolute impotence, which may then loop back into a renewed assertion of nihilistic power."[11] Revolutions tend to follow a predictable order. At first, the revolutionaries renounce all authority and all established structures. Once the authorities are overthrown and the structures demolished, the revolution enters a new phase. New authorities and new structures are imposed. Most revolutions, however, had some criteria for their new societies—the French Revolution's Enlightenment rationalism, the Russian Revolution's Marxist economics, the Iranian Revolution's commitment to Islam. A postmodernist revolution, rejecting all such absolutes, would be arbitrary, self-consciously constructing a society governed only by the nihilism of its power.

"Theoretical extremity," "rage," "nihilistic power"—such recurrent themes of postmodernism do not bode well for maintaining a free, democratic society. Most people do not realize that the tenets of postmodernism have been tried before in a political system. Social constructivism, cultural determinism, the rejection of individual identity, the rejection of humanism, the denial of the transcendent, power reductionism, the rejection of reason, and the revolutionary critique of the existing order are tenets not only of postmodernism but of *fascism*.

As has been mentioned and as I demonstrate in another book, *Modern Fascism: Liquidating the Judeo-Christian Worldview*,[12] many of the ideas that came together in the fascism of the 1930s survived World War II and continued to develop in postmodernist thought. Fascists taught that reality is a social construction, that culture determines all values. Particular cultures and ethnic groups therefore constitute their own self-contained worlds, which should be kept uncontaminated, although these groups will often compete with each other. Individuality is a myth; particular human beings can only find fulfillment when they lose themselves in a larger group. "Humanistic values" are a myth; there are no absolute transcendent moral laws by which the culture can be judged. These are

"Jewish"—i.e., Biblical—ideas that are responsible for the alienation, guilt, and instability of Western culture. Strength, not love
and mercy, must be the true expression of a culture's will to power.
Collective emotion, not abstract reason (another "Jewish" contribution), must be cultivated as the culture's source of energy.

"National Socialism" would institute a controlled, state-
directed economy that would work for the good of the nation. The
state would solve all of the people's problems. The organic state,
conceived as the source of all values and of all good, would acquire
a mystical status, taking on the role of God and receiving the devo-
tion of all of its members. As in the ancient pagan societies, before
the alienation brought into the West by the Bible, the culture
would be fully integrated with nature and with the gods.

Many people at the time saw fascist ideology as liberating.
But its social constructivism and cultural determinism, put into
practice, meant totalitarian oppression. Its rejection of the individual meant the extinction of liberty. Its rejection of objective moral
values meant that there could be no restraints on the actions of the
state, resulting in eugenics programs, secret-police terrorism, and
the euthanasia of the handicapped and "unwanted." Its ideological hostility to the Judeo-Christian tradition led to the co-opting of
the church by syncretistic theologies, the suppression of confessional Christianity, and mass extermination of the Jews.

To react against the modern is in many ways to revert to the
primitive, the barbaric. The fascism of the 1930s was never a conservative movement (despite Marxist propaganda), but it was a
reaction against the objectivity, rationalism, and alienation of the
"modern world," a reaction structurally parallel to that of the postmodernists. Fascism, like postmodernism, had its origins in romanticism, with its primitivism and subjectivity, and existentialism,
with its rejection of absolutes and its "triumph of the will." Hitler
may have failed because he was ahead of his time.

CONTEMPORARY DEMOCRACY

Postmodernist ideas may have troubling political implications, but
surely these ideas are held mainly by sequestered academics and the
lunatic fringe. Few ordinary people believe in the "social construction of reality" and other esoteric postmodernist ideology. It seems

hardly likely America would give up its democratic freedoms for some Marxist, post-Marxist, or fascist totalitarianism.

As a matter of fact, I have great confidence in American institutions and in the compelling strength of democracy and free-market economics. Nevertheless, there are reasons to be concerned about the health of American democracy.

As we have seen, the relativism of the academic world is now shared by 66 percent of Americans (including 72 percent of the "next generation" and 53 percent of evangelicals).[13] Charles Colson points out the political implications of relativism:

> Nowhere is the existence of an absolute standard more vital than in politics and government. In the West, nations built sound political structures on the belief that ultimately man's laws were to be but a reflection of God's immutable, moral laws. . . . But if there is no truth—no objective standards of what is good or just and, therefore, no standard of what is unjust—then the social contract is always threatened by the whim of the moment. And tyranny, either from the unrestrained passions of the majority or from a ruthless dictator, inevitably follows.[14]

As Colson points out, tyranny comes not only from dictators; there can also be a tyranny "of the majority."

A democratic tyranny, operating without moral restraints, can unleash the "passions" of the majority and thus perpetrate every kind of evil. Today moral questions are often resolved by opinion polls, which are then translated into public policy. Centuries-old moral and legal sanctions against abortion have crumbled in favor of the "mother's right to choose." The question of the morality of euthanasia is being put to a vote in state ballots. When a society accepts no moral absolutes, there is no higher tribunal than subjective opinions. On the shifting sands of public opinion—often unconsidered, changeable, and vulnerable to manipulation—laws are enacted. But laws divorced from morality become what postmodernists say they are, an arbitrary imposition of power.

The American Constitution foresaw the possibility of unjust laws and the tyranny of the majority. The writers put into place a

Clinton, a "new Marxist" president, will appoint more with no belief in absolutes.

mechanism to ensure that the laws passed by the majority are checked against an objective legal code. Objective, learned, and independent judges would ensure that no laws conflict with the absolutes set forth in the Constitution.

The court system, culminating in the Supreme Court, judges laws according to the absolutes of constitutional law. But this system can only work if society and the courts believe in absolutes. Today postmodernist legal theory teaches that the Constitution is not a document setting forth absolute principles, but an organism that must be continually reinterpreted as society evolves. Judicial activists assume the power to extrapolate new rights never mentioned in the Constitution to address the needs of society. Following this reasoning, the Supreme Court legalized abortion, striking down all laws restricting abortion in the name of a newly inferred "right to privacy."

The extrapolation of new rights.

Traditionally, the judicial system was responsible for interpreting laws, but the new judicial activists, without the hindrance of legislators or absolute guidelines, are making laws. The most divisive issues of today's "culture wars" have been precipitated by this judicial activism. Besides legalizing abortion, the courts have allowed pornography to flourish, given special rights to homosexuals, upheld the feminist agenda, and cast prayer and Bible reading out of the schools.

As Judge Alex Kozinski acknowledged, "Judges who get into the habit of playing legislator find it tempting to start treating all laws—including the Constitution—as merely a springboard for implementing their own sense of right and wrong."[15] Personal opinions replace absolutes. The judge's opinions, however, become law for everyone. As well-educated members of the intellectual establishment, their sense of right and wrong is likely to be that of their postmodernist peers.

This judicial activism, which can cancel laws passed by democratically-elected legislatures, concentrates immense power in the hands of a tiny, unelected minority. "It's a sign of the times," observes John Leo, "that reformers now routinely skip the legislative process and take their issues directly to court."[16] Here the "reformers" are likely to get what they want without having to first persuade Congress or the American public.

The tyranny of bureaucracy poses another potential threat to

American democracy. Neil Postman has described how the emerging information technologies are forming a new social order, which he describes as a "technopoly." He foresees an ideological conflict between the values of democracy, with its transcendent moral underpinnings, and the new technological order, which lacks them. Those who control the information, he observes, exercise political power. Since information is controlled by technical means, political power will reside in the hands of technical experts.[17]

Already "experts" entrenched in the nation's bureaucracies set policies with the force of law, apart from any kind of democratic process. Postman describes the new breed of experts as so specialized that they are ignorant about everything outside their specialty. Experts claim exclusive authority in areas that before have always been seen as universal human concerns—raising children, solving personal problems, making ethical decisions. Wrapped in the mantle of the social sciences (the "Queen of the Sciences" according to postmodernism) and armed by technical machinery such as standardized tests, statistics, and opinion polls, experts are deferred to in the courts, in legislative committees, and in the media.[18]

The nation's educational curriculum is determined not by local school boards, nor even by classroom teachers, but by the bureaucracy of the state boards of public instruction. The educational bureaucracies not only control what teachers teach. They also control what teachers are taught (by strict licensing requirements and detailed requirements for teacher-training programs). The effect is to ensure that all schools follow the latest educational theories, including those proven ineffective. Attempts to reform the schools end up only giving even more power to the educational bureaucracies, who require even more teacher education courses, impose even more stifling controls on local school districts, and insist on even more experimental methodology.

Thus many of the society's most important decisions are made not by ordinary citizens but by an unelected elite. Hospitals farm out questions of medical ethics to committees of "experts." Courtroom decisions hinge on the testimony of "expert witnesses" (who can usually be found to represent both sides of a case). Congressional committees listen to the testimony of "experts" in drafting legislation designed to solve society's problems. In most cases, the experts are brought in to answer questions that ordinary human beings have always been competent to answer: Is this fair? Is this right or wrong? Will this work? When the experts become permanently entrenched in governmental bureaucracies and receive the authority to set policies with the status of law, the democratic process becomes more and more irrelevant.

Disillusioned by the corruption and ineffectiveness of their legislators, Americans are tragically acquiescing in their loss of self-government. Americans, once zealous of their rights and fiercely protective of their liberties, now for the most part seem content to let the experts and the courts make their decisions for them.

The increasing triviality of politics—as elections are decided by marketing techniques, mass technology, and the image manipulation of "spin doctors"—further erodes democracy. An apologist for postmodernism, Walter Truett Anderson, gleefully describes the phoniness of contemporary politics:

> We can also see an increasing theatricality of politics, in which events are scripted and stage-managed for mass consumption, and in which individuals and groups struggle for starring roles (or at least bit parts) in the dramas of life. This theatricality is a natural—and inevitable—feature of our time. It is what happens when a lot of people begin to understand that reality is a social construction. The more enterprising among us see that there is much to be gained by constructing—and selling to the public—a certain reality, and so reality making becomes a new art and business. And a very big business, if you consider how much money is spent (and made) in fields such as advertising and public relations and political campaigning.[19]

Running for office becomes indistinguishable from advertising, P.R., and big business. Political persuasion is a matter of "selling" a particular construction of reality. Postmodernist politicians play a role, present an image, and manufacture theatrical events. This trivialization of democracy is inevitable, says Anderson, "when a lot of people begin to understand that reality is a social construction."

That the postmodernist worldview permeates contemporary politics is evident in other ways as well. The postmodernist view

Slick Willie!

that objective data can be organized and interpreted to fit practically any "paradigm" has given us the "spin doctor." A politician
hires an "expert" to interpret anything that happens so that it
places the candidate in the best possible light. Political promises are
no longer meant to be kept—that old-fashioned view assumes that
truth is some sort of an absolute. Rather, political promises are
"performative," meant to achieve a momentary result, to sway an
audience or "make a statement." Once the moment has passed, the
result has been obtained, and the politician faces "new realities,"
he or she openly abandons the promise. Those who believe in the
social construction of reality can easily justify manufacturing evidence and programmatic lying.

The cynicism and transparent phoniness of postmodernist
politics have profoundly disillusioned ordinary Americans, further
eroding democracy. Today only a fraction of those registered even
bother to vote. Access to the media, so necessary to political success, costs so much that only entrenched incumbents and chal-
lengers with enormous wealth can afford to run for political office.
The segmentation of society has eroded the impact of political parties, which traditionally provided an entrance point on the local
level for citizens wanting to get involved in politics. Today the
major political parties must satisfy diverse and often incompatible
"interest groups" to run a national election, resulting in ideological distortion and policy paralysis. As a result, few Americans
actively engage in self-government. If democracy ceased to exist,
many people would not even notice.

Is the outlook really so bleak? It is surely true that the collapse
of communism, the end of the Cold War, was a great victory for
democracy. The ideals of freedom sent millions of ordinary people
into the streets, defying the tanks and the KGB. For all their pretensions to "construct reality," the totalitarian regimes could not
control the men and women whose faith and demands for "truth"
started a democratic revolution. While American democracy lan-
guishes, democracy is sweeping away former dictatorships in Latin
America and Africa. Principles of the free-enterprise economy are
even more successful, bringing prosperity to poor nations, rewarding individual initiative and making socialism from Sweden to
China obsolete.

Democracy and a free economy may well represent the true

postmodern, as opposed to postmodern*ist*, society. Classical Marxists in fact criticize the postmodern world—with its freedom, diversity, and prosperity—as being nothing more than an advanced stage of capitalism.[20] They see Ronald Reagan as the archetypal postmodern President, with his actor's mastery of the media, his nostalgic sentiments, his *laissez faire* policies, and his sanctioning of prosperity (which they call "greed"). For them the postmodern economy with its consumerism, marketing, and emphasis on money rather than social labor (the sign rather than the signified) represents capitalism at its most threatening.

Maybe these unrepentant Marxists are right, in which case democracy and free enterprise represent the true conditions of postmodernity. In that case, the collectivism and radicalism of postmodernist ideology will prove to have been not an alternative to modernism, but its death throes.[21] In the meantime, we can expect the worldview that gave us a free society (namely that of the Bible) and the postmodernist worldview to conflict, competing with each other for the soul of the new millennium.

Even today postmodernist alternatives challenge the triumph of freedom in the former Communist states. While newly freed nations of the Soviet Empire struggle to make democracy and a free economy work, the postmodernist forces of tribalism threaten them with anarchy or fascism. Democracy, however, should not be written off. It has proven its strength and its validity. For democracy to succeed, however, it needs an infrastructure—a worldview grounded in the Bible. While many in the Western democracies abandon that worldview, many in the East are now discovering it.

[handwritten margin note: Amen! (I wondered when hed finally say it)!]

THE POSTMODERNISTS MEET THE RUSSIANS

In 1988 a conference on "Literature and Social Values: Soviet and American Views" brought American critics and theorists together with their Soviet counterparts. Russian writers and university professors came to California to meet with some of the most distinguished American postmodernist critics. In 1990 the postmodernists visited the by-then-defunct Soviet Union. Their exchange of ideas baffled both sides.

American postmodernists were astonished that the Russians actually believed in concepts such as "absolute values," "truth," and "humanism." Even more astonishing to the American post-modernists was that the Russians insisted on basing these absolutes on *religion*:

> The Soviets asserted repeatedly their belief in absolute values in literature. . . . [That] went along with an appeal to a spiritual absolute and to a tradition of religious spiritualism in Russia that guarantees the high value of certain works. This was, to me at least, by far the most surprising feature of what the Soviet participants had to say. Nor was this impression contradicted by the papers we heard from a quite different set of Soviet scholars in the follow-up conference in Moscow two years later. A large number of the papers we heard there were written from a deeply religious perspective.[22]

The tone of these comments by J. Hillis Miller, one of the most distinguished and influential deconstructionist critics, is especially revealing. He is *incredulous* that anyone today might think in these terms. Certainly, no one in America thinks along these lines—at least, no one who *counts*:

> This firmly held though not altogether coherent set of assumptions was a great surprise to me. . . . Nothing at all like the Soviets' views about literature exists today among literary scholars in the United States except among certain extremely conservative critics—for example, members of the National Association of Scholars or others who appeal to the "Western tradition" as against multicultural study, women's studies, and the study of minority literatures. But that analogy would by no means be exact, since the American conservative view does not usually appeal so overtly to religion as the mediator of absolute values.[23]

Needless to say, the Russians, so recently freed from Communist tyranny, were even more astonished at what the Americans were saying. "After listening to you," said Feliks Kuznetsov, secretary of the Union of Soviet Writers, "I will take away with me the impression that we have come to a deeply atheistic country."[24]

It seems odd that the American scholars do not see the connection between the Russians' suffering under communism and their embrace of absolute spiritual values. Certainly, the Americans knew that Russian artists were persecuted. "Americans gasped a little," says Miller, "when a Soviet colleague said that a supposedly 'antirevolutionary' writer may have 'been shot by mistake, a tragic mistake,' just as we gasped during our visit to the Soviet Union two years later when, in a museum, we were shown a painting for which the artist was executed." Miller's response to these atrocities is to make a little joke: "At least that demonstrates that art is taken seriously in the Soviet Union!"[25] Quite. Art is certainly not taken so seriously in the United States, either by the government or the artists or postmodernist critics. Art so dangerous to tyranny that it provokes arrest, art taken seriously enough to die for, is art that testifies to absolutes.

Miller expresses a worry that the Russians' insistence on objective truth might lead to a resurgence of authoritarianism.[26] Postmodernists are fond of associating belief in absolutes with tyranny, but such a connection defies logic. (Which is most favorable to tyrants—the belief that wielding power is the only value, or the belief that absolute values transcend society and are the means by which society and its power can be judged?) It also, rather impudently, denies the experience of those who actually suffered through Communist straitjackets and gulags.

While Milan Kundera, author of *The Unbearable Lightness of Being*, fled communism for the West (why, if the West is so oppressive?), another Czech writer, Vaclav Havel, stayed home. The KGB later arrested him for writing plays that criticized communism. (If literature is only an expression of existing power structures, how could he protest?) A KGB agent—not a critic—interrogated him, and they put him in an objectively real prison of concrete and steel. This was no prison house of language. Rather than binding him, language for Vaclav Havel expressed freedom, and he used it to attack lies and to testify to the truth. (If there is no truth, there can be no lies, or rather everything is a lie. What is there to go to prison for? Should Havel have changed with the circumstances, embracing the "lightness of being," drifting with the winds as the collaborators did? Why should we admire someone like Havel for standing up for the truth if in fact there is no truth?)

Those who were interrogated, consigned to concentration camps, or executed were not persecuted because they held to "postmodernist" beliefs, but because they held to absolutes. They insisted upon the very concepts now under attack in the West— truth, individual freedom, a moral law above the society that insures human rights—all of which are grounded objectively and absolutely in the person of God.

Another cruelly persecuted author, Alexander Solzhenitsyn, has observed that what was taken from the East by force is being rejected in the West by its own free will.[27]

EVERYDAY POSTMODERNISM

*M*ost Americans believe they have individual identities. They believe in an objective world, that truth is not just a social construction. Postmodernist ideology is alien to the way most people think and live. Although it may be influential in intellectual circles, it would seem to have little to say to the ordinary American trying to raise a family and pay the bills.

Certainly, the American heritage of common sense should fend off the excesses of postmodernist ideology. Individuality and democracy have deep roots in American culture and will not easily be surrendered. Besides, many Americans are modernists and even premodernists. The leaven of Christian faith should mitigate the relativism and nihilism encouraged by the more radical postmodernists.

Nevertheless, postmodern worldviews and postmodern culture surround us. Ordinary Americans cannot avoid these. Postmodernism shapes our lifestyles, the way we make a living, how we educate our children, and how we approach our personal problems and those of society.

THE POSTMODERN MENTALITY

Leith Anderson has observed that the new generation tends to think unsystematically. As a result, people often hold ideas that logically contradict each other. Anderson, a megachurch pastor, gives the example of a young man who says that he believes in Reformed theology, the inerrancy of Scripture, and reincarnation.[1] He doesn't grasp that Christianity is incompatible with reincarnation, which rests on a very different worldview. Even when this is pointed out to him, he shows no interest in revising his beliefs. Because he does not think in systematic terms, he does not see how different systems clash. He "likes" the Bible, and he also "likes" the thought of coming back in a different life.

The religious implications of this way of thinking will be discussed in the next chapter. But holding mutually contradictory ideas has become characteristic of the contemporary mind-set. Some politicians claim to be politically conservative, but liberal on social issues. Health, fitness, and organic food fanatics sometimes ravage their bodies by taking drugs. Many who personally consider abortion morally wrong are also "pro-choice." Many people fail to think through their positions and make little effort to be consistent.

With no absolute canons of objective truth, the rational is replaced by the aesthetic. We believe in what we *like*. Those unused to thinking in terms of absolute, objective truth still have opinions and strongly held beliefs. In fact, their beliefs may even be more difficult to dislodge, since they admit no external criteria by which these can be judged and shown to be wrong. Since their beliefs are a function of the will, they cling to them willfully. Since their beliefs will tend to have no foundation other than their preferences and personality, they will interpret any criticism of their beliefs as a personal attack. Since "everyone has the right to their own opinion," they do not mind if you do not agree with them, but they will become defensive and sometimes angry if you try to change their opinions.

Engage practically anyone in a discussion of some controversial issue, and the problem of postmodernism shows itself. To the contemporary mind, both in academia's ivory towers and in the local coffee shop, there are no absolutes. People do not accept the same authorities, methodologies, or criteria. Persuasion becomes impossible if everyone exists in a self-contained world, speaking a language incomprehensible to outsiders. "That may be true for you, but it isn't true for me."

POSTMODERN BUSINESS

Even businesses are being redesigned along postmodernist lines. Companies are turning away from hierarchical structures, with their clear lines of authority and rationalized central planning. Unity, objective organization, and clear-cut authority are *modernist* values. Instead, companies decentralize, "empowering" their employees to make decisions as part of quality-control *groups*. Thus, the postmodernist values of diversity, the rejection of authority, and emphasis upon groups invade what one might think would be the last bastion of conservatism, the business world.

I am not presuming to criticize postmodern business practices. The new ways of organizing businesses may be effective, perhaps necessary adaptions to postmodern culture. Modernism has failed across the board, and we should not expect modern business paradigms to fare any better. My point here is simply to show that postmodernism pervades everything, and none of us can escape it.

The factory symbolizes the modern economy. The industrial revolution gave birth to the modern era. Scientific knowledge found practical expression in manufacturing technology. As factories churned out cloth, steel, tools, and automobiles, living standards skyrocketed. To be sure, the industrial revolution was not without its cost and controversies, but both capitalists and Marxists, entrepreneurs and labor unions focused on the factory and the business of production.

The computer symbolizes the postmodern economy. Today computers have taken over much of the operation of factories. Human beings sit in front of computer screens processing information. Workers no longer have to perform mindlessly repetitive tasks on the assembly line but have access to megabytes of information once available only to the front office. This allows for "decentralized decision-making." The new technology also allows customized manufacturing to the specific needs of the customer. The modern factories were geared to mass production. The postmodern factories allow companies to manufacture for specific *groups*.

Manufacturing itself is giving way to "service industries." Production of tangible objects is increasingly either automated or farmed out to inexpensive labor overseas (part of the "globaliza-

tion" of the economy, another postmodern touch). Many companies now produce something intangible. "Goods and services," of
course, have always been intrinsic to an economy, but today services are gaining the upper hand. Many new service-oriented companies exist sheerly to help other companies deal with the new
technology. Consulting agencies have become Fortune 500 companies by producing nothing more than information.

There is a difference, by the way, between "knowledge" and
"information." Knowledge is substantial and tangible. Information
is fleeting and ever-changing. The premodern and the modern value
knowledge; the postmodern is obsessed with data.

The modern economy saw people as producers; the postmodern economy sees them as consumers. The American economy
is now "market-driven," which means not only that companies
must have up-to-the-minute information about their customers, but
that they must aggressively advertise what they sell. "Market-
research" gives pollsters and social scientists (two postmodernist
professions) big clout in industry. Advertisers now have at their dis-
posal a vast array of information media with which to make their
pitch. Television commercials give access to a mass audience, but
the new information technology—cable TV, faxes, fiber optics—
also allows for a "targeted" audience, pitching products to specific
groups of consumers (in accord with the segmentation of postmodern society).

In line with the postmodernist slogan that everything is a text,
advertisers have turned the world into a gigantic billboard, making commercials out of everything from sporting events to shopping
carts. Company logos have themselves become fashion statements,
so that people wear hats and T-shirts that advertise some product,
turning themselves into unpaid shills for the ad-men. The centrality of advertising in today's economy bolsters the postmodernist
obsession with rhetoric, style, and image.

THE NEW CLASS

We still have blue-collar workers, and we still have a middle class,
both oriented to the production of tangible goods. The new economic climate, however, has given rise to a new social class geared
to a less tangible product—information, advice, therapy. The New

Class includes educators (from elementary school teachers to university professors), communicators (journalists, artists, television producers, advertisers), planners (management consultants, pollsters, marketing specialists), and those in the "helping professions" (psychologists, social workers, government bureaucrats, and—significantly—clergy). The important role of information in the contemporary economy means that the New Class has great influence and social status.

Politically, business interests and the middle class have tended to be conservative, with blue-collar laborers and the poor favoring liberal candidates. The New Class, despite its affluence and establishment credentials, tends to be liberal, both politically and socially. There are certainly major exceptions, but the New Class tends to value change for the sake of change, social engineering, and moral permissiveness.

Such opinions and attitudes have become "class markers," I.D. tags that tell who belongs and who does not belong to this new elite. As the sociologist Peter Berger points out:

> The symbols of class culture are important. They allow people to "sniff out" who belongs and who does not; they provide easily applied criteria of "soundness." Thus a young instructor applying for a job in an elite university is well advised to hide "unsound" views such as political allegiance to the right wing of the Republican party (perhaps even to the left wing), opposition to abortion or to other causes of the feminist movement, or a strong commitment to the virtues of the corporation.[2]

If the young instructor hides any conservative views and gets the job, the social pressure to abandon them later will be enormous. Those views may well change as the instructor becomes indoctrinated into the new culture of the faculty lounge. People have noticed that conservative politicians tend to become more and more liberal to the extent that they participate in the social life of Washington, D.C., an enclave of the New Class. In the postmodernist climate, political and moral beliefs no longer indicate honest conviction but solidarity with a group.

Hansfried Kellner describes the concern of the New Class with "lifestyle engineering." The very concept of "lifestyle," the idea that life is to be expressed in a wide variety of "styles," is post-modernist. Kellner points out how these new professions claim expertise in areas formerly outside the jurisdiction of "experts," applying the technocratic mentality to aspects of life that resist rationalization. "How does one achieve 'mental health,'" Kellner asks, "and how does one determine that it *has* been achieved? Or a satisfactory 'work choice'? Or a situation of greater 'social justice,' or more adequate 'quality of life'?"[3] Yet such vague and slippery concepts make up the New Class stock in trade.

Kellner points out that the traditional professions—medicine, law, engineering—involve mastery of a specific body of knowledge and the application of an intrinsic logic. A doctor diagnosing and treating a disease and an engineer designing a bridge "embodied a rational understanding of the world and the implementation of rational means of dealing with the world." That is, they presuppose an objective order in existence. Different medical doctors, grounded in objective science and a standardized methodology, examining the same patient will tend to give a similar diagnosis and course of treatment. They exemplify modernism.

The new professions, on the other hand, have no universally recognized body of knowledge and no generally accepted methods, although they invoke the jargon and the statistics of science. "Most of the new professionals have been trained in social sciences and the humanities, [which] . . . do not possess unified and unequivocally validated bodies of knowledge, as compared with the natural sciences. Competing and conflicting theories, approaches, and methods exist side by side."[4] For example, if you need psychiatric help, you might be treated by a Freudian, a Jungian, a humanist, or a behaviorist. Your treatment might consist of telling about your childhood, recording your dreams, getting in touch with your feelings, or exposing yourself to operant conditioning. The philosophies behind these psychological theories are incompatible—Freud and the behaviorists cannot both be right—and the methodologies are untestable.[5]

Kellner shows how the New Class and the Business Class have come together to form what he calls the "New Capitalism."[6] Once stodgy and conservative business executives, concerned with production and high finance, now read pop psychology paperbacks, try to upgrade their "management styles," hire expensive consultants to conduct feel-good workshops for their employees, and redesign their companies according to the latest social science research and postmodernist "paradigms."

The media, consisting wholly of communicators, takes New Class values for granted. Since the educators run the universities and the public schools, they expose every student to their principles. Social scientists' values and slogans have reached beyond the confines of the New Class to permeate all of society. A therapist counseling a homosexual would generally not condemn his "lifestyle" as morally wrong. Rather, the counselor would try to make him feel good about himself, to accept his "lifestyle choices" and help him get into a support group. Today this approach, omnitolerant and anti-judgmental, operates throughout the culture.

THE FATE OF SCIENCE

Even the traditional modernist professions are changing to fit the postmodernist paradigms. The natural sciences remain the bedrock of modernism. Contemporary science, though, sees the new physics, with its logic-bending subatomic particles and unimaginable black holes, complicating the old materialistic assumptions of an orderly, mechanistic natural law. Mathematics, the epitome of rationalism, is now engaged with "chaos theory," the study of randomness and *dis*order. The history of science, as pioneered by Thomas Kuhn, suggests that science is not so much an uninterrupted march towards greater and greater truth, but a succession of *paradigms*, humanly devised imaginative models that organize the known data, but which must be continually revised as more data is discovered.[7]

This new science by no means proves, as some imply, that there is no order in the universe—to find a mathematical order even in disorder proves the opposite; the mysteries of the new physics are being unveiled by rigorously objective methods. Christians have nothing to fear from the new sciences and should be grateful to them for overturning the mechanical clock-work universe of Enlightenment materialism and for restoring a sense of wonder at the unfathomable mystery of God's creation. Kuhn's understanding of scientific paradigms is particularly useful for creationists, who can show that the theory of evolution is not a scientific truth, but a conceptual and culturally conditioned model that neither accounts for all the data nor can be expected to last forever.

The impact of the new sciences on the culture as a whole, however, has meant a profound shift away from the modernist idea that science offers clear explanations and neat solutions. The antirationalism and environmentalism of contemporary culture have in fact promoted a widespread distrust of science. In the popular mind, for better and for worse, science no longer provides absolute truth.

If science is changing, so are its practical applications such as medicine. Modern medicine involves a highly trained expert meeting individually with a patient, whose symptoms are scientifically analyzed and who is cured by means of modern technology. Despite the way modern medicine has dramatically improved and extended our lives, the fashion today is to question, in the postmodern way, the doctor's "authority." Patients become "consumers," who demand a choice in their therapies. They suspect medical technology, though it has saved countless lives. They abhor medication and life-support systems. Although the simplest surgeries would be impossible without life-support machines and although we in countless ways owe our lives to technology, many people say that they would rather die than "be kept alive by some machine."

Hostile to science, many put their faith in "alternative medicine," in natural foods and herbal medicine, Taoist acupuncture and Hindu meditation, all of which owe more to premodern paganism than to modern science. Medicine merges with psychology in "holistic" therapies, some of which teach that the body determines the mind, employing drugs and exercises to solve mental problems. Others teach that the mind determines the body, prescribing meditation, biofeedback, and relaxation techniques to fight disease.

In the meantime, the medical industry, like other businesses, is reorganizing according to the postmodernist paradigms. Instead of a one-on-one relationship with a doctor, we now have health maintenance organizations in which *groups* of physicians contract with *groups* of patients. Even many psychologists are abandoning the modernist treatment of individuals in favor of *group* therapies.

EDUCATION

The postmodernist emphasis on groups shows up also in education. Students engage in "collaborative learning." Instead of each individual student learning the lesson and doing the homework, students work together in groups, collaborating to receive a group grade. Of course, grading itself becomes problematic to postmodernists. Giving grades implies that some work is better than other work and that some students are academically better than others. This is "judgmental," not to mention hierarchical and nonrelativist. Grading implies objective standards and absolute values. This is all anathema to postmodernists. They can avoid grades with "Outcome Based Education."

Leith Anderson describes other shifts in the theory and practice of education:

> The old approach was more theoretical, time-and-place oriented, deductive, linear, sequential, process-oriented, long-term, and standardized (everyone fit into the same schedule and curriculum).[8]

This unified, rationalistic approach characterizes modernism. Classical education was more oriented to content than to process, but it too, being grounded in language, was open to abstract ideas and sequential thinking.

Modern education, however, is by now dismissed as "the old approach."

> The new approach is more practical, experiential, inductive, rooted in relationships with models and mentors, short term (like field trips, seminars, and retreats), interactive, hands-on, product-oriented, issue driven, and customized (offering options that fit individual needs).[9]

Such features of postmodern education are not all bad, any more than the features of modern education were all good. But they reflect the postmodernist worldview. In the absence of absolutes, postmodernist education focuses on the tangible and the experiential. Instead of students learning primarily from *language*—from books and the mental disciplines of reading and writing—the new curriculum relies on *images*—computer screens and VCRs—and on manufacturing elaborate but entertaining experiences, such as interactive games and field trips. The high priority on relationships and on "customized" instruction exemplifies the postmodernist obsession with diversity and group identity.

SOCIAL POLICY

Just as the social engineers have taken over education, postmodernist ideology molds other government policies and attempts at social reform as well. Marvin Olasky has described how efforts to help the poor have shifted.[10] In the classical model of welfare, aid to the poor was primarily handled by the church. Those who were helped and those who did the helping had a personal relationship. The charity aimed at lifting people out of their economic problems by attending to spiritual as well as material needs. Moral reform and character building—through work, responsibility, and spiritual transformation—enabled people to escape poverty.

In the modern model of welfare, the government played a larger role. Reaching its high point with the New Deal, modern welfare offered a rational plan to provide temporary help and employment for the indigent. Like the classical model, modern welfare restricted itself to those truly in need. Accepting welfare was embarrassing. Both the system and the recipients were geared towards getting people off of welfare and into the economic mainstream as soon as possible. As with modernist art and architecture, modernist welfare was rational, efficient, and minimalistic.

The postmodern model of welfare began with the Great Society of the 1960s. Its principle is *entitlement*. People began to see welfare benefits as *rights*. They no longer viewed the poor as individuals who must be helped to improve their lot. Rather, the poor are an aggrieved *group*, made so by the society. Thus they have no individual responsibility. "Welfare rights" groups were established, led not by poor people but by affluent New Class activists. Entitlement programs multiplied. The stigma against taking welfare payments diminished.[11]

Rather than ending poverty, postmodern welfare made it permanent. The poor acquired a new status, as a subculture, a protected group. Social mobility ground to a halt. The work ethic diminished. Economic incentives to marry evaporated.[12] Traditional values fell apart. In cities drugs and violence drove out the middle class, further increasing unemployment and turning poverty-stricken neighborhoods into war zones. The postmodern approach to welfare, by subsidizing and therefore perpetuating poverty, debased and shackled those it pretended to help, all in the name of diversity, group identity, cultural determinism, and relative values.

Today the group entitlement mentality has spread far beyond the welfare system. The middle class too demands its share of "entitlement programs." Retirees, students, farmers, small businesses, protected industries, artists, college students, art lovers, city dwellers, and anyone who can afford a lobbyist all demand federal money based on their group identity. The federal government now pays money so middle class students can get a college education. Social Security finances retirement for everyone. Now we are told that all Americans are "entitled" to federally controlled health care.

Our growing dependency on the government, judging from the track record of the welfare system, may be similarly catastrophic to our national character.

THE GLOBAL ENVIRONMENT

Many of our social problems are both a cause and an effect of postmodernism. In the meantime, the nation as a whole finds itself caught up in the problems of "the global community."

Airplanes have made travel easy, quick, and routine—erasing distance. Telephones, faxes, and computer networks have made communication instantaneous. Satellites enable the whole world to watch the same television programs. Free trade has created a "global economy." An automobile may have been designed in Japan, assembled in the United States with parts manufactured in Mexico, and the end product sold in Saudi Arabia. Labor and capital, imports and exports, flow across borders as if they did not exist.

On one hand, the world has drawn closer together. The market economy has triumphed over socialism. The decisive defeat of communism vindicates American ideals, and the rest of the world, for the most part, realizes this. When children in Bulgaria, Nigeria, and Singapore wear blue jeans and Air Jordans, listen to rock 'n' roll music, and eat McDonald's hamburgers, they emulate American culture, exulting in its ideals of freedom and individuality. To be sure, contemporary American culture is not what it should be, and it would be tragic for other countries to lose their cultural heritage to American pop culture. Still, no one can deny that the world looks more and more like America.

Not only are capitalism and democracy taking hold globally, but so is Christianity—not so much in the post-Christian West, but in the Third World. It may not be too much to hope for that the postmodern world might enjoy an era of prosperity, freedom, and spiritual vitality.

On the other hand, in other ways the world is splitting apart. The ethnic hatreds, militant nationalism, and civil wars that dominate the so-called "new world order" flow from postmodern tribalism. The postmodernist obsession with group identity and cultural determinism is global in scope. Not only American society but the whole world has segmented into mutually antagonistic groups.

If we are each inextricably bound into our own cultural worlds, if there are no universals to make us part of a common humanity, and if there are no moral absolutes to regulate the way we treat our fellow human beings, then we must retreat into our own tribes. It makes perfect sense to "cleanse" our land of groups that do not belong, groups that are so defined by their own cultures that they are intrinsically alien to us. It becomes difficult to recognize them as individual human beings. It becomes easy to kill them.

The purest example of the shift from the modern to the postmodern, in both its positive and its negative implications, exists in Eastern Europe. Marxism was imminently modern in its hostility to religion, its embrace of science, and its grand scheme to unify humanity and to solve all of society's problems by "rational" planning. In practice, Marxism was unspeakably evil, oppressive, and inhuman. In a fitting irony, the ideology that reduced all human issues to matters of economics met its end in the economic sphere. The Soviet Union did unify the vast reaches of Eastern Europe and northern Asia, bringing hundreds of diverse cultures into the Communist Empire. It did so by suppressing all native traditions and all religions and by requiring, with the aid of secret police, strict adherence to Marxist-Leninist ideology.

With the disintegration of communism, modernism died and the postmodern era began.[13] The persecution of Christianity came to an end, and thousands returned to Christ. Occupied nations, such as the Baltic states, won their independence. Freedom was real.

Sadly, Russia and the other former members and satellites of the Soviet Union immediately had to face the dark side of the postmodern era, the alternative of postmodern*ism*. Lacking the "totalizing" ideology and state power of communism, the components of the Soviet Union came apart. That is not bad in itself—nations deserve their independence. But the independent nations themselves kept segmenting, dissolving into ever-smaller ethnic groups, implacably hostile to their neighbors. Armenians and Kazhakstanis began slaughtering each other; Georgia split from Russia and then itself erupted into civil war. In Eastern Europe, the Czechs and Slovaks split into two countries; in what was once Yugoslavia, Serbs, Croats, and Bosnians shocked the world with their genocidal violence.

As if this were not bad enough, the countries freed from communism had to face other temptations of postmodernism. The global information network presented them with alluring images of Western consumerism. The pop culture beckoned with its rock 'n' roll and Hollywood values. Fruits of the global economy were dangled before their eyes, but the legacy of socialism—by eliminating private property, meaningful currency, and the work ethic—kept them from participating in the free market. Since their Christian heritage had been all but exterminated, many were left with the postmodernist dictum that there are no absolutes. The new freedom of the press led to a boom in pornography. The removal of the police state meant an explosion of crime. Instead of rebuilding their cultures, many went money-mad, embracing materialism and the lust for consumer goods, turning to prostitution as an easy way to earn hard currency.

Which face of the postmodern era will prevail in the former Soviet Union, the opportunity to restore the values ravaged by modernism or the anarchy of moral relativism? Which face will prevail in the United States? The East and West, for all of their differences, face the same question.

In the meantime, despite the demise of the Cold War, the world is not a safe place. Modern wars featured global confrontations between powerful nations united with their allies. Vast military forces, armed with high-tech weapons of mass destruction, met each other on fields of battle. There is little prospect of such a war now, with America the only remaining superpower. The postmodern brand of warfare, however, is terrorism.

The terrorist cell is in fact a model of postmodernism and its dangers. A group is segmented from the rest of society, insulated by its own self-identity. The group recognizes no values that transcend its own. Fueled by a sense of victimization, self-righteousness, and group solidarity, the terrorist cell will have no qualms about blowing up buildings or machine-gunning innocent bystanders.

Such bystanders are not seen as individuals, but as members of a group—as Americans or Bosnians or Jews. They share a collective guilt. Group responsibility, group injury, group blame constitute the mind-set of both postmodernism and terrorism. Again, as Benjamin Barber points out, terrorists see "war not as an instrument of policy but as an emblem of identity, an expression of community, an end in itself."[14]

Postmodernism manifests itself throughout our everyday life, from our newspapers to our children's education, from the way we work to the way we spend leisure time. Its most insidious influence, however, is in our spiritual lives.

PART FOUR

POSTMODERN RELIGION

SPIRITUALITY WITHOUT TRUTH

*E*ver since the Enlightenment and throughout the modern age, scholars have expected religion to die out. It hasn't happened. "Modern man," it was said (this was before feminism), was incapable of believing in the supernatural.

The twentieth century opened with a theological battle between the so-called modernists and the fundamentalists. With the Scopes Trial of 1925, the media caricatured the fundamentalists, and the intellectual elite ridiculed them. The modernists seized the denominational structures of most mainline churches, including the seminaries, and emerged triumphant. Ever since, modernist theologians have been "demythologizing" the Bible in an effort to make Christianity palatable to the twentieth-century mind. They assume that "modern man" is so oriented to the scientific method and the triumph of the "secular city" that he simply cannot believe in miracles, divine revelation, and a God unseen.

Seminaries began studying the Bible, not as the authoritative Word of God, but as any other ancient document, using the historical-critical methodology of "modern scientific scholarship." This approach assumed that the miracles of the Bible did not occur and must be accounted for in nonsupernatural ways. Rather than seeing the Bible as authoritative, it held that Bible statements should be received "critically," as reflecting the culture and preoccupations of an ancient people. According to the modernist approach, what the Bible says is not necessarily true. Rather, theological liberals put their confidence in the alleged truth about

Scripture as uncovered by the Biblical critics, garbed in the infallible robes of modern scientific rationalism.

Liberals designed their theology to accommodate modern thought and culture, turning the church away from its preoccupation with an otherworldly salvation to a concern with society's tangible problems. The church's traditional concern for good works shifted into political activism designed to usher in the centrally planned utopia modernists expected. The church's traditional concern for spirituality switched to psychology, using the very same methods and assumptions of the secular "social scientists." Churches began to sponsor encounter groups, and pastors began counseling their flock to help them to "self-realization."

Now the political utopianism and the psychological naiveté of liberal theology—while still dominating most mainline seminaries—seem curiously dated. Far from appealing to modern man, the liberal churches have plummeted in membership. If the liberals were right, there is really no need for a church. If the Bible is a myth and we do not really need to be saved, as the liberals so earnestly preached, why not sleep in on Sunday mornings? Ironically, the conservative and fundamentalist churches began to grow, addressing the genuine spiritual needs that modernist churches denied.

Of course, the "modern man" the liberals tried to appeal to did not really exist. This new breed of humanity, so scientific, so rational, was a projection of modern philosophy, a myth created by a tiny number of intellectuals who wanted to attribute their own scientism and rationalism to the whole human race. Ordinary people faced their limitations and their guilt as they always have, and many of them found faith in the Word of God. The theological liberals squandered their Christian heritage in a futile attempt to gain favor with modernist intellectuals. After awhile modernism itself, with its supreme overconfidence and manifest failures, became a mockery. The fall of modernism dragged down liberal theology with it. For that, we can be eternally grateful.

The postmodern era holds promise for Bible-believing Christians. But it also holds new and different perils. Modernist heresies have floundered, but now postmodernist heresies replace them. Rationalism, having failed, is giving way to *ir*rationalism— both are hostile to God's revelation, but in different ways. Modernists did not believe the Bible is true. Postmodernists have cast out the category of truth altogether. In doing so, they have opened up a Pandora's box of New Age religions, syncretism, and moral chaos.

The fundamentalist churches could easily define themselves against the modernists—the battle lines were clearly drawn. Today the issues are more complex and more insidious. Tragically, the postmodernist mind-set is gaining a foothold *within* evangelical churches.

TRUTH OR DESIRE

To review, postmodernism assumes that there is no objective truth, that moral values are relative, and that reality is socially constructed by a host of diverse communities. These beliefs by no means rule out religion, as modernism tended to. But the religions and the theologies they promote are very different from both Biblical orthodoxy and modernism.

Before, in both the modern and the premodern eras, religion involved beliefs about what is real. There either is a God, or there is not. Jesus was either the incarnate Son of God, or He was just a man. Miracles happened, or they did not. Some Christians vehemently disagreed with each other: Is there such a place as Purgatory? Does Mary intercede for us in Heaven? Are some predestined to damnation? But these were disagreements over questions of fact. Today religion is not seen as a set of beliefs about what is real and what is not. Rather, religion is seen as a preference, a choice.[1] We believe in what we like. We believe what we want to believe.

Where there are no absolute truths, the intellect gives over to the will. Aesthetic criteria replace rational criteria. Listen to the way people today discuss religion. "I really like that church," they will say. Agreeing with that church or believing in its teaching scarcely enters into it. People discuss tenets of faith in the same terms. "I really like the Bible passage that says, 'God is love.'" Fair enough and amen. There is much to like in Christianity—God's love for us, Christ's bearing our sins, His grace and help.

But then we start hearing about what the person does *not* like. "I don't like the idea of Hell." This is certainly an appropriate response—who could possible "like" Hell? But our natural distaste for this horrible doctrine is surely beside the point. The issue is not whether we like it, but whether there is such a place. Reality seldom takes into account our personal preferences, even in the most trivial facets of everyday life. That there might actually be a Hell, a realm of punishment and torment that lasts forever, is a momentous concept, staggeringly important.

To determine whether or not there is such a hideous existence beyond the grave—and to find out how we can be delivered from such a fate—a Christian must turn to the source of everything that we can know about spiritual reality, the revealed Word of God. The Christian must not necessarily expect to "like" the information thus uncovered. In fact, Christians must be leery of wholly pleasant theologies void of hard edges or challenging demands. Such a faith is nothing more than wish-fulfillment and seductive fantasies.

Today even conservative and evangelical ministers seldom mention Hell. Certainly "people don't like to hear about that," and we do not want to scare them away. But people have never liked to hear about Hell. The difference is that today, unlike any other time in history, many people are *unwilling* to believe (as if belief were a function of the will) what they do not *enjoy* (as if aesthetic considerations determined questions of fact).

This completely different way of thinking about religion—that it is a matter not of what is true but of what one likes and what one wants—explains why the cults take in so many intelligent and well-educated people. The Church of Scientology, for example, teaches that aliens from outer space entered our universe millions of years ago and fought a galactic war. These aliens affected us in our past lives. We can solve our problems by hooking up to an electronic box and by being counseled by a Scientologist (at great expense), who will remove the negative "engrams" accumulated in our past lives. Thus we become "clear" spiritual beings.

People who think of themselves as too sophisticated to believe in the Gospel of John can believe in this? Scientology, in fact, especially attracts affluent business executives, successful movie stars, and well-educated young professionals. For all of its scientific rhetoric, scientology makes no pretense of giving real evidence for the existence of these space aliens and previous lives. Scientologists may reject the possibility of revelation from God, but be quite willing to accept revelation from founder L. Ron Hubbard.

But postmodern religions do not require evidence or plausibility. Hubbard was originally a successful science fiction novelist. Many people tremendously enjoy the aliens and galactic conflicts that are the staple of science fiction. Would it not be even better if these were real? The doctrines of scientology are fascinating, imaginatively stimulating, even entertaining. Why not choose to believe them?

Talk to a member of any cult, and notice how the person describes and evaluates its teachings in completely subjective and pleasure-oriented terms: "The Maharishi is really *cool*." "Transcendental Meditation gives me a natural high." "The Reverend Moon makes me feel good about myself." Liking something and wanting it to be true are the only criteria for their beliefs.

A Christian would explain these cults' popularity in more depth by saying that their followers have been ensnared by Satan. We need to realize that Satan seduces us by appealing to our *desires*. Satan lures us by promising precisely what we like and what we want. (Of course, by demonic irony, what he actually gives is what we do *not* like and what we do *not* want, namely, Hell.) In light of "the desires of the sinful nature" (Romans 13:14), we dare not make the satisfaction of our desires our prime spiritual authority.

[margin handwritten note: Eve saw that the tree was "to be desired to make one wise."]

MORALITY OR DESIRE

For postmodernists, morality, like religion, is a matter of desire. What I want and what I choose is not only true (for me) but right (for me). That different people want and choose different things means that truth and morality are relative, but "I have a right" to my desires. Conversely, "no one has the right" to criticize my desires and my choices.

Although postmodernists tend to reject traditional morality, they can still be very moralistic. They will defend their "rights" to do what they want with puritanical zeal. Furthermore, they seem to feel that they have a right not to be criticized for what they are doing. They want not only license but approval.

Thus tolerance becomes the cardinal virtue. Under the postmodernist way of thinking, the principle of cultural diversity means that every like-minded group constitutes a culture that must be considered as good as any other culture. The postmodernist sins are

[bottom handwritten note: The issue of separation will certainly be heating up!]

"being judgmental," "being narrow-minded," "thinking that you have the only truth," and "trying to enforce your values on anyone else." Those who question the postmodernist dogma that "there are no absolutes" are excluded from the canons of tolerance. The only wrong idea is to believe in truth; the only sin is to believe in sin.

The morality of desire has wreaked havoc with sexuality. The birth control pill divorced sex from procreation. Soon sex was detached from marriage. Men and women now routinely live together without being married. Women who want to have a child now do so without bothering about having a husband. The sexual revolution devastated the family. Society now sees the fulfillment of sexual desires as a right which no one can criticize.

Now the AIDS plague, in which the immune system turns against the body and destroys it, challenges sexual permissiveness. AIDS is an imminently postmodern disease, not only as a sort of macabre self-deconstruction, but because it is caused by the legacy of the '60s—the sexual revolution, gay rights, and drug abuse. While many are turning back to sexual morality, others are fleeing from AIDS into brands of sex not only detached from the family but from human beings altogether. Pornography, phone sex, and ultimately the technological promise of "virtual sex"—in which people will be able to strap themselves into a body condom and plug into a 3-D sexual fantasy[2]—threaten the ultimate dehumanization of sexuality. Despite all consequences, people cling tenaciously to the ethic of desire.

Postmodernist morality has a curious tenet—the concept of collective responsibility and collective guilt. As the group-oriented ideology minimizes the individual, it also minimizes personal responsibility. If the culture shapes the individual, then the culture must be responsible for what individuals do. As a result, blame falls on the culture rather than on individuals. Moral status is determined not by one's actions, but by one's membership in a group. A young white male is thus encouraged to feel collective guilt for the way white people have mistreated "people of color" through the centuries and for the way men have historically oppressed women. He may have never owned slaves, massacred Indians, or abused women, yet he should feel guilty for what his ancestors did. To atone for this guilt, he may plunge into liberal or radical politics. In the meantime, government and businesses set up affirmative action programs to redress "historical injustices," compensating the victims of the past by rewarding their descendents, who themselves may not have suffered any injustice.

Of course, even the concept of collective guilt assumes the existence of objective moral standards. Calls for "justice" imply a standard of right and wrong, of people getting what they deserve. C. S. Lewis points out that even people who deny the existence of right and wrong react in ways that belie that belief when someone takes their seat on the bus or treats them unfairly.[3]

Honest postmodernists themselves recognize the dilemma of advocating "justice" while denying that moral absolutes exist. Steven Connor warns against

> underestimating the effect of the postmodern abandonment of the universal horizon of value and morality. It will not do simply to assume the continuation of values and morality, in the hope that these will naturally persist among postmodern persons of good will who will automatically agree about what value and morality are.[4]

He points out the contradiction of postmodernists denying moral certainty in the West while championing moral struggles in the Third World. Such inconsistency, he says, asserts "the cultural relativity of certain values, and does not cope with the a priori denial of the possibility of any universal value."[5]

> Indeed, when inspected closely, it becomes apparent that the postmodern critique of unjust and oppressive systems of universality implicitly depends for its force upon the assumptions of the universal right of all not to be treated unjustly and oppressively.[6]

Connor does not resolve this dilemma; he ends his book on postmodernism by calling for the forging of "new and more inclusive forms of ethical collectivity," "the creation of a common frame of assent."[7] But to do so would be to abandon the very assumptions of postmodernism.

The only consistent position for postmodernists is that all talk of morality, *including their own*, only masks the will to power.

Calls for justice, liberation, and the end to oppression can only be rhetorical devices. Groups that lack power must seize it by any means and use it against their oppressors. That the latter will now be victims of oppression is only fitting. The naked exercise of power, unrestrained by moral limits, is a formula first for terrorism and then for totalitarianism.

On both the political and the individual level, the ethics of desire amounts to *the will* (what I choose) *to power* (what I want). Politically, the ethics of desire means ruthless power struggles between competing groups. In the United States, this manifests itself in feminists seeking to imprison pro-life demonstrators, gay activists disrupting church services, the "Borking" of conservative candidates, and overt terrorism. In the former Soviet Empire, it manifests itself in civil war and ethnic cleansing. For individuals, the ethics of desire means selfishness, promiscuity, and moral abandon. "I must have the power to do what I want, and you do not have the power to stop me."

Without a moral framework, society disintegrates into warring factions and isolated depraved individuals. The result is a replay of the violence, perversion, and anarchy described in the book of Judges, which at once diagnoses the moral collapse of ancient Palestine and precisely defines postmodernist ethical theory: "everyone did what was right in his own eyes" (Judges 21:25 NKJV).

THE NEW RELIGIONS

Whereas modernism sought to rid the world of religion, postmodernism spawns new ones. Unconstrained by objectivity, tradition, reason, or morality, these new faiths differ radically from Christianity. They draw on strains of the most ancient and primitive paganism.

Even the deconstructionists speak in mystical terms. They have been compared to the medieval practitioners of "negative theology" who refused to say what God is, maintaining that they could only say what God is *not*. More precisely, they are like the monks of Zen Buddhism who undercut rationality itself, obliterating all distinctions to achieve the enlightenment of Nirvana, the state of cosmic nothingness. The deconstructionists dissolve every positive statement, every rational argument, every truth claim—destroying form, they say, so as to open up what lies beyond the possibilities of representation. What lies beyond the final eclipse of absolutes will be beyond our imagining, conditioned as we are by rationalist categories. The inadequacies of language will be left behind, and the alienation of the isolated individual supposedly will be healed in a mystical reconciliation of nature, psychology, and culture.[8] (Postmodernists naively assume the best, lacking the doctrine of original sin, which would predict that destroying all form would release horrific evil.)

Postmodernism, in its rejection of objective truth, has clear affinities with Hinduism and Buddhism, which teach that the external world is only an illusion spun by the human mind. The Eastern religions also provide the basis for more popular brands of spirituality. As the postmodernist Walter Truett Anderson points out:

> The rush of postmodern reaction from the old certainties has swept some people headlong into a worldview even more radical than that of the constructivists. Many voices can now be heard declaring that what is out there is only what we *put* out there. More precisely, what *I* put there—just little me, euphorically creating my own universe. We used to call this solipsism; now we call it New Age spirituality.[9]

New Age religions, for all of their pagan trappings, have in common the idea that the self is divine, that *you* are God, the creator of your own universe. As old as the Serpent's lie to Eve (Genesis 3:5), this idea now finds its way into self-help books, motivational tracts, and pop psychology ("You create your own reality").

The New Age movement, like postmodernism, exists in bewildering diversity, yet with common themes. New Age gurus may be "channelers" of ancient Egyptian warriors or extraterrestrial life forms. They may teach the beneficent powers of crystals or promote herbal medicine. They may do pseudoscientific research into extrasensory perception, or they may put on robes to practice Tibetan meditation. They may throw the *I Ching*, or they may practice witchcraft. For all of their differences, they will all assert the dogma that the self is god, that the objective universe is an illusion, and that truth is relative.

The New Age religions are, of course, little more than a revival of the old paganism. Behind the craze for horoscopes, E.S.P., and channeling lurks old-fashioned divination, magic, and demon possession. With the eclipse of Christianity, primitive nature religions come creeping back in all of their superstition and barbarism. These are, of course, adjusted to the contemporary imagination. Feminists, in reacting against "patriarchal" religions such as Christianity, try to restore goddess-worship. Environmentalists stress how the whole planet constitutes a single interdependent ecosystem. It is as if we are all individual cells of a larger organism, a living being long worshiped as Mother Earth, the goddess Gaia.

The pagan faiths, at least in their modern reincarnations, are morally permissive. Computer hackers, the cyberpunks, cultivate what they call "techno-erotic paganism," using their modems to enter the electronic realm of "cyberspace." Here on their interconnected computer screens, they attain a sort of global communion that enables them both to carry on quasi-theological conversations and to tap into pornographic E-mail.[10] The new religions are often tied to moral rebellion. The revival of goddess worship may relate to homosexuality as well as to feminism. Scholars have shown how in ancient times homosexuality was associated with goddess worship.[11] Many ancient religions also practiced infanticide. Whether or not abortion is a form of Molech worship, its acceptance signals a profound shift away from the presuppositions of a transcendent ethical religion back to a darker, more barbaric ethical consciousness.

The next major new religion, however, will probably not be one of the old forms of overt paganism, but rather a syncretic hybrid. In a postmodernist and increasingly consumer-centered world in which truth is relative, people will pick and choose various aspects of the different faiths according to what they "like." George Barna predicts that "left to their own devices, adults will be less impressed by, and less accepting of, Christianity's most basic and important beliefs. Instead, as adults continue their search for truth and purpose, they will become syncretistic."

> As elements of Eastern religions become more prolific, the most appealing aspects of Christianity (which will be the lifestyle elements, rather than the central spiritual tenets) will be

wed to the exotic and fascinating attributes of Eastern faiths. The result will be a people who honestly believe that they have improved Christianity, and who would even consider themselves to be Christian, despite their creative restructuring of faith.[12]

Barna goes on to observe that "those who feared the takeover of communism railed against the dangers of America becoming a godless nation. They need not fear: we will become just the opposite, a nation filled with many gods."[13]

Biblical Christians will find themselves in exactly the position of the ancient Israelites and the early church—having to hold on to their faith in the midst of hostile pagan neighbors. They will also face the same temptations. Many of the Israelites fell into syncretism, going so far as to erect pagan altars in the Temple of the one true God. Many in the early church fell into heresy as they attempted to combine Christianity with Gnostic philosophy and Manichean mystery cults. The pressure to follow the practices, values, and beliefs of pagan neighbors has always been intense. But God's Word is clear:

> Be careful not to be ensnared by inquiring about their gods, saying, "How do these nations serve their gods? We will do the same." You must not worship the LORD your God in their way, because in worshiping their gods, they do all kinds of detestable things the LORD hates. They even burn their sons and daughters in the fire as sacrifices to their gods. See that you do all I command you; do not add to it or take away from it. (Deuteronomy 12:30-32)

SOCIETY'S OPTIONS

Can a society exist for long without a moral and religious consensus? Societies divided against themselves into fragmented and warring factions, lacking any cohesive frame of reference, are by definition unstable. Societies that fly apart eventually reassemble themselves in a different way. Presently, in this postmodernist moment, we are in the demolition phase, when not only traditional values but modern values are being taken apart. What comes next, when the pieces of society are put together again into a new design, remains to be seen. There are, however, signs of new kinds of secularized religions that herald new kinds of societies.

Sir Arnold Toynbee, in his magisterial analyses of world civilizations, has argued that successful societies have some sort of religious consensus. When this consensus is lost, new objects of worship will rush in to fill the spiritual vacuum. According to Toynbee, when a society loses its transcendent faith, it turns to three alternatives, which he frankly terms "idolatries": nationalism, ecumenicalism, and technicalism. 3

Under the first option, nationalism, a transcendent universal faith gives way to the "deified parochial community."[14] In this model, each little group considers itself to be divine. The particular culture or subculture idolizes itself. The community becomes the source of moral values, which extend only to members of that community. Outsiders are enemies, to whom moral considerations do not apply. Toynbee shows how this happened with ancient Athens and Sparta, in the rise of Renaissance nationalism after the medieval consensus collapsed, and in the fascism of Mussolini and the National Socialism of Hitler.[15]

Toynbee's model is startlingly prophetic of postmodernism and postmodernist society. When Eastern Europe lost its Marxist consensus, new nationalisms emerged—"deified parochial communities" that are at each other's throats. The loss of a democratic consensus in the United States has led to racial politics, militant interest groups, and subcultures that simmer with hostility towards each other.

Another option to the loss of a transcendent religious consensus is the "deified ecumenical empire."[16] This model idolizes unity while still accommodating great diversity. When Rome lost its localized ancestral religion and turned into a vast empire, it instituted emperor worship. The empire itself, in the person of its ruler, became a god. Rome insisted that everyone under its rule burn incense and offer prayer to Caesar. Under this one condition, Rome could tolerate people of all religions. But Christians claimed that there was only one true faith and refused to worship the emperor. Consequently, the Romans excluded them from this pluralistic society and put them to death. Otherwise, the society held together by deifying itself. The divinized Roman empire was "ecumenical," that is, worldwide. Religions seek to be universal in scope. Rome advanced its faith by conquering everyone in sight, bringing everyone into the fold with evangelistic (and murderous) zeal, uniting the whole known world.

Ancient Rome was not the only society to try to forge an idolized ecumenical community. Toynbee sees a similar pattern in ancient Egypt, Sumeria, Persia, and more recently in the Ottoman Empire, the Imperial Dynasties of China, and even the trappings of the worldwide British Empire.[17] He also sees a resurgence of ecumenism in his own time (the years after World War II) with the high hopes being invested in the United Nations and the utopian schemes for a single world government.

"Unity," of course, is a modernist value. The ecumenical idolatry may be a function of late modernism, a response to the lack of religious consensus that began with the Enlightenment and reached its peak in the twentieth century. Modernist theologians led the way with their appropriately termed "ecumenical movement," an attempt to unite all churches by obliterating their distinct beliefs. Many churches jettisoned orthodoxy in favor of vague sentiments and left-wing one-world politics.

The concern for "unity" may be a modernist value, but it remains a postmodernist option. The ecumenical movement, having failed to unify all Christian churches, now works to unite all world religions, which again means obliterating their distinct beliefs in favor of a new faith alien to them all. These theologians embrace the postmodernist principle of relativism while trying to formulate a more or less arbitrary framework for embracing all cultures and religions. This may be a harbinger of what is to come. Certainly, the value of "tolerance" above all, as Toynbee shows, is a defining characteristic of ecumenical communities.[18] So is intolerance for those, such as Christians, who dissent.

Despite the postmodernist preference for diversity, environmentalists, New Age theologians, business gurus, rock stars, and other champions of the new consciousness are speaking again of "global unity." (We are all dependent on a single ecosystem. We are all cells in "Gaia," the single global organism that constitutes the earth. American businesses are part of an interdependent global economy. We are the world.) The term "globalization," in fact, may be the new buzz word for this emerging postmodernist ecumenicalism. The word suggests both cultural relativism and an over-arching though ill-defined global unity.

The worship of unity inevitably results, says Toynbee, in a loss of liberty. Individuality, by definition, must be suppressed if there is to be unity. Yet the prospect of a unified society taking upon itself all of the attributes and responsibilities of the gods—defining our values and taking care of all of our needs—remains attractive. Toynbee saw the modern welfare state as a particular example of the deified community. The state poses as the ultimate provider of food, jobs, health, and everything else its people need, with its citizens trading their freedom for security. Toynbee wrote in the 1950s, "It looks as if the ecumenical welfare state may be the next idol that will be erected in a still discarded Christianity's place."[19]

This vision of an omni-benevolent and omnipotent state still allures many in the West (particularly in America, which has not yet fully implemented the welfare state so as to experience its failures). Nevertheless, the colossal collapse of Soviet communism, the ultimate welfare state, the most flagrant deified ecumenical empire, may render this option obsolete.

The third alternative to a transcendent religious faith, according to Toynbee, is the "idolization of the invincible technician."[20] He traces how technology developed to the point of taking on the functions of a religion. The divine attributes of omniscience and omnipotence were ascribed to technology.

Certainly, science as such defines the modern, not the postmodern world. But Toynbee is concerned not so much with the impact of scientific knowledge as with the ascendency of technique, with the mastery of nature and with a lifestyle made possible by machines. Postmodernist anti-intellectualism may well slow the pursuit of scientific knowledge, but the appetite for television, computers, and as yet unimagined electronic technology will be insatiable. The technicians who invent these products will form a new priesthood with knowledge inaccessible to the laity—to whom the technology will be as incomprehensible as magic. The masses may be totally uninterested in objective science, but they will build their lives and their values around technology.

Toynbee seems to have predicted what Neil Postman now describes as taking place throughout contemporary society—the advent of "technopoly," a condition in which technology acquires a monopoly over all of culture. Technology's preoccupation with process over content, Postman argues, results in moral and spiritual confusion and alters our whole capacity for thought. "Abetted by a form of education that in itself has been emptied of any coherent worldview," he writes, "technopoly deprives us of the social, political, historical, metaphysical, logical, or spiritual basis for knowing what is beyond belief."[21]

Technology, needing constant revision to be "up to date," is inherently opposed to tradition.[22] This is appropriate in the sphere of technology. A brand-new computer is likely to be better than an old one. But what is valid in one realm is not necessarily valid in others. Though traditions in all cultures have always served an important social function (such as to preserve moral values and create stable families), technology trashes them all. In the Middle Ages, scholastic theology inappropriately applied its methodology to realms outside its ken, such as science. Today the reverse has happened. People apply the technological mind-set to everything, including theology and ethics.

Whereas modern society was aggressively secular, postmodern society assigns religious functions to itself. Postmodernists reduce theological, moral, and human mysteries to matters of technical expertise. Postman shows how technical experts have become the new priests:

> In Technopoly, all experts are invested with the charisma of priestliness. Some of our priest-experts are called psychiatrists, some psychologists, some sociologists, some statisticians. The god they serve does not speak of righteousness or goodness or mercy or grace. Their god speaks of efficiency, precision, objectivity. And that is why such concepts as sin and evil disappear in Technopoly. They come from a moral universe that is irrelevant to the theology of expertise. And so the priests of Technopoly call sin "social deviance," which is a statistical concept, and they call evil "psychopathology," which is a medical concept. Sin and evil disappear because they cannot be measured and objectified, and therefore cannot be dealt with by experts.[23]

People, feelings, ideas, values all must be *quantified*. The technological mind-set must reduce everything to numbers. We are in the
age of statistics—opinion polls, standardized tests, and "assessment
instruments" which purport to measure everything from the quality of our work to our psychological condition. We evaluate not in
terms of right and wrong, but by circling a number on a ten-point
scale.

Traditional symbols, such as those of religion, are not repu-
diated; rather, they are trivialized.[24] Statistics reduce beliefs to opinions and moral standards to personal preferences. Technological
reproduction and ceaseless visual representation work against any
concept of mystery or the sacred. The Biblical concept of holiness
means literally "set apart"; technology brings everything into
view—sex, suffering, personality, the inner life—rendering everything profane, which means literally "common."

It is no accident that the electronic media love to portray sex,
which was once kept secret and private, and violence, which was
once hidden as being too horrible. The new visual media will portray everything that can be seen. What cannot be seen—God, faith,
goodness, spirituality—is outside its ken and will be ignored. If not
ignored, spiritual reality will be visualized in terms of the new
media, and thus trivialized. When God is to be treated in a movie,
He will be played by George Burns, and the movie will be a comedy. Religious images still have a powerful emotional resonance,
but they will be employed without reference to their meaning. The
latest sex symbol calls herself Madonna, the title of the Virgin
Mary. She flaunts a crucifix as part of her sexy wardrobe and makes
a steamy video in which a statue of a saint comes alive, and they
have sex in a church. The media repeats profanity and blasphemy
so often that after awhile it no longer shocks. The public gets used
to it, whereupon, as Postman says, the symbols are drained of their
significance.[25]

In a technopoly people "make no moral decisions, only practical ones."[26] Because they lack transcendent notions of good and
evil, they fall back on the only standard they have, that of technology: What *works*? People reduce the value-of-human-life issue
to a question of health care costs. They justify killing the sick, the
handicapped, and children in the womb in quantifiable economic
terms—polls show that a majority of people would not want to be

kept alive on a machine; euthanasia would keep hospital costs down; abortion would help trim the welfare rolls. People turn to "experts" to resolve their ethical dilemmas, entrusting end-of-life decisions to hospital ethics boards. Many who wish to commit suicide want a doctor's supervision, enlisting the counsel, support, and aid of someone such as Dr. Kevorkian, a new kind of priest who administers a different kind of last rites.

We are currently in the midst of a profound transition, away from the premodern and the modern into uncharted waters. Whether the new world disorder will move in the direction of "deified parochial communities," "a deified ecumenical empire," or "the idolization of the invincible technician" is not clear. Currently, we see signs of all three—of fierce group identity, globalized schemes for enforced unity, and an unfettered technopoly. There is, of course, one more option—recovering transcendent faith.

Toynbee approvingly quotes a letter he received from Edwyn Bevan, who recognizes the connection between anarchy and tyranny. Bevan's bleak forecast of the world's future carries with it one specific ray of hope:

> Anarchy is essentially weak, and in an anarchic world any firmly organized group with rational organisation and scientific knowledge could spread its dominion over the rest. And, as an alternative to anarchy, the world would welcome the despotic state. . . . But there *is* the Christian Church . . . a factor to be reckoned with. It may have to undergo martyrdom in the future world-state, but as it compelled the Roman world-state in the end to make at any rate formal submission to Christ, it might again, by the way of martyrdom, conquer the . . . world-state of the future.[27]

POSTMODERN CHRISTIANITY

The state of Christianity in the postmodern society is hard to assess. Christianity has not only survived the modern era, contrary to the expectations of modernist intellectuals, it seems to be thriving in the postmodern era. Liberal, modernist churches are withering on the vine while conservative and evangelical churches flourish. Polls report that as many as 94 percent of Americans believe in God, 80 percent claim to be Christians, and over 43 percent go to church every Sunday.[1]

And yet, if these figures are correct, why is Christianity almost invisible in contemporary culture? Why is moral and intellectual relativism so rampant when 70 percent of all Americans believe that "The Bible is the written word of God and is totally accurate in all it teaches"?[2]

Although we live in the age of the "megachurch" and the church growth movement, the percentage of Americans going to church is about the same as in the 1980s, and Protestant membership has actually declined.[3] Contemporary Christians, who often seem to be at peace with an ungodly culture, lack staying power, spiritual commitment, and fidelity to Biblical moral standards.[4] Many churches do well in quantity while doing poorly in quality.

The end of the modern era opens up genuine opportunities for Biblical Christianity. However, instead of squarely facing the postmodern condition, many Christians succumb to the postmod-ern*ism* plaguing the rest of the culture. Conservative and evangelical Christians did well, for the most part, in avoiding the temptations of modernism. Now with their modernistic enemy defeated, they are letting their guard down, naively giving in to the new cultural climate. Many supposedly conservative churches now alter not only their style but their message in an attempt to appeal to contemporary society.

It does not have to be this way. The church can be postmodern without being postmodern*ist*. Christians can take advantage of the death of modernism to confess the historic Biblical faith to a lost and confused generation. To be relevant to the postmodern era, the church must simply proclaim the truth of God's Word, the validity of God's law, and the sufficiency of the gospel of Jesus Christ.

EVANGELICAL POSTMODERNISM

In many ways, the church cannot help but be caught up in postmodern changes. We have seen how postmodern society is highly segmented, with different groups splitting off into their own subcultures. The clearest example of this phenomenon may lie in the conservatives' own camp. Christians today have their own schools, their own colleges, their own bookstores, their own entertainment industry, and their own media. Postmodernists claim that since there can be no universal consensus, people who share a language and a worldview must form their own self-contained communities. This is certainly happening in contemporary Christianity.

Christians who decry the Christian subculture should realize that the alternative may be cultural extinction. Christianity has been excommunicated from the culture at large—systematically excluded from the schools, the intellectual establishment, and the media. The establishment of Christian schools, publishers, arts groups, broadcasters, businesses, and so on may be one of the great achievements of the twentieth-century church. As postmodernist pressures intensify, having counter institutions already in place may prove invaluable for Christians to stage an effective resistance.

Christians should use their bases to make forays into the culture at large and exert their influence at every level. They should certainly resist the temptation to remain in the security of the "Christian ghetto." They may find themselves accepted, though, only up to a point. Usually, people do not choose to live in a ghetto.

The Jewish ghettos and the Black ghettos were means of exclusion, and Christians can expect to be excluded from an increasingly godless world. The Jews of the Warsaw Ghetto and the Blacks of Harlem in the 1920s were shut out of the mainstream, but this did not prevent them from having a rich, vibrant cultural life of their own. Christians might aspire to do as well.

The problem is not that Christians have their own parallel institutions, but that these institutions are sometimes so similar to secular ones. The mind-set cultivated by the evangelical subculture often startlingly resembles that of secular postmodernism.

The postmodernist rejection of objectivity pervades the evangelical church. "We have a generation that is less interested in cerebral arguments, linear thinking, theological systems," observes Leith Anderson, "and more interested in encountering the supernatural."[5] Consequently, churchgoers operate with a different paradigm of spirituality. "The old paradigm taught that if you have the right teaching, you will experience God. The new paradigm says that if you experience God, you will have the right teaching."[6] Not only is objective doctrine minimized in favor of subjective experience; experience actually becomes the criterion for evaluating doctrine.

Anderson, a megachurch pastor and church growth consultant, says that pastors will increasingly have to deal with people such as the young man we discussed earlier who says that he believes in the inerrancy of Scripture, Reformed theology, and reincarnation. To say that belief in reincarnation is inconsistent with belief in the Bible may hardly register. The new generation (he might have said the postmodernist generation) simply does not think in systematic terms. The young man *likes* the Bible, John Calvin, and Shirley MacLaine. Each is meaningful to him. He can live with the contradictions.[7]

This downplaying of doctrine and objective thinking helps explain why 53 percent of evangelical Christians can believe that there are no absolutes (as compared to 66 percent of Americans as a whole).[8] Certainly, the evangelical tradition has always cultivated the emotions and stressed an experiential religion, as opposed to mere "head knowledge." This openness to personal feelings and experience is a point of contact with postmodernism, which has gone on to exaggerate the role of subjectivity beyond anything that a "hot gospeler" of the nineteenth century would ever recognize.

Similarly, evangelicals have tended to emphasize the role of choice in salvation. People are urged to make a "decision for Christ," a commitment regularly described as a function of the human will. This terminology corresponds well to the postmodernist mind-set, which understands religion and morality in terms of choice, not truth.

When evangelicals dig into their own substantial theological heritage, however, they find more to this "decision theology" than they had realized. For Luther, Calvin, St. Augustine, and many other Biblical theologians, the human will is in bondage to sin, so that our choices drive us away from God. In salvation we do not choose God; He chooses us. We are not saved by our wills, but by God's grace which transforms our sinful wills by the power of the Holy Spirit. Then and only then can we be said to have freedom of the will and are enabled to "choose Christ." Even theologians such as Arminius, Wesley, and Aquinas, who believed that the human will is free and must cooperate in the process of salvation, did not view salvation as a sheerly autonomous choice.

Evangelicalism, having perhaps neglected its theology, thus seems attractive to postmodernists for its warm emotionalism and its exaltation of choice. Other practices evangelicals have followed for years (such as Bible studies and prayer groups) suddenly have a new resonance for postmodernists (with their fondness for support groups and the cultivation of group identity). While such traditions of evangelicalism might be good ways of attracting postmodernists in order to evangelize them, sometimes the conversion has gone in the other direction.

We have seen how postmodernism is open to popular culture and to frank commercialism. Art, politics, and ideas—lacking connection to objective reality—are all pitched to the tastes of the consumer. Rhetoric and mass-marketing replace rational persuasion. Postmodernism encourages a consumer mentality, catering to what people like and want. This carries over, as we have seen, into religion. When truth is no longer a factor, one chooses a religion like any other commodity—do I like it? Does it give me what I want?

Charles Colson tells about an evangelical church that decided it needed to grow in membership. The pastor first commissioned a market survey. It found that many people were turned off by the term "Baptist." The church changed its name. The survey showed that people wanted accessibility, so the church put up a new building off the freeway. It had beamed ceilings, stone fireplaces, and no crosses or other religious symbols that might make people feel uncomfortable. Then the pastor decided to stop using theological language. "If we use the words *redemption* or *conversion*," he reasoned, "they think we are talking about bonds." He stopped preaching about Hell and damnation and shifted to more positive topics. Sure enough, the church grew. "There's a spirit of putting people over doctrine," gushed one member. "The church totally accepts people as they are without any sort of don'ts and dos."[9] In abandoning its doctrine and its moral authority and in adjusting its teaching to the demands of the marketplace, the church embarked on a pilgrimage to postmodernism.

Instead of preaching that leads to the conviction of sin and salvation through the cross of Jesus Christ, churches preach "feel-good" messages designed to cheer people up. Some have described postmodernist culture as a "therapeutic culture," in which a sense of psychological well-being, not truth, is the controlling value.[10] The contemporary church likewise faces the temptation to replace theology with therapy.

Since postmodern thought is impatient with transcendent spiritual beliefs, the focus shifts to the here and the now, to the tangible. People have little interest in Heaven; they want health and wealth now. Since postmodernists are oriented to power, they will be drawn to power churches which promise miracles to solve every problem, political clout, exponential numerical growth, and success after success.[11] (Luther was thinking of something similar when he contrasted the "theology of glory," based on power and pride, with the "theology of the cross," based on our own humility and the suffering of Jesus Christ.)[12]

Colson severely criticizes the feel-good theologies of the "hot-tub religion" and the capitulation to popular culture of the "McChurch." Consumerism in the church, he says, dilutes its message, changes the church's character, perverts the gospel, and negates the church's authority.[13]

Even more serious than church consumerism (although usually accompanying it), evangelical theology itself has in some circles capitulated to postmodernist ideology. This new theology, as developed by academic theologians and as evident in countless evangelical bookstores and pulpits, has been described as a "megashift" away from classical Protestantism to a completely different (and essentially postmodernist) understanding of the gospel.[14]

Megashift theology attempts to soften the hard edges of Biblical orthodoxy and to accommodate contemporary society's values and mind-set. Michael Horton explains the new theology through a series of contrasts.

Whereas classical Christianity stresses the transcendence of God and His immutability, omnipotence, and omniscience, the new model stresses the immanence of God, who is dynamic, capable of change, and in partnership with His creation. Classical Christianity sees the whole human race as implicated in Adam's Fall. As such, we are all corrupt and condemned. Sin is a condition. The new model denies the universal Fall. We are not guilty for Adam's sin, except as we follow Adam's poor moral example. Sin is an act.

Classical Christianity teaches that our problem is our condemnation, that we all stand under the wrath of God. The new model teaches that our problem is essentially ignorance—we do not know how much God loves us.

Classical Christianity teaches that there is no salvation apart from faith in the atoning work of Jesus Christ. The new model teaches that many are saved apart from faith in Christ, that the Holy Spirit can bring salvation even to people who do not know Christ, who is presented not so much as our sacrifice but as our example.

Classical Christianity teaches that our eternal state is immortality in either Heaven or Hell. The new model teaches that the wicked are annihilated, but that otherwise Heaven will be open to all.[15]

The new model reflects a number of postmodernist tenets: downplay of absolutes; distrust of transcendence; preference for "dynamic change" over "static truth"; desire for religious pluralism so that people of other cultures and religions are saved; the downplay of God's authority over us; the tone of tolerance, warm sentiments, and pop psychology. For all of its nice thoughts, however, megashift theology strikes at the very foundation of any faith that can call itself evangelical—the good news that Jesus Christ died on the cross to atone for our sins and to offer us the free gift of salvation. At stake is the gospel itself.

The megashift theologians understand Christ's death on the cross as God's way of showing how much He loves us. In this view, Christ does not atone for our sins, since our sins are nothing more than our individual acts. Jesus is not our sacrifice; rather, He is our example. He shows us how we should love each other. His death on the cross makes us feel sorry for Him, and when we really realize how much He suffered, it makes us feel God's love. This motivates us to change our lives and to love others.

Evangelism, according to this model, does not involve proclaiming God's judgment against sinners and His gracious offer of salvation through faith in Jesus Christ. Rather, evangelism simply educates people as to how much God loves them. God really does not want to punish anyone; He wants all to feel good about themselves, to lead a full life, to be happy. Those who turn away from God will miss out on this abundant life, though the Holy Spirit may well bring them to Heaven even though they never knew Christ.

Although this theology turns God into a warm, fuzzy therapist, it is essentially a teaching of moralism and despair, focusing on human works. Its facile optimism gives no comfort to tormented souls and includes no efficacious provision for the forgiveness of sin. "If righteousness could be gained through the law, Christ died for nothing!" insists the book of Galatians (2:21), which solemnly warns against trying to please men by devising some other gospel (1:6-10).

Michael Horton, a searching critic of this pseudo-evangelical theology, shows its human-centered inversion:

> Before, God existed for his own happiness, but the new god exists for ours. Instead of sinners having to be justified before a good and holy god, we are now ourselves the good guys who demand that God justify himself before us. Why should we believe in him? How will believing in him make me happier and more fulfilled than believing in Karma or the latest ideological bandwagon?[16]

The arrogance and superficiality of those who would come before God demanding consumer satisfaction, treating the Holy One of Israel as if He were a mere choice among many options, is grotesque.

Horton squarely faces the fact that God's revelation may not be what we want or like:

> Let's face it, there are a lot of things we find in the Bible that we do not like one bit. There is a great deal in the Christian message that offends us. God is supposed to exist to see to it that I get what I want; that I'm happy. The cross is supposed to show people how much God loves us and wants us to imitate Christ's love and compassion. It is there to boost our self-esteem and show us how much we're worth. But how can hell make people happy? How can it reform people? We just don't seem to be asking the questions the Bible answers these days. According to Scripture the universal issue is not "How can I be happy?" but "How can I be saved?"[17]

THE CONFESSIONAL OPTION

The British anthropologist Ernest Gellner has studied the fragmentation of contemporary culture and how it needs, as all cultures do, a religion, an overarching worldview to provide values and meaning. He concludes that there are now only three religious alternatives: postmodern relativism, rationalist fundamentalism, and religious fundamentalism.

Gellner himself advocates what he calls "rationalist fundamentalism," a principled return to the ideals of the Enlightenment. Like religious fundamentalism, this avowedly dogmatic rationalism believes in absolute, transcendent truths. It agrees with relativists, however, in rejecting revelation and intellectual certainty.

"Postmodern relativism," however, Gellner finds almost contemptible. After a trenchant critique of the postmodernists, he summarily dismisses them:

> To the relativists, one can only say—you provide an excellent account of the manner in which we choose our menu or our

wallpaper. As an account of the realities of our world and a guide to conduct, your position is laughable.[18]

Gellner, while a confirmed secularist, is far more respectful to religious fundamentalists:

The fundamentalists deserve our respect, both as fellow recognizers of the uniqueness of truth, who avoid the facile self-deception of universal relativism, and as our intellectual ancestors. Without indulging in excessive ancestor-worship, we do owe them a measure of reverence. Without serious, not to say obsessional monotheism . . . , the rationalist naturalism of the Enlightenment might well never have seen the light of day. In all probability, the attachment to a unique Revelation was the historical pre-condition of the successful emergence of a unique and symmetrically accessible Nature. . . . Without a strong religious impulsion towards a single orderly world, and the consequent avoidance of opportunist, manipulative incoherence, the cognitive miracle would probably not have occurred.[19]

Gellner sees religious fundamentalism not only as the revered ancestor of modernism, but as a legitimate option for the contemporary world.

Unfortunately, the particular brand of religious fundamentalism that he studies and that he sees as having the most vitality is *Islamic fundamentalism*. Christianity (at least the version he is familiar with in England) must seem to him so vitiated, so compromised and obedient to the rest of the culture, that he does not take it seriously. Christians do need to be aware that Islam is becoming their major religious competitor across the world. The church in Africa already faces intense struggle and persecution from Islam. No longer only a Middle Eastern religion, Islam extends throughout Africa and Asia, is a powerful presence in the former Communist states, and is making inroads in Western Europe and the United States. A militant, uncompromising Islam may emerge as the most potent postmodern religion, against which timid rationalists, wishy-washy relativists, and eager-to-please Christians may prove impotent.

Gellner's own position, which he terms in refreshing candor "rationalist fundamentalism," dogmatically embraces objective reason and the scientific method. Gellner, like more and more scholars and thoughtful people who are waking up to the consequences of postmodernism, is trying desperately to go back to the values of the Enlightenment and to reinstitute modernism. The effort, I believe, is futile. Gellner easily refutes postmodernism by rational analysis, but that is hardly the point. Those who reject rationalism altogether will hardly be swayed by Gellner's logic, impeccable as it may be. The momentum of the culture is building in a very different direction. Postmodernist relativism may be "laughable," but it cannot so easily be dismissed.

For Christianity to be a viable alternative to modernism (now discredited), postmodernism (a formalized anarchy under which few people can live for long), and, for that matter, Islamic fundamentalism, it must get its house in order. It cannot sell out to modernism, as in liberal theology, nor to postmodernism, as in megashift theology. Both liberalism and megashift evangelicalism surrender to the culture. Selling out to the dominant culture is, ironically, not a formula for success but for failure. The liberal churches tried to appeal to "modern man" by embracing modernism, but in doing so they made themselves irrelevant and doomed themselves when the intellectual climate changed. Evangelical churches that uncritically embrace postmodernism risk the same fate. In capitulating to the spirit of the age, both syncretic theologies refuse to minister to the genuine spiritual needs of the human beings lost in either the labyrinth of modernism, which denies them the supernatural, or postmodernism, which denies them truth.

"We do not yet know what the future holds," writes Diogenes Allen, "but it is clear that a fundamental reevalution of the Christian faith—free of the assumptions of the modern mentality that are generally hostile to a religious outlook—is called for."[20] Allen points out that the postmodern era makes possible a recovery of the Christian orthodoxy that has been under attack ever since the Enlightenment: "No longer can Christianity be put on the defensive, as it has for the last three hundred years or so, because of the narrow view of reason and the reliance on classical science that are characteristic of the modern mentality."[21]

Thomas Oden believes that classical Christian orthodoxy will reemerge in the postmodern era. For Oden, the collapse of communism marks the collapse of modernism, and he finds great significance in the survival and vindication of the Russian Orthodox church, whose traditions have changed little since the first centuries. Oden describes liberal Protestantism, with which he was once associated, as futile. He notes how theologians in every tradition are returning to the Bible, studying the early church, and recovering the wisdom and spirituality of the church fathers. "Postmodern Christians," he writes, "are those who, having entered in good faith into the disciplines of modernity, and having become disillusioned with the illusions of modernity, are again studying the Word of God made known in history."[22]

Oden believes that the postmodern*ists* are actually hypermodernists, pushing modernist skepticism to its ultimate limits. Instead of offering a genuine alternative to modernism, as Christian orthodoxy does, the cultural relativists represent nothing more than the death throes of modernism. While I hope he is right, I believe that Oden, like Gellner, underestimates the postmodernists, whose ideas now permeate the entire culture. I also suspect that he is too sanguine about the triumph of classical Christianity, which must surely face great opposition in an increasingly relativistic society. Nevertheless, Oden issues a stirring call for Christians to accept the death of modernism and to engage the new era by recovering their doctrinal and spiritual heritage.

Gellner sees some kind of "fundamentalism," whether rationalistic or religious, as the preferable option (indeed the only option) to relativism. The term "fundamentalism," though, is a relic of the disputes over modernism. The term has fallen into disrepute even among those to whom Gellner would assume it applies. Besides, in the postmodern world it has the connotations associated with Islamic fundamentalism, with its authoritarian mullahs and its hand-chopping austerity. This is not what Christians, who have a very different concept of law, culture, and grace, would want to convey.

The churches that resisted the regime of Adolf Hitler, that first postmodernist state, referred to themselves as the "confessional" churches. They confessed their faith against a syncretic church and against the police state, taking their stand on the Word of God and Christian doctrine, as expressed in their historic confessions of faith.[23] In their honor and in recognition that many of the issues will be exactly the same, we might speak of cultivating a "confessional Christianity."

Christians, if they are to be an alternative to postmodern relativism, need to confess their faith, in word and deed. This means knowing what that faith is.

Christians in every church body might begin by returning to their own doctrinal heritage. Lutherans, Calvinists, and other historical churches have formal written confessions of what they believe. Anglicans, Catholics, and the Orthodox have rich and rigorous theological traditions. Other denominations have less strictly defined doctrinal positions, but they still have their confessions of faith and their Bible-based heritage, which they should reclaim. In doing so, they might regain their vitality and testify to a core of Biblical truth that will stand as a blazing witness to the relativistic culture. Biblical churches with doctrinal integrity will have a stronger witness than muddled, eager-to-please-everyone congregations that do not stand for anything in particular.

Confessionalism should not mean "dead orthodoxy," the insistence on some kind of doctrinal purity at the expense of a warm, personal faith. The goal should be "live orthodoxy," a faith that is both experiential and grounded in truth, with room for both the feelings and the intellect. At times in church history doctrine has been overemphasized, but that will hardly be a danger in a society whose every tendency is to deny truth altogether.

Emphasizing doctrine will highlight the doctrinal differences between the various Christian traditions, but this need not mean destructive religious warfare. The various traditions need to be recovered before they can be either appreciated or challenged; once they are reestablished, debates about which theologies are most in accord with Scripture could resume, because theology would be taken seriously again. Vibrant theological debate would invigorate the church. The ecumenical method of unity—extinguishing all characteristic beliefs—has failed, but rigorous confessionalism, combined with an awareness of who the church's real enemies are, could be not only edifying but unifying. The unity of the church, after all, as the Apostle Paul clearly states, encompasses diversity, one Body consisting of diverse organs (1 Corinthians 12). This synthesis of unity and pluralism sounds almost postmodern.

APPROPRIATING POSTMODERNISM

Michael Horton's plea for a return to Reformation theology and Thomas Oden's project of recovering the theology of the early church both amount to a call for a new Christian confessionalism. The postmodern intellectual climate should theoretically make room for that. As a spokesman for postmodernism puts it, "The idea that all groups have a right to speak for themselves, in their own voice, and have that voice accepted as authentic and legitimate is essential to the pluralistic stance of postmodernism."[24] Surely this should include Christian communities, who share the same beliefs and the same theological language. If postmodernism seeks to bring the marginal into the center, surely Christianity has been consigned to the margins of modern thought. Furthermore, as Oden points out, the church is one of the few institutions that really is global, multicultural, and multi-generational.[25]

Confessional Christians can even join in the postmodern demolition of modernism, which still has a stronghold in the theological establishment. There is an urgent need, for example, to challenge the historical/critical approach to Scripture, which has vitiated the authority of the Bible throughout the mainline denominations. Postmodern criticism can show how the supposedly scientific and objectively historical Biblical scholarship, with its rejection of the supernatural and its naturalistic speculations about the Biblical text, is in fact not objective or scientific at all. The tools of postmodern scholarship could expose how the historical/critical method, for all of its pretensions to objectivity, merely masks the modernistic worldview, and that going beyond the language of the Biblical text is sheer speculation. Some scholars have already started this process, but much remains to be done before liberal Biblical scholarship is fully dismantled.

Confessional Christians can also appropriate the insights of postmodern scholarship by taking sin seriously and emphasizing the epistemological implications of the Fall. Human reason *is* inadequate, as the postmodernists say; but Christians base their beliefs not on reason but on revelation. We *are* wholly dependent upon language, as the postmodernists say; but Christians base their faith on God's language, that is, the Bible as the Word of God. Postmodernists say that meaning can only be determined from within an "interpretive community." For Christians, the church is their interpretive community.[26]

Although Christians can make use of postmodern scholarship, after a point they will have to challenge that scholarship. Christians, while questioning exclusive dependence on reason, do believe in absolute truths. Since God reveals Himself in language, language is not intrinsically deceptive; rather, language is revelatory and can express truth. God—not culture—is the origin of meaning, truth, and values. As the author of existence, God is authoritative. Thus, certain absolute truths and transcendent values are universal in their scope and application.

Christians will be in a position to address the dilemmas that postmodernists, if they are honest, are facing. "From now on, postmodern theorists will urge, there are no absolute grounds of value which can compel assent," observes Steven Connor. "But in such a situation, questions of value and legitimacy do not disappear, but gain a new intensity."[27] Postmodernism cannot answer those questions, however urgent and intense they are. David Harvey, confronting the superficiality and commercialism of the postmodernist way of thinking, urges "a counterattack of narrative against the image, of ethics against aesthetics" and a "search for unity within difference."[28] But to do so requires a transcendence that postmodernism cannot account for.

In an address to Congress, Václav Havel, the playwright who rose from a Communist prison to become the President of free Czechoslovakia, spoke for both the East and the West:

> We still don't know how to put morality ahead of politics, science, and economics. We are still incapable of understanding that the only genuine backbone of our actions—if they are to be moral—is responsibility. Responsibility to something higher than my family, my country, my firm, my success.[29]

But to what—or to Whom—are we responsible? What—or Who— is higher than everything that we can see? As Postman says, it is not enough to be liberated from a flawed theory—we need a better theory, but technopoly gives no answer.[30] Christianity, on the other hand, can give an answer.

Postmodern Christians must not, however, expect to fare particularly well at the hands of postmodernists. Christians will be excoriated for "thinking they have the only truth." They will be condemned for their intolerance, for "trying to force their beliefs on everybody else." Christians can expect to be excluded from postmodernists' invocations of tolerance and pluralism. As the culture becomes more and more lawless and brutal, Christians may even taste persecution. The church may or may not grow in such a climate. I suspect that it will shrink to a faithful remnant. But the Church of Jesus Christ cannot be overcome by the gates of Hell, much less by a culture (Matthew 16:18).

CONCLUSION:
"When the Foundations Are Destroyed"

The Word of God anticipates the dilemma of our age and for our church in the profound question of Psalm 11:3: "When the foundations are being destroyed, what can the righteous do?" Our whole modern era has been engaged in destroying foundations and in trying to erect some new foundation on the rubble.

Our Lord Himself spoke of foundations: "Everyone who hears these words of mine and puts them into practice is like a wise man who built his house on the rock." He who rejects the foundation of God's Word, on the other hand, "is like a foolish man who built his house on sand" (Matthew 7:24, 26). Sands, of course, keep shifting. The history of modern thought consists of a succession of foundations—the rationalism of the Enlightenment, the emotionalism of Romanticism, the will-power of Existentialism. In times of crisis, however, when "the rain came down, the streams rose, and the winds blew," each of these humanly built foundations collapses "with a great crash" (Matthew 7:27).

Today we see the rejection of *all* foundations. The various projects of modernism involved destroying foundations and replacing them with foundations of a different kind. Today the modern has become obsolete, and the futility of this never-ending cycle of demolition and reconstruction has become evident. The postmodernists pose a completely different alternative. Perhaps we can build without foundations.

Those who defend postmodernism and those who criticize it agree that the essence of postmodernism is that it is "anti-foundational."[1] Whereas the various kinds of modernism, beginning with the Enlightenment, sought, in David Harvey's words, to "totalize chaos," postmodernism seeks to live with the chaos, to avoid foundational judgments altogether.[2]

Christians can accept and take part in the postmodernists' critique of the endless succession of humanistic foundations. But the church is "built on the foundation of the apostles and prophets, with Christ Jesus himself as the chief cornerstone" (Ephesians 2:20). "Each one should be careful how he builds," warns the Apostle Paul. "For no one can lay any foundation other than the one already laid, which is Jesus Christ" (1 Corinthians 3:10-11).

WHAT CAN THE RIGHTEOUS DO?

But "when the foundations are being destroyed"—*all* foundations—"what can the righteous do?" How can the church that claims to have one exclusive foundation function in an age in which all foundations are being trashed? In the past people argued about what is right and what is wrong, what is true and what is false. Today people dismiss the very concepts of morality and truth. How can Christians promote "righteousness" in such an age? How can Christians testify to the truth of Christ? How can they proclaim the gospel to people who deny that they are sinners and who think that everybody is saved?

Church growth experts have studied ways to communicate Christianity to what is, in effect, the postmodern society. Leith Anderson, for example, says that contemporary people have problems paying attention when someone talks about abstract ideas. Such ideas, however, can be brought down to earth by expressing them in stories and by emphasizing practical applications. He further suggests that since contemporary people tend not to think in a systematic way or pay close attention to rational argumentation, ideas can best be approached issue by issue and through the influence of relationships. Role models, mentors, and friends shape people's thinking—for better or worse—more than objective reasoning.[3]

The young man who says he believes the Bible but who also

believes in reincarnation might come back to orthodoxy through a Bible study focusing on the specific issue of life after death. As he reads the Word of God, the Holy Spirit will be at work. In the meantime, by forming close relationships with a pastor whom he respects and solid Christians whom he loves, the young man will likely come under the influence of their orthodoxy.

Such suggestions about how to communicate with the postmodern mind-set can be useful. Jesus, after all, communicated in parables, not abstract treatises. Jesus certainly "discipled" his disciples.

Some of the church-growth research points to different applications than are usually made. Postmodern people, it is agreed, are group-oriented. This insight has led to the "metachurch" structure, in which enormous and impersonal "megachurches" are broken down into small groups for personal fellowship. To me, the appeal of small, personal groups shows the continued relevance of small churches.

The postmodern mind is open to the past. Church growth researchers often overlook this fact. From the historic preservation movement to the nostalgia of popular culture with its TV reruns, historical fiction, and "retro" fashions, contemporary people are fascinated and attracted to the past. Only a modernist would dismiss something because it is "old-fashioned." The traditions of the church—including traditional forms of worship—may have more appeal than we realize, especially to a generation that lacks traditions but yearns for them.

Churches are right to seek ways to communicate with and appeal to contemporary society. They must remember, however, that while they need to reach out to postmoderns, they dare not leave them where they found them. A newly organized church may have to market itself to the unchurched "consumers"; but once they are brought in, the church should challenge that consumer mind-set. The church may have to appeal to people's emotions, but it then must teach them how to think Biblically.

Church growth experts such as Anderson argue that churches need to change in step with the culture in order to attract members. The purpose of the church, however, is not so much to change as to change lives. Certainly, some changes might be in order if the church has been perpetuating some unnecessary stumbling blocks to evangelism. Potential barriers to outreach—a too-intrusive ethnic identity, inaccessible facilities, unfriendliness, failure to communicate with the outside world—need to be addressed.

The temptation, though, is to change the character and the teaching of the church in order to be more popular with potential members. The desire to be a "megachurch" often leads to "megashift" theology. Changes in style tend, often inadvertently, to produce changes in content. Revising worship services to make them more emotional and entertaining can only teach the congregation subjectivity and spiritual hedonism.

"Do not conform any longer to the pattern of this world," writes the Apostle Paul, "but be transformed by the renewing of your mind" (Romans 12:2). This text alone is enough to shoot down the argument that the church must change according to prevailing social trends. "The pattern of this world" is not to determine church ministry. This rules out every kind of syncretism, liberalism, and "megashift" theology. Rather, Christians are to "be transformed" by the Holy Spirit and their *minds* are to be renewed by the Word of God.

Making disciples requires moral, intellectual, and spiritual *discip*line, certainly alien to human nature, especially today. But to think that people today are incapable of understanding Christian truth or of having their minds transformed is to underestimate the Holy Spirit and the power of God.

True church growth—whether quantitative or qualitative—will come not through social science research and marketing techniques, but, as Tom Nettles points out, through revival and reformation;[4] not through human ingenuity, but through the action of God. In the meantime, the church must hold fast to its Biblical identity.[5]

In particular, the church must stand firm on the two foundational concepts now under attack: morality and truth. "The ultimate proof of the sinner," said Luther, "is that he doesn't know his own sin. Our job is to make him see it."[6] Proclaiming God's Law can bring conviction of sin; at that point, our job is to proclaim the gospel of salvation in Jesus Christ.

This proclamation requires a commitment to truth. "The church of the living God," says the Apostle Paul, is "the pillar and bulwark of the truth" (1 Timothy 3:15 RSV). The church is to be a "pillar"; that is, it must support truth and hold it up by its teachings and by its actions.[7] This truth, the text makes clear, is not merely the knowledge of human reason, but it is the far richer truth of "the mystery of godliness," namely the incarnation, glorification, and efficacy of Jesus Christ (1 Timothy 3:16), who is Himself the Truth (John 14:6).

THE LESSONS OF HISTORY

Destroying the foundations is not a new idea. The question raised in Psalm 11 has applied to God's people throughout the ages.

The slaves in Egypt had few supports for their faith and were at the mercy of their pagan overseers until Moses came with the Word of God and mighty acts of deliverance. When the children of Israel came into the promised land, their neighbors' paganism sorely tempted them. In fact, the Israelites did succumb to syncretism. They conformed to the behavior patterns of the Canaanites to the extent of sacrificing their own children (Jeremiah 7). God's judgment was severe. He sent against them the Babylonian Empire, which destroyed their nation and carried them off into captivity. Their foundations were literally destroyed as the Babylonians razed the walls of Jerusalem and demolished the Temple, the holy place of sacrifice, the center of their faith.

Yet God remained with His people in their exile and brought them back together. Again they would be sorely tried by their surrounding cultures, by the Greek empires, by the Romans. When Jesus came, He was to be the chief cornerstone of the foundation (Ephesians 2:20), but He was also the stone the builders rejected (Matthew 21:42).

The Roman Empire was, to say the least, a pluralistic society. Though they had lost their ancient virtues, Romans were supremely tolerant. The only people they could not tolerate were the Christians. During the persecutions Christians who refused to recant their faith had their legal rights suspended and could be instantly put to death—under a legal system otherwise scrupulously fair.

According to historian Stephen Benko, in his study of the anti-Christian propaganda in imperial Rome, one of the main reasons the early Christians were persecuted so cruelly was that they claimed to possess exclusive truth. In its decay Roman culture had become something like postmodernist culture, advocating cultural relativism (under Roman control, of course) and the validity of all religions (as long as everyone burned incense to Caesar). The Christians' refusal to acknowledge the deity of the Emperor was bad enough. But what galled the ancient Romans and whipped them into a murderous rage, as Benko shows, was that these low-life presumptive slaves claimed to possess the *only* truth.[8]

The church, however, did not try to conform to the pattern of the world. It refused to compromise its principles. Far from being popular and socially acceptable, Christianity was despised. Evangelism efforts were complicated by the fact that those who became Christians faced the death penalty. (Now *there's* a problem in church marketing.) Thousands of Christians were martyred. Nevertheless, the Holy Spirit kept bringing people to Christ. Eventually the whole Roman Empire in all of its power and glory bowed before the lordship of Christ.

Throughout its history, the church has always had two options—to go along with the times or to counter them. One could argue that the most vital theological movements in church history have been those which went *against* the trends of their time.

During the Enlightenment of the eighteenth century, many in the church decided to go along with the Age of Reason. They jettisoned belief in miracles and the supernatural and reinterpreted Christianity in rationalistic terms. This was the first version of liberal Christianity. And yet the eighteenth century was also marked by a religious movement that went *against* its times. The Methodist movement in the English-speaking world and the Pietist movement within Lutheranism countered Enlightenment rationalism with a supernatural, emotional spirituality. In America the Age of Reason was accompanied by the Great Awakening.

Many in the nineteenth century reacted against Enlightenment rationalism in favor of the emotionalism, subjectivity, and self-exploration of romanticism. This movement spawned a different theological liberalism, a debased form of pietism which presented Christianity as nothing more than a set of feelings. And yet nineteenth-century romanticism was countered by theological movements that went squarely against the spirit of the age. The Oxford movement in England stressed the relevance of traditional liturgies and objective dogma to a feeling-obsessed age. This was also the time of the Catholic revival, which brought ex-romantics such as Gerard Manley Hopkins and Francis Thompson to Christianity. Lutheran theologians such as C. F. W. Walther and Reformed theologians such as Charles Hodge and Charles Spurgeon combined personal piety with doctrinal rigor.

Twentieth-century existentialism inspired yet another brand of liberal theology, draining Christianity of its objective content. Yet the most flourishing religious movements of the twentieth century have challenged the assumptions of the times. In America modernism was countered by fundamentalism. Evangelicals have stressed the proclamation of the gospel and upheld the authority of the Bible. The confessional churches survived the church struggle of Hitler's Germany, Polish Catholicism undermined communism, and Eastern Orthodoxy outlasted Soviet rule.

Neil Postman has argued that education should be "thermostatic." When the room gets too cold, the thermostat clicks on the heat; when it gets too hot, the thermostat makes the air conditioner kick in. The thermostat keeps the temperature in balance by countering the prevailing climate. Postman says that education needs to do the same. When the culture is static and hidebound, education can loosen up people's thinking. When the culture is in a state of constant change, education needs to be a force for stability. In a visual television-oriented environment, schools more than ever need to stress reading and writing.[9]

The church too needs to be "thermostatic." In a cold, cerebral age, the church needs to draw on its rich and comprehensive spiritual heritage to cultivate human emotions, without compromising its theological integrity. In an emotional, subjective age, the church needs to cultivate objective thinking. In the postmodern age, the thermostatic church will need to emphasize morality and truth.

Father Jerzy Popieluszko, the Polish priest martyred by the Communists, put it well: "A Christian must be a sign of contradiction in the world."[10] The church under communism endured the most intense persecution of the twentieth century. Though many church bureaucrats collaborated with the Communists, the Christians who practiced their faith did not compromise, risking arrest by the KGB. Believers within the Eastern Orthodox church in Russia maintained their ancient liturgies and their third-century theology. Conservative Protestants—Baptists, Pentecostals, the Calvinists, and Lutherans of Eastern Europe—also resisted the atheistic indoctrination and intimidation.

For those who eventually brought down the monolith of communism, ending the modern era, the issue was always "truth." The theme of the dissidents, over and over again, from Solzhenitsyn to the Christian martyrs, from Václav Havel to the Solidarity activists, was their insistence on truth, not lies.[11]

Such an emphasis on truth and such moral heroism must ring hollow to the postmodern relativists in the West. In fact, when Solzhenitsyn gave the commencement address at Harvard in 1978, he began by invoking Harvard's motto "Veritas" (Latin for "truth"). His speech excoriated the West's immorality, materialism, and godlessness. It ruffled the feathers of the intellectual establishment, provoking outrage among the academics and sparking indignant editorials in the liberal media. "He believes himself to be in possession of The Truth," editorialized the *New York Times* in the ultimate postmodernist condemnation, "and so sees error wherever he looks."[12] Michael Novak may be more to the point when he calls Solzhenitsyn's address "the most important religious document of our time."[13]

Solzhenitsyn's address raises postmodern issues in a distinctly Christian way. Its very title alludes to the postmodern condition: "A World Split Apart." He affirms traditional cultures against the all-encompassing mass culture of Western secularism. He dissects the West's materialism and concern for comfort and pleasure, which has drained away our capacity for courage and sacrifice. He deplores the way our laws have been divorced from morality. "Society has turned out to have scarce defense against the abyss of human decadence, for example against the misuse of liberty for moral violence against young people, such as motion pictures full of pornography, crime, and horror."[14] He blasts the irresponsibility of the news media and the West's "TV stupor."[15] "Your scholars are free in the legal sense," he observes, "but they are hemmed in by the idols of the prevailing fad."[16] He attacks "humanism which has lost its Christian heritage"[17] and cites the obsolescence of the "ossified formulas of the Enlightenment."[18]

At the heart of his analysis is worldview criticism and a Christian view of history:

On the way from the Renaissance to our days we have enriched our experience, but we have lost the concept of a Supreme Complete Entity which used to restrain our passions and our irresponsibility. We have placed too much hope in politics and social reforms, only to find out that we were being deprived of our most precious possession: our spiritual life. It is trampled by the party mob in the East, by the commercial one in the West.[19]

Both the communist East and the secularist West are plagued by the same spiritual sickness.

Solzhenitsyn, like the postmodernists, believes that the modern era is over and that we are on the threshold of something new:

If the world has not approached its end, it has reached a major watershed in history, equal in importance to the turn from the Middle Ages to the Renaissance. It will demand from us a spiritual blaze; we shall have to rise to a new height of vision, to a new level of life, where our physical nature will not be cursed, as in the Middle Ages, but even more importantly, our spiritual being will not be trampled upon, as in the Modern Era.[20]

Despite his devastating critique of both the East and the West, heightened by the events that have unfolded since his address in 1978, Solzhenitsyn is not pessimistic. He ends, "No one on earth has any other way left but—upward."[21] He challenges us to begin "a spiritual blaze."

THE LORD IS IN HIS HOLY TEMPLE

"When the foundations are being destroyed, what can the righteous do?" The psalm goes on to give the answer, shifting the issue away from what human beings can do, to a confession of faith: "The LORD is in his holy temple; the LORD is on his heavenly throne" (Psalm 11:4).

Human beings may destroy foundations, but that has no effect whatsoever on the sovereignty of God. He rules. He transcendently and objectively reigns in Heaven. Furthermore, He is present not only in Heaven, but on earth. He is not only on His heavenly throne; He is in His holy Temple—that is, in His Church. No matter what the culture does, the children of God have this absolute security, that God is in control and that He is present with them.

The psalm shifts the issue away from what human beings can do to what God is going to do. It describes the horrible judgment God has in store for "the wicked and those who love violence" (Psalm 11:5): "On the wicked he will rain fiery coals and burning sulfur; a scorching wind will be their lot" (11:6). Absolutes are real. The consequences for violating them are apparent in this world and the next. Absolutes have their objective being in the character of God Himself: "For the LORD is righteous, he loves justice" (Psalm 11:7).

When the foundations are destroyed, God's people can expect to be targeted. "For look, the wicked bend their bows; they set their arrows against the strings to shoot from the shadows at the upright in heart" (Psalm 11:2). That the enemies of the faith are shooting "from the shadows" suggests the subtlety of the attacks. But instead of running away and hiding, instead of "flee[ing] like a bird to your mountain," the believer relies on a foundation that will never be shaken: "In the LORD I take refuge" (Psalm 11:1).

With this knowledge, Christians can agree with the post-modernists on the transience of human knowledge, culture, and history. "Jesus Christ," on the other hand, "is the same yesterday and today and forever" (Hebrews 13:8).

All men are like grass, and all their glory is like the flowers of the field; the grass withers and the flowers fall, but the word of the Lord stands forever. (1 Peter 1:24-25)

NOTES

CHAPTER ONE: *"There Are No Absolutes"*

1. Charles Colson, "Reaching the Pagan Mind," *Christianity Today*, 9 November 1992, p. 112.
2. George Barna, *The Barna Report: What Americans Believe* (Ventura, CA: Regal Books, 1991), pp. 83-85.
3. *Ibid.*, pp. 292-94.
4. George Gallup and Sarah Jones, *100 Questions and Answers: Religion in America* (Princeton, NJ: Princeton Research Center, 1989), p. 120.
5. Andrew M. Greeley, "Sex and the Single Catholic: The Decline of an Ethic," *America*, 7 November 1992, p. 344.
6. *Ibid.*
7. James R. Kelly, "Abortion: What Americans *Really* Think and the Catholic Challenge," *America*, 2 November 1991, p. 314.
8. Kim Lawton, "The Doctor as Executioner," *Christianity Today*, 16 December 1991, p. 50.
9. Leith Anderson, *A Church for the Twenty-first Century* (Minneapolis: Bethany House, 1992), p. 17.
10. George Barna, *The Frog in the Kettle: What Christians Need to Know About Life in the Year 2000* (Ventura, CA: Regal Books, 1990), p. 123.

CHAPTER TWO: *From the Modern to the Postmodern*

1. Diogenes Allen, *Christian Belief in a Postmodern World* (Louisville, KY: Westminster/John Knox Press, 1989), p. 2.
2. Thomas C. Oden, *Two Worlds: Notes on the Death of Modernity in America and Russia* (Downers Grove, IL: InterVarsity Press, 1992), p. 32.
3. See Thomas C. Oden, *After Modernity . . . What?: Agenda for Theology* (Grand Rapids, MI: Academie Books, 1990).
4. James Nuechterlein, "The Last Protestant," a review of Peter Berger, *A Far Glory: The Quest for Faith in an Age of Credulity*, in *First Things*, March 1993, p. 42. Nuechterlein is paraphrasing the position of Peter Berger, which he goes on to criticize.
5. For example, Aristotle distinguished between what is good in itself and

what is good because it leads to other goods. Life, virtue, and beauty are good in themselves; money is good insofar as it is a means to a good end, enabling one to live, do good deeds, and enjoy beauty. Such weighing of ends and means led, among other things, to the concept of a liberal arts education (the study of what is good in itself) as opposed to a technical education (the study of skills that lead to other social goods). See Aristotle's *Nichomachean Ethics*. For a good modern introduction to Aristotelian thinking, see the various works of Mortimer Adler, a neo-Aristotelian philosopher who recently has become a Christian.

6. See Michael J. Gorman, *Abortion and the Early Church* (Downers Grove, IL: InterVarsity Press, 1982) for the widespread practice of abortion in the Greco-Roman world and for the response of the early church.

7. See K. J. Dover, *Greek Homosexuality* (Cambridge, MA: Harvard University Press, 1978).

8. For a more detailed account of the Enlightenment and romanticism, including literary and religious implications, see my book *Reading Between the Lines* (Wheaton, IL: Crossway Books, 1990), pp. 169-90.

9. See Nancy R. Pearcey and Charles B. Thaxton, *The Soul of Science: A Christian Map to the Scientific Landscape* (Wheaton, IL: Crossway Books, 1994), pp. 106-07.

10. Cited by David Harvey in *The Condition of Postmodernity* (Cambridge, MA: Basil Blackwell, 1989), p. 39, quoting from Charles Jencks, *The Language of Post-Modern Architecture* (London: Academy Editions, 1984), p. 9.

11. Harvey, *Condition of Postmodernity*, p. 38.

12. Oden, *Two Worlds*, p. 79. Ihab Hassan, one of the leading scholars of postmodernism, also believes that postmodernism is an intensification of tendencies already present in modernism. See Steven Connor, *Postmodernist Culture: An Introduction to Theories of the Contemporary* (Oxford: Basil Blackwell, 1989), pp. 111-14.

13. Harvey, *Condition of Postmodernity*, p. 27.

14. *Ibid.*, p. 9.

15. *Ibid.*, p. 11.

16. See Pearcey, *Soul of Science*, pp. 192-93. For other intellectual influences on the postmodernist, see Harvey, p. 9.

17. Ihab Hassan, "The Culture of Postmodernism," *Theory, Culture and Society*, 2 (1985): 123-24.

18. The first instance of the word *postmodernism* cited by the *Oxford English Dictionary* is dated 1949 from a book on architecture. I have found an even earlier use of the term, a book of Christian apologetics by Bernard Iddings Bell entitled *Religion for Living: A Book for Postmodernists*, published by Harper in 1940. The first citation of the term as a broader description of culture is from Toynbee's *An Historian's Approach to Religion* in 1956. We will be drawing on Toynbee in more detail in subsequent chapters. Toynbee, who focused on the central role that religion plays in civilizations, often championed Christianity, although he drew back from Christianity's exclusivist claims in favor of universalism based on the supposed commonalities in all of the world's "higher religions." See *An Historian's Conscience: The Correspondence of Arnold*

J. Toynbee and Columba Cary-Elwes, *Monk of Ampleforth*, ed. Christian B. Peper (Boston: Beacon Press, 1986).

19. Arnold J. Toynbee, *A Study of History* (London: Oxford University Press, 1948), 5:399.
20. *Ibid.*, pp. 404-11.
21. *Ibid.*, pp. 412-31.
22. *Ibid.*, pp. 432-39.
23. *Ibid.*, pp. 439-40.
24. Patricia Waugh, *Postmodernism: A Reader* (London: Edward Arnold, 1992), p. 5.

CHAPTER THREE: *Constructing and Deconstructing Truth*

1. Walter Truett Anderson, *Reality Isn't What It Used to Be: Theatrical Politics, Ready-to-Wear Religion, Global Myths, Primitive Chic, and Other Wonders of the Postmodern World* (San Francisco: Harper & Row, 1990), p. 6.
2. *Ibid.*, pp. x-xi.
3. Patricia Waugh, ed., *Postmodernism: A Reader* (London: Edward Arnold, 1992), p. 5.
4. David Harvey, *The Condition of Postmodernity* (Cambridge, MA: Basil Blackwell, 1989), p. 9.
5. See Waugh, *Postmodernism*, p. 6.
6. Quoted in Harvey, *Condition of Postmodernity*, p. 9.
7. Waugh, *Postmodernism*, p. 6.
8. *Ibid.*
9. For another explanation of deconstruction from a Christian perspective, one which gives a lucid account of the thought of Jacques Derrida and other specific theorists, see Alan Jacob, "Deconstruction," in *Contemporary Literary Theory: A Christian Appraisal*, ed. Clarence Walhout and Leland Ryken (Grand Rapids, MI: Eerdmans, 1991), pp. 172-98. See also Roger Lundin, *The Culture of Interpretation: Christian Faith and the Postmodern World* (Grand Rapids, MI: Eerdmans, 1993) for a sustained study of deconstruction and related academic issues.
10. See Harvey, *Condition of Postmodernity*, pp. 50-51.
11. Thomas C. Oden puts it well in *Two Worlds: Notes on the Death of Modernity in America and Russia* (Downers Grove, IL: InterVarsity Press, 1992), p. 79, "By deconstruction, we mean the dogged application of a hermeneutic of suspicion to any given text, where one finds oneself always over against the text, always asking the skeptical question about the text, asking what self-deception or bad faith might be unconsciously motivating a particular conceptuality."
12. Steven Connor, *Postmodernist Culture: An Introduction to Theories of the Contemporary* (Oxford: Basil Blackwell, 1989), pp. 217-18.
13. Quoted from *American State Papers, Great Books of the Western World*, ed. Robert Maynard Hutchins (Chicago: Encyclopaedia Britannica, 1952), 43:1.
14. Connor, *Postmodernist Culture*, pp. 233-34.
15. Waugh, *Postmodernism*, p. 4.

16. Connor, *Postmodernist Culture*, p. 33.
17. Waugh, *Postmodernism*, p. 1.
18. Connor, *Postmodernist Culture*, pp. 232-34.
19. *Ibid.*, pp. 32-33. Connor is quoting and paraphrasing the postmodern scientific theorist Jean-François Lyotard.
20. *Ibid.*, p. 154.
21. Quoted in Anderson, p. 50. Compare Dostoevsky: "If God is dead, everything is permitted."
22. This is the title of one of his novels. See my discussion of the novel in my book *Reading Between the Lines* (Wheaton, IL: Crossway Books, 1990), pp. 209-10. For a sustained exploration and advocacy of this disconnected "lightness of being," see Henry S. Kariel, *The Desperate Politics of Postmodernism* (Amherst: University of Massachusetts Press, 1989).
23. Harvey, *The Condition of Postmodernity*, pp. 351-52.
24. Connor, *Postmodernist Culture*, pp. 9-10.
25. R. Rorty, quoted in Harvey, *The Condition of Postmodernity*, p. 56.
26. C. S. Lewis, *Miracles* (New York: Macmillan, 1947), pp. 19-21.
27. See Connor, *Postmodernist Culture*, pp. 204-11.
28. Dick Hebdige, "A Report on the Western Front: Postmodernism and the 'Politics' of Style," *Block*, 12 (1986/7), pp. 4-26. Cited and discussed in Connor, *Postmodernist Culture*, p. 210.
29. See also Kenneth Myers, *All God's Children and Blue Suede Shoes: Christians and Popular Culture* (Wheaton, IL: Crossway Books, 1989), who shows how the television mind-set is permeating every level of our culture, even the "high culture" of the art world and the universities.
30. See Philip Elmer-Dewitt, "Cyberpunk!" *Time*, 8 February 1993, pp. 59-65.
31. The questions are raised by Connor, pp. 35-36.
32. Lewis, *Miracles*, p. 109.
33. C. S. Lewis, *Mere Christianity* (New York: Macmillan, 1960), p. 19.
34. See my discussion of Schaeffer in "The Fragmentation and Integration of Truth," in *Francis A. Schaeffer: Portraits of the Man and His Work*, ed. Lane T. Dennis (Wheaton, IL: Crossway Books, 1986), p. 48.
35. See Francis Schaeffer, *The God Who Is There*, in *The Complete Works of Francis A. Schaeffer* (Wheaton, IL: Crossway Books, 1984), 1:103-05.
36. For a thoughtful account of hermeneutics from a Christian point of view, see Roger Lundin, "Hermeneutics," in Walhout and Ryken, eds., *Contemporary Literary Theory*, pp. 149-71.
37. I am indebted for this point to James W. Voelz, a professor at Concordia Seminary, who developed it in his paper "Multiple Signs, Levels of Meaning and Self as Text: Elements of Intertextuality," which was delivered at the Society of Biblical Literature Convention in San Francisco, November 1992.

CHAPTER FOUR: *The Critique of the Human*

1. Quoted in Walter Truett Anderson, *Reality Isn't What It Used to Be: Theatrical Politics, Ready-to-Wear Religion, Global Myths, Primitive*

Chic, and Other Wonders of the Postmodern World (San Francisco: Harper & Row, 1990), p. 51.

2. David Harvey, *The Condition of Postmodernity* (Cambridge, MA: Basil Blackwell, 1989), p. 44.

3. *Ibid.*

4. See David Michael Levin, *The Opening of Vision: Nihilism and the Postmodern Situation* (New York: Routledge, 1988), pp. 405-08.

5. From Heidegger's essay on Nietzsche, quoted in Levin, p. 3.

6. *Ibid.*, p. 24.

7. *Ibid.*

8. Patricia Waugh, *Postmodernism: A Reader* (London: Edward Arnold, 1992), p. 1.

9. Quoted in Charles Colson, *The Body* (Dallas: Word, 1992), p. 175.

10. Simopekka Virkkula, "One Man's War," *Books from Finland*, 24 (1990): 45-50. The article is a review of Pentti Linkola's book *Johdatus 1990-luvun a jatteluun* [*Introduction to the Thought of the 1990s*] (Helsinki: WSOY, 1989).

11. Quoted in Colson, p. 176.

12. For a critique of the overpopulation scare and a Christian response to environmental issues, see E. Calvin Beisner, *Prospects for Growth: A Biblical View of Population, Resources, and the Future* (Wheaton, IL: Crossway, 1990).

13. Levin, *Opening of Vision*, pp. 4-5.

14. David Horowitz, "The Queer Fellows," *American Spectator*, January 1993, p. 43.

15. N. P. Ricci, "The End/s of Woman," in Arthur Kroker, ed. *Ideology of Power in the Age of Lenin in Ruins* (New York: St. Martin's Press, 1981), p. 302. This book is fascinating as an attempt by the academic left to come to terms with the collapse of communism. The various essays demonstrate that American Marxists are bloody but not bowed, perplexed at the failure of socialism but still defiant in their revolutionary ideology.

16. Michel Foucault, "Nietzsche, Genealogy, History," in *Foucault Reader*, ed. Paul Rabinow (New York: Pantheon, 1984), pp. 78-79.

17. Ricci, *"End/s of Woman,"* p. 303.

18. Jean-Françoise Lyotard, as summarized by Steven Connor, *Postmodernist Culture: An Introduction to Theories of the Contemporary* (Oxford: Basil Blackwell, 1989), p. 37.

19. See Victor Farias, *Heidegger and Nazism*, tr. Paul Burrell (Philadelphia: Temple University Press, 1989), p. 253. For the connection between Heidegger's Nazi ideology and his philosophy, see Tom Rockmore, *On Heidegger's Nazism and Philosophy* (Berkeley: University of California Press, 1992).

20. Gene Edward Veith, *Modern Fascism: Liquidating the Judeo-Christian* (St. Louis: Concordia Publishing House, 1993).

21. David H. Hirsch, *The Deconstruction of Literature: Criticism after Auschwitz* (Hanover, NH: Brown University Press, 1991), p. 165. His entire book is a telling critique of postmodernism in light of its ties to fascism.

22. See Neil Postman, *Teaching as a Conserving Activity* (New York: Delacorte Press, 1979), pp. 47-70.

23. See Neil Postman, *Amusing Ourselves to Death: Public Discourse in the Age of Show Business* (New York: Viking, 1985).

24. Neil Postman, *Technolopoly: The Surrender of Culture to Technology* (New York: Vintage Books, 1993), pp. 73-82.

25. Harvey, *Condition of Postmodernity*, p. 61.

26. Quoted in Connor, p. 171.

27. Rudy Rucker, quoted in Philip Elmer-Dewitt, "Cyberpunk!" *Time*, 8 February 1993, p. 59, an article exploring Cyberpunk ideology.

28. Kroker, *Ideology of Power*, p. 16.

29. Harvey, *Condition of Postmodernity*, p. 53.

30. *Ibid.*, p. 52.

31. See *Ibid.*, p. 46.

32. Cited in *Ibid.*, pp. 5-8.

33. Arthur Kroker, *Panic Encyclopedia: The Definitive Guide to the Postmodern Scene* (New York: St. Martin's Press, 1989), p. 73.

34. See Harvey, *Condition of Postmodernity*, pp. 113-14, 117.

35. See the theology of Charles Williams (C. S. Lewis's friend), who relates the unity and diversity of the Trinity to a wide range of issues, from social orders to human love. See Mary McDermott Shideler, *The Theology of Romantic Love: A Study in the Writings of Charles Williams* (Grand Rapids, MI: Eerdmans, 1962).

CHAPTER FIVE: *Playing with Conventions—Art and Performance*

1. Terry Eagleton, "Awakening from Modernity," *Times Literary Supplement*, 20 February 1987. Quoted in David Harvey, *The Conditions of Postmodernity* (Cambridge, MA: Basil Blackwell, 1989), p. 9.

2. Jameson's analysis is discussed in Steven Connor, *Postmodernist Culture: An Introduction to Theories of the Contemporary* (Oxford: Basil Blackwell, 1989), p. 44.

3. *Ibid.*, p. 158.

4. *Ibid.*, p. 239.

5. Harvey, *Conditions of Postmodernity*, p. 7.

6. For the postmodernist embrace of kitsch, see Connor, p. 238.

7. See Harvey, *Conditions of Postmodernity*, p. 51.

8. See Connor, *Postmodernist Culture*, p. 44.

9. *Ibid.*, pp. 44-45. He quotes Jameson.

10. Harvey, *Conditions of Postmodernity*, p. 58.

11. *Ibid.*

12. Charles Newman in a review of the state of the contemporary novel in *The New York Times*, 17 July 1987, quoted in Harvey, p. 58.

13. Quoted in Connor, p. 134.

14. *Ibid.*, pp. 98-99.

15. *Ibid.*, p. 138.

16. *Ibid.*

17. See Heiner Stachelhaus, *Joseph Beuys*, tr. David Britt (New York:

Abbeville Press, 1991), for a description and photographs of the performance.

18. See Connor, *Postmodernist Culture*, p. 240.
19. Alastair Mackintosh, "Warhol," in *Contemporary Artists*, 3rd ed. (Chicago: St. James Press, 1989), p. 1013.
20. Gerard Malanga, quoted in David Bourdon, *Warhol* (New York: Harry N. Abrams, 1989), p. 138.
21. Mackintosh, *Contemporary Artists*, p. 1013.
22. Bourbon, *Warhol*, p. 140.
23. Connor, *Postmodernist Culture*, p. 186.
24. *Ibid.*, p. 132.
25. See *Ibid.*, pp. 149-153.
26. See my article, "Patronizing the Patrons," in *Philanthropy, Culture, & Society*, April 1993, pp. 1-8.
27. Connor, *Postmodernist Culture*, p. 148.
28. Roberta Smith, "At the Whitney, a Biennial with a Social Conscience," *New York Times*, 5 March 1993, p. C27.
29. Harvey, *Conditions of Postmodernity*, p. 51.
30. Quoted in Connor, p. 136.
31. See *Ibid.*
32. *Ibid.*, p. 143.

CHAPTER SIX: *Towers of Babel—The Example of Architecture*

1. See Steven Connor, *Postmodernist Culture: An Introduction to Theories of the Contemporary* (Oxford: Basil Blackwell, 1989), pp. 66-70.
2. Francis Schaeffer discusses this point in relation to the beauty of the Concorde airliner in *How Shall We Then Live?: The Rise and Decline of Western Thought and Culture* (Old Tappan, NJ: Fleming H. Revell, 1976), pp. 196-97.
3. See David Harvey, *The Condition of Postmodernity* (Cambridge, MA: Basil Blackwell, 1989), p. 39; Charles Jencks, *The Language of Post-Modern Architecture* (London: Academy Editions, 1984).
4. See Connor, *Postmodernist Culture*, pp. 70-75.
5. Robert Venturi, et al., *Learning from Las Vegas* (Cambridge, MA: MIT Press, 1977).
6. O. B. Hardison, Jr., *Disappearing Through the Skylight: Culture and Technology in the Twentieth Century* (New York: Viking, 1989), pp. 113-15; Connor, *Postmodernist Culture*, p. 74.
7. See Connor, *Postmodernist Culture*, pp. 73-74.
8. See the discussion in Hardison, *Disappearing Through the Skylight*, pp. 115-16.
9. See *Ibid.*, p. 116.
10. See Harvey, *The Condition of Postmodernity*, p. 83.

CHAPTER SEVEN: *Metafiction—TV, Movies, and Literature*

1. See my discussion of this issue in my book *Reading Between the Lines: A Christian Guide to Literature* (Wheaton, IL: Crossway Books, 1990), pp. 17-25.

2. See Arthur Kroker and David Cook, *The Postmodern Scene: Excremental Culture and Hyper-Aesthetics* (New York: St. Martin's Press, 1986), p. 268.
3. Steven Connor, *Postmodernist Culture: An Introduction to Theories of the Contemporary* (Oxford: Basil Blackwell, 1989), p. 176.
4. For a hilarious and devastating satire of these kinds of programs from an explicitly Christian point of view, see Walker Percy's "The Last Donahue Show," in *Lost in the Cosmos: The Last Self-Help Book* (New York: Washington Square Press, 1983), pp. 48-59.
5. David Harvey, *The Condition of Postmodernity* (Cambridge, Mass.: Basil Blackwell, 1989), p. 48.
6. *Ibid.*
7. Connor, *Postmodernist Culture*, p. 179.
8. *Ibid.*, pp. 176-77.
9. Cited in *Ibid.*, p. 168.
10. *Ibid.*, p. 123. Postmodernists also talk about "metahistory" (historical studies of historical studies) and "metanarratives" (overarching stories that encompass all other stories told by a culture).
11. *Ibid.*, pp. 123-25.
12. John Barth, "Life-Story," in *The Norton Anthology of American Literature*, 3rd ed., ed. Nina Baym et al. (New York: W. W. Norton, 1989), 2:2144-45, 2151-52.
13. *Ibid.*, p. 2152.
14. Carlo Fruttero and Franco Lucentini, with Charles Dickens, *The D. Case, or the Truth About the Mystery of Edwin Drood*, tr. Gregory Dowling (New York: Harcourt, Brace, Jovanovich, 1992).
15. Marvin Olasky, *Prodigal Press: The Anti-Christian Bias of the American News Media* (Westchester, IL: Crossway Books, 1988), pp. 59-71.
16. Bobbie Ann Mason, "Big Bertha Stories," in *Literature: An Introduction to Fiction, Poetry, and Drama*, 5th ed., ed. X. J. Kennedy (New York: Harper Collins, 1991), pp. 428-429.
17. Quoted in Harvey, p. 58.

CHAPTER EIGHT: *The New Tribalism*

1. The point is made with similar illustrations in David Harvey, *The Condition of Postmodernity* (Cambridge, MA: Basil Blackwell, 1989), pp. 87-88.
2. Philip Elmer-Dewitt, "Cyberpunk!" *Time*, 8 February 1993, p. 62.
3. Leith Anderson, *A Church for the Twenty-First Century* (Minneapolis: Bethany House, 1992), p. 33.
4. See Kenneth A. Myers, *All God's Children and Blue Suede Shoes: Christians and Popular Culture* (Westchester, IL: Crossway Books, 1989), pp. 17-23.
5. This definition of culture does not even appear in the *Oxford English Dictionary*, published in 1933, the authoritative guide to the history of English words, although the second edition of 1989 does define it.
6. For this point and for the way postmodernism has extended and altered

the concept of civil rights, see David Horowitz, "The Queer Fellows," *American Spectator*, January 1993, pp. 42-48.

7. Steven Connor, *Postmodernist Culture: An Introduction to Theories of the Contemporary* (Oxford: Basil Blackwell, 1989), p. 228. Notice the metaphor involved in the term "marginal." It is based on the line of thought that sees all of culture as a "text." The text of a book consists of the words on the page. Something jotted down in the margin is not part of the main text. Similarly, "marginal groups" are excluded from the official cultural "text," although they do exist along the edges.

8. *Ibid.*, pp. 188-89.

9. *Ibid.*, p. 229.

10. See Shelby Steele, "The Recoloring of Campus Life," in *The Norton Reader*, ed. Arthur Eastman et al. (New York: W. W. Norton, 1992), pp. 554-66.

11. See Michelle Maglalang, "US Faces Bigger Problems Than Loss of Meaning," *Milwaukee Journal*, 2 July 1993, p. A9.

12. Benjamin Barber, "Jihad vs. McWorld," *Atlantic Monthly*, March 1992, p. 53.

13. *Ibid.*, p. 62.

14. *Ibid.*, pp. 59-60.

15. *Ibid.*, p. 60.

16. Tom Strini, "PBS Series Shows Dance as a Link Between Cultures, a Human Mirror," *Milwaukee Journal*, 9 May 1993.

CHAPTER NINE: *The Politics of Power*

1. David Horowitz, "The Queer Fellows," *American Spectator*, January 1993, pp. 42-48. See also a similar discussion applied to Hollywood values in K. L. Billingsley, *The Seductive Image: A Christian Critique of the World of Film* (Wheaton, IL: Crossway, 1989), pp. 112-13.

2. Steven Connor, *Postmodernist Culture: An Introduction to Theories of the Contemporary* (Oxford: Basil Blackwell, 1989), pp. 243-44.

3. *Ibid.*, p. 212.

4. I am indebted to Dr. Paul Busiek for his research on the influence of Gramsci on the American Left. See, for example, Carl Boggs, *Gramsci's Marxism* (London: Pluto Press, 1976), and S. Steven Powell, *Covert Cadre: Inside the Institute for Policy Studies* (Ottawa, IL: Green Hill Publishers, 1987).

5. For this phenomenon throughout contemporary society, see Charles Sykes, *A Nation of Victims: The Decay of the American Character* (New York: St. Martin's Press, 1992).

6. John Leo, "Today's Campus Politics Seems Right Context for Meeting on Rage," *Milwaukee Journal*, 6 July 1993, p. A9.

7. Stanley Fish, "There's No Such Thing as Free Speech and It's a Good Thing, Too," in *Debating P. C.: The Controversy over Political Correctness on College Campuses*, ed. Paul Barman (New York: Laurel, 1992). See the discussion of this article in Roger Lundin, *The Culture of Interpretation: Christian Faith and the Postmodern World* (Grand Rapids, MI: Eerdmans, 1993), pp. 24-25.

8. Lundin, *Culture of Interpretation,* p. 25.

9. Fish, "There's No Such Thing," p. 244. Quoted in *Ibid.*

10. Arthur Pontynen, "Oedipus Wrecks: PC and Liberalism," *Measure,* February 1993, p. 2.

11. Connor, *Postmodernist Culture,* p. 213.

12. Gene Edward Veith, *Modern Fascism: Liquidating the Judeo-Christian Worldview* (St. Louis: Concordia Publishing House, 1993).

13. George Barna, *The Barna Report: What Americans Believe* (Ventura, CA: Regal, 1991), pp. 83-85.

14. Charles Colson, *The Body: Being Light in Darkness* (Dallas, TX: Word, 1992), p. 163.

15. Quoted in John Leo, "Judge-made Law Foments Strife," *Milwaukee Journal,* 29 March 1993, p. A9.

16. *Ibid.*

17. See Neil Postman, *Technopoly: The Surrender of Culture to Technology* (New York: Vintage Books, 1993), pp. 82-90.

18. *Ibid.,* pp. 85-90.

19. Walter Truett Anderson, *Reality Isn't What It Used to Be: Theatrical Politics, Ready-to-Wear Religion, Global Myths, Primitive Chic, and Other Wonders of the Postmodern World* (San Francisco: Harper & Row, 1990), pp. 5-6.

20. This is basically the argument of David Harvey, *The Condition of Postmodernity* (Cambridge, MA: Basil Blackwell, 1989).

21. Thomas Oden characterizes the postmodern*ism* of the deconstructionists and other radical contemporary thinkers as "ultra-modernist," pushing the skepticism inherent in all modernism to its extreme. He argues that the "ultra-modernists" will soon pass away as part of the death of modernity. See, for example, *After Modernity—What?: An Agenda for Theology* (Grand Rapids, MI: Academie Books, 1990), p. 77, *et. passim.*

22. J. Hillis Miller, "Literature and Value: American and Soviet Views," *Profession 92,* 1992, p. 25.

23. *Ibid.* The National Association of Scholars is an organization of academics concerned about the coercive effect of "politically correct" ideologies on the life of the university and upon scholarship. The group is not anti-minority, nor is it as conservative or as marginal as Miller implies.

24. *Ibid.,* p. 22.

25. *Ibid.*

26. *Ibid.,* p. 26.

27. This is the argument of Solzhenitsyn's "Templeton Address: Men Have Forgotten God," in *In the World: Reading and Writing as a Christian,* ed. John H. Timmerman and Donald R. Hettinga (Grand Rapids, MI: Baker, 1987), pp. 388-97.

CHAPTER TEN: *Everyday Postmodernism*

1. Leith Anderson gave the example in a presentation, "Facing the Future," at the Evangelical Press Association Convention, St. Paul, Minnesota, 12 May 1993.

2. Peter Berger, "The Class Struggle in American Religion," *Christian Century*, 25 February 1981, p. 198.
3. Hansfried Kellner, "Introduction," *Hidden Technocrats: The New Class and the New Capitalism*, ed. Hansfried Kellner and Frank W. Heuberger (New Brunswick, NJ: Transaction Publishers, 1992), p. 3.
4. *Ibid.*, p. 3. See also Neil Postman's discussion of the social sciences in *Technopoly: The Surrender of Culture to Technology* (New York: Vintage Books, 1993) and William Kirk Kilpatrick's critique of contemporary psychology in *Psychological Seduction* (Nashville: Thomas Nelson, 1983). All of these critics of the social sciences—Postman, Kilpatrick, Berger, Kellner—are themselves distinguished social scientists. They still see value in their fields despite their criticisms.
5. See Walker Percy's discussion of this point in *Lost in the Cosmos: The Last Self-Help Book* (New York: Washington Square Press, 1983), p. 11.
6. See Kellner, "Introduction," *Hidden Technocrats*, pp. vii-ix. The entire book documents this thesis.
7. See Nancy R. Pearcey and Charles B. Thaxton, *The Soul of Science: A Christian Map to the Scientific Landscape* (Wheaton, IL: Crossway Books, 1994).
8. Anderson, "Facing the Future," p. 44.
9. *Ibid.*
10. Marvin Olasky, "Culture of Irresponsibility?" *World*, 23 May 1992, p. 7. See also Olasky's book *The Tragedy of American Compassion* (Wheaton, IL: Crossway, 1992).
11. *Ibid.*, pp. 168-70.
12. *Ibid.*, pp. 185-88.
13. See Thomas Oden, *Two Worlds: Notes on the Death of Modernity in America and Russia* (Downers Grove, IL: InterVarsity Press, 1992).
14. Benjamin Barber, "Jihad vs. McWorld," *Atlantic Monthly*, March 1992, p. 60.

CHAPTER ELEVEN: *Spirituality Without Truth*

1. See Walter Truett Anderson, *Reality Isn't What It Used to Be: Theatrical Politics, Ready-to-Wear Religion, Global Myths, Primitive Chic, and Other Wonders of the Postmodern World* (San Francisco: Harper & Row, 1990), pp. 7-9.
2. See Philip Elmer-Dewitt, "Cyberpunk!" *Time*, 8 February 1993, pp. 59-65.
3. C. S. Lewis, *Mere Christianity* (New York: Macmillan, 1960), pp. 17-20.
4. Steven Connor, *Postmodernist Culture: An Introduction to Theories of the Contemporary* (Oxford: Basil Blackwell, 1989), pp. 242-43.
5. *Ibid.*
6. *Ibid.*, p. 243.
7. *Ibid.*, p. 244.
8. *Ibid.*, p. 212.
9. Anderson, *Reality Isn't What It Used to Be,* p. 13.
10. Elmer-Dewitt, "Cyberpunk!" p. 64.
11. See Daniel F. Greenberg, *The Construction of Homosexuality* (Chicago:

University of Chicago Press, 1988), p. 99. Greenberg's book is important in its demonstration of the *cultural* foundations of homosexuality.

12. George Barna, *The Frog in the Kettle: What Christians Need to Know About Life in the Year 2000* (Ventura, CA: Regal Books, 1990), p. 121.
13. *Ibid.*, p. 122.
14. Arnold Toynbee, *An Historian's Approach to Religion* (New York: Oxford University Press, 1956), p. 211.
15. *Ibid.*, pp. 211-15.
16. *Ibid.* See also pp. 43-58.
17. *Ibid.*, pp. 43-58.
18. See *Ibid.*, pp. 250-53.
19. *Ibid.*, p. 219.
20. *Ibid.*, pp. 220-38.
21. Neil Postman, *Technopoly: The Surrender of Culture to Technology* (New York: Vintage Books, 1993), p. 58.
22. See *Ibid.*, p. 185.
23. *Ibid.*, p. 90.
24. *Ibid.*, p. 185.
25. See *Ibid.*, pp. 164-80.
26. *Ibid.*, p. 79.
27. A letter from Edwyn Bevan, quoted in Arnold J. Toynbee, *A Study of History* (London: Oxford University Press, 1948), 5:9-10.

CHAPTER TWELVE: *Postmodern Christianity*

1. George Gallup, Jr., and Robert Bezilla, "U.S. Religious Composition Changes; Fervor Constant," Princeton Religion Research Center (1993), Religious News Service, in *Reporter: News for Church Leaders*, August 1993, p. 16. The statistics on Americans who claim to be Christian are taken from an earlier Gallup poll cited by Charles Colson, *The Body* (Dallas: Word Publishing, 1992), p.46.
2. George Barna, *The Barna Report: What Americans Believe* (Ventura, CA: Regal, 1991), pp. 292-94.
3. Bill Hall, "Is the Church Growth Movement Really Working?" in *Power Religion: The Selling Out of the Evangelical Church*, ed. Michael Horton (Chicago: Moody Press, 1992), pp. 142-43.
4. See Colson's discussion of this point, *The Body*, p. 31.
5. Leith Anderson, *A Church for the Twenty-First Century* (Minneapolis: Bethany House, 1992), p. 20.
6. *Ibid.*, p. 21.
7. Leith Anderson gave the example in a workshop, "Facing the Future," at the Evangelical Press Association convention, 12 May 1993, St. Paul, MN.
8. Barna, *Barna Report,* pp. 83-85, 292-94.
9. Colson, *The Body,* pp. 43-44.
10. See Roger Lundin, *The Culture of Interpretation: Christian Faith and the Postmodern World* (Grand Rapids, MI: Eerdmans, 1993), pp. 5-6.
11. For the various manifestations of the power mentality in the church, see

Michael Horton, ed., *Power Religion: The Selling Out of the Evangelical Church* (Chicago: Moody Press, 1992).

12. See, for example, Alister E. McGrath, *Luther's Theology of the Cross* (Oxford: Basil Blackwell, 1985).

13. Colson, *The Body,* pp. 44-47. The term "hot-tub religion" is from J. I. Packer.

14. See Robert Brow, "The Evangelical Megashift," *Christianity Today,* 19 February 1990, pp. 12-14.

15. "Theology at a Glance," *Modern Reformation,* January/February 1993, p. 33.

16. Michael S. Horton, "How Wide Is God's Mercy?" *Modern Reformation,* January/February 1993, p. 8.

17. Michael S. Horton, "What Is the Megashift?" *Modern Reformation,* January/February 1993, p. 1.

18. Ernest Gellner, *Postmodernism, Reason and Religion* (London: Routledge, 1992), p. 96.

19. *Ibid.,* pp. 95-96.

20. Diogenes Allen, *Christian Belief in a Postmodern World* (Louisville, KY: Westminster/John Knox Press, 1989), p. 2.

21. *Ibid.,* p. 2.

22. Thomas C. Oden, *Two Worlds: Notes on the Death of Modernity in America and Russia* (Downers Grove, IL: InterVarsity Press, 1992), p. 53. See also his book *After Modernity—What?: Agenda for Theology* (Grand Rapids, MI: Academie Books, 1990).

23. I tell their story—and it is an inspiring and instructive one—in my book *Modern Fascism: Liquidating the Judeo-Christian Worldview* (St. Louis: Concordia Publishing House, 1993.)

24. David Harvey, *The Condition of Postmodernity* (Cambridge, MA: Basil Blackwell, 1989), p. 48.

25. Oden, *Two Worlds,* p. 54.

26. James W. Voelz, "Multiple Signs, Levels of Meaning and Self as Text: Elements of Intertextuality," Society of Biblical Literature convention, San Francisco, November 1992.

27. Steven Connor, *Postmodernist Culture: An Introduction to Theories of the Contemporary* (Oxford: Basil Blackwell, 1989), p. 8.

28. Harvey, *Condition of Postmodernity,* p. 359.

29. Quoted in Neil Postman, *Technopoly: The Surrender of Culture to Technology* (New York: Vintage Books, 1993), p. 82.

30. *Ibid.*

CHAPTER THIRTEEN: *Conclusion—"When the Foundations Are Destroyed"*

1. David Harvey, *The Condition of Postmodernity* (Cambridge, MA: Basil Blackwell, 1989), p. 9.

2. *Ibid.,* p. 11.

3. Leith Anderson, *A Church for the Twenty-First Century* (Minneapolis: Bethany House, 1992), pp. 45-46.

4. Tom Nettles, "A Better Way: Church Growth Through Revival and

Reformation," in *Power Religion: The Selling Out of the Evangelical Church*, ed. Michael Horton (Chicago: Moody Press, 1992), pp. 161-87.

5. For a challenging exposition of what this means and how the church can live its faith in the postmodern world, see Charles Colson, *The Body* (Dallas: Word, 1992).

6. Quoted in *Ibid.*, p. 191.

7. See Colson's discussion of this passage, *Ibid.*, pp. 183-200.

8. Stephen Benko, *Pagan Rome and the Early Christians* (Bloomington: Indiana University Press, 1984), pp. 58-59.

9. Neil Postman, *Teaching as a Conserving Activity* (New York: Delacorte Press, 1979).

10. Quoted in Colson, *The Body*, p. 213.

11. See Colson's stirring account of the church under communism and the role of Christians in its fall, *Ibid.*, pp. 201-31. Notice the recurring emphasis upon "truth."

12. "The Obsession of Solzhenitsyn," *New York Times*, 13 June 1978, reprinted in *Solzhenitsyn at Harvard: The Address, Twelve Early Responses, and Six Later Reflections*, ed. Ronald Berman (Washington, DC: Ethics and Public Policy Center, 1980), p. 23.

13. Michael Novak, "On God and Man," in *Solzhenitsyn at Harvard*, p. 131.

14. Aleksandr I. Solzhenitsyn, "A World Split Apart," in *Ibid.*, p. 9.

15. *Ibid.*, p. 13.

16. *Ibid.*, p. 11.

17. *Ibid.*, p. 18.

18. *Ibid.*, p. 19.

19. *Ibid.*

20. *Ibid.*, p. 20.

21. *Ibid.*

SCRIPTURE INDEX

INDEX